UP CLOSE AND PERSONAL.

GEEZERS

ON CAMP WITH THE

SAS

UP CLOSE AND PERSONAL.

GEEZERS

ON CAMP WITH THE

SAS

MONICA LAVERS

Orphans
Publishing

First published in Great Britain in 2021 by
Orphans Publishing
Enterprise Park, Leominster
Herefordshire HR6 0LD

www.orphanspublishing.co.uk

A Cataloguing in Publication record for this book
is available from the British Library

Hradback: 978-1-903-36044-6
Also available in ebook

Printed and bound by Clays Ltd, Elcograf, S.p.A.

AUTHOR'S NOTE

I did not set out to write a book when I went to work as part of garrison support, even though, for a deeply secret organisation, the SAS probably have more books written about them than any other unit in the British Army. Indeed, I assumed I would not be allowed to, so the thought never entered my head. I eventually wrote this book as a personal memoir, having been deeply struck by how Margaret Thatcher, in her later years, had dementia to such an extent that she could not remember being Prime Minister. I did not want to forget my short time working with the most famous elite regiment in the world.

There are strict rules about what can be said and written about UK Special Forces, and the MOD never comments either to confirm or deny any details of operations or training. I have to thank the Defence Security Media Advisory service (DSMA) and the Ministry of Defence for their unparalleled guidance and patience in helping me to get this book acceptable for publication. It is a long, detailed and very meticulous process and took eleven months, but national security is paramount, plus the personal security of the Regiment members and Headquarters. The reader may find, therefore, a certain lack of detail in some areas, but it is necessary. We must protect our most elite regiments and I hope you will appreciate that I need to skate around certain issues. What matters most are the personal stories of these extraordinary people. Although I have, of necessity, changed their identities, everything that is written here is an entirely true and honest account of events between 2015 and 2018.

Monica Lavers, 2020

We are the Pilgrims, master; we shall go
Always a little further; it may be
Beyond that last blue mountain barred with snow,
Across that angry or that glimmering sea,
White on a throne or guarded in a cave
There lies a prophet who can understand
Why men are born: but surely we are brave,
Who take the Golden Road to Samarkand.

JAMES ELROY FLECKER

1

They call themselves 'geezers', and a geezer is outside the hangar now, pressing his face to the window then peering through a chink in the curtain covering the door, trying his security pass and pushing the door, flitting from one to the other like a persistent dog trying to get attention. We're closed. When he catches sight of me, he holds his palms together in a prayer gesture then claps a fist over his heart for good measure.

I recognise him immediately – it's Christopher 'Kip' Formby, the chief instructor whose gravelly Northern Irish accent makes 'How are you?' sound like a death threat. He's ignoring the 'Closed' sign on the door, because he thinks that sort of thing doesn't apply to him. I hear a beep as his pass is pressed against the security pad, a push of the door, then the beep, beep again. Another push, then a rattle. I have the key and, for now, the power.

He's a difficult man to like, but at least you know where you are with Kip Formby. Bullish, self-obsessed and arrogant, he's a top counter-terrorism instructor and weapons expert and he doesn't much mind who knows it.

He's the opposite of humble and unassuming – everything his renowned regiment should be – he even drops hints about his regimental identity when he's out in town just in case anybody should think he's merely an ordinary person.

I pull back the makeshift curtain. Outside is the usual colourless, miserable scene of shipping containers, Portakabins and parked cars belonging to men out of the country for months, weeds growing up around them – and Kip Formby in combats and a thick jacket, his dog beside him. The sky is so low, it feels like a lid. Snow clouds, they say. I tap the imaginary watch on my wrist and shake my head and he responds with a dramatic scowl and arms spread, mouthing *What the fuck?*

Oh well, it's nearly Christmas, and it's freezing and cheerless out there, so I decide to give him the benefit of the doubt. I'm winding things down anyway, emptying bins and sorting our monthly racking registers and fire extinguisher records. Honestly, you wouldn't believe the stuff we do in this store. The place is massive and there are only two of us working here, Craig and me, and God knows where Craig is this afternoon. I take pity on Kip because most of camp has gone away now for Christmas, with only us poor remnants of the civilian staff left in case something bad happens somewhere in the world and supplies are needed. We had several emergencies last year, and yours truly was speedily packing crates with foot powder and toilet paper. Elite soldiers need toilet paper like anybody else.

I flick the door lock and an explosion of wind blasts in, like a thousand football fanatics crowding the gates until they give way. 'Come on in then,' I say, taking care not to sound too welcoming, and I walk off quickly, pulling up my collar. For days now, people on camp have been muffled up, grey, shapeless bundles shuffling along with their hands pushed down deep into their pockets, hunched against the bitter wind. We lose all our characteristics in the cold. In the rain, we scurry and fiddle with umbrellas. In the sun, we grow upright again and relax. But in the bone-cold, shoulders buried in our necks, heads covered, we're like ghosts.

A kingpin of his squadron by reputation if nothing else, everybody has heard of Kip. Playing against the huge, hulking, handsome, strong and silent geezer type, Kip Formby is short, stocky, serious and talks about himself without pausing for breath. I first met him when I worked in the kitchens down the road. 'Down the road' is what everyone calls the training camp, hidden away in the beautiful hills and woods of the countryside. The squadrons who were training there didn't really say much to staff in the kitchens. Straight off The Area – the hilly place where they train – filthy and wet and still wearing their gun holsters strapped to their legs, they shuffled along like a wartime ration queue snaking down the corridor, slab-faced, craning their necks around one another as they got nearer to the hotplate, hope fading as the mountain of chicken breasts or huge tray of steak pie diminished to the last portion. That was the thing about the 2-2 guys: elite and special they may be, but there's always an air of resignation and patience about them. Nobody complained about anything – except Kip.

One particular time when he wasn't on the list for a free lunch and had to fork out £1.94, which was the price of lunch, if you can believe it, he was so livid he pushed right behind the girl on the till, found me in the pastry room in the middle of some argy-bargy with Kayleigh, a girl I worked with, and demanded to know where the boss was so he could get his meal for free. I pointed him straight to the Warrant Officer in charge of catering. Seconds later out he came from the office, announcing stone-faced that he'd sorted it, and just to make his point he piled his tray with as much food as he could lay his hands on, which wasn't exactly the spirit of the place. It was a pyrrhic victory. I was used to his tantrums, so the next day I hovered around when the rest of his table had gone back onto The Area and told him gently that it was wrong of him to throw his weight about like that: we'd been given our instructions and he shouldn't undermine us. It wasn't my place to speak to him about this, but I'm not exactly the wilting type. To his credit he looked at the floor as I spoke, nodding like a priest hearing confession, then said, 'Fair enough.' Seconds later I was called away to wash some dishes, so it didn't get discussed any further. Anyway, it must have sunk in because the following day he marched into the cookhouse, headed for the charity box and rather ostentatiously stuffed a twenty-pound note into it, saying, 'Sorry for being an obnoxious shit.' That became a major topic of conversation on the camp, on and off, for the next few weeks.

That's what it's like there: like a spilled cup of coffee, a tiny bit of gossip leaks into every corner and crevice and you're still finding the stains in unlikely places, months later.

Kip gets himself and his dog inside, follows me down the narrow, dark corridor, peeling off his wet jacket, then gazes upwards and turns a complete circle, momentarily struck by how the corridor opens out as if into a cathedral.

'I've never been down here,' he says, surprised by the unexpected vastness of the place. He sounds like landed gentry who have lived on the estate for decades and only just realised that there are dozens of staff toiling away below stairs.

'Your luck's in. I couldn't leave you out there on a day like this, could I?' I say, adding, 'Oh, and you brought your dog.' I like dogs but this one marks its territory every time it comes in here and Kip just laughs about it.

'Yeah, well, what's one more little bitch in here?' he says, walking away with a mirthless chortle. That's his idea of a joke, and it sounds like he's been saving it up for a suitable moment. He goes off like an inquisitive toddler, peering into boxes, lifting stuff up and spoiling my ironic but innovative 'Padlock Recognition Area'. I hope he doesn't need something complicated.

'Hey, I've been wanting these for my NVGs!' he exclaims, picking up a small box of anti-static cleaning wipes for glasses. 'Can I have two packs?'

'You can't just take stuff,' I say. 'It's not a free shop.'

He puts his hands on his hips.

'Surely if it's urgent?'

He's trying it on. 'C'mon, Kip, how can it be urgent? You didn't even want them until you just saw them!' I say. 'Anyway, you can get night vision goggle cleaner from your own storeman – or even from the pound shop.'

He's already casting around at the rest of the shelves, inspecting canisters of gun oil.

'Yeah, but I'd have to go there,' he mutters over his shoulder. He can't even be bothered to turn and look at me.

'What did you actually come in for, anyway?' I ask, picking up some delivery notes and starting to arrange them on the table. 'I thought you'd be full-on with Selection down there?'

'No, I teach the final phase.' He turns around, hands on hips, then takes a deep breath as if he's about to burst into an operatic aria. His face looks like he's expecting trouble but he does at least look at me this time.

'I don't suppose you've got bubble-wrap?'

So that's why he's here.

'And some packing tape and a couple of brown boxes?' I ask, softening. He's about to tell me his marriage has fallen apart.

'Fifteen years and three kids,' he mutters. 'The missus wants to go home to her mum. Hates Hereford, same old story. And she's taking the kids.' He slaps a hand on the bubble-wrap. 'And I'm helping her to fucking pack! Moving back to her family, then I'm moving into one room on camp. One fucking room!'

His voice is low, almost talking to himself. It's a shock to see him like this, no longer the 'obnoxious shit' or figure of fun he's usually seen as. I lower the clipboard and cross my hands over it. These guys might be elite and special and all that, but their relationships are terrible. I want to hear his story. He leans against the wall, slumped, sinking, almost liquefied. He's undeniably good-looking and I don't suppose this would be news to him. His Irish looks, the black hair and blue eyes are stunning and he's clean-shaven, which is quite unusual round here. Combats is all I've ever seen him in – today he wears a green base layer and his security pass has been shoved into his breast pocket. His body is like most of the other geezers, not bulging with muscles but wiry, with the good bum they all have from carrying those heavy backpacks on the hills. His face, on the other hand, serving no useful purpose to a soldier, is weathered, lined on the forehead, eyes wrinkled more than usual from squinting in the sun or creased against a blizzard. Many of these guys look a decade older than they are. Their lives are relentless. They miss their kids' birthdays, Father's Day, wedding anniversaries. I know men who come home from eight months away only to sort their kit and be sent somewhere else the very next day.

'Someone else?'

'God, no,' he says, looking at the floor. He seems miles away. 'Well, not me, anyway.'

I wait, listening to the creaking of the hangar, the noise of a helicopter outside, the familiar sound of the garrison fire engine, off for a cruise around camp.

'D'you know Mike Peller?' he asks suddenly.

'Er, don't think so. Who does he play for?'

I know perfectly well who Mike Peller is. He's bedded every wife here, and their sisters too. Kip doesn't reply but his eyes shoot up, as mine do, as a strong gust of wind hits the hangar. It sounds like someone's dropped a bomb on us.

I rub my freezing hands together. It'll be dark soon. The dim corners of this clanking, cheerless coffin of a place seem appropriate in a strange sort of way. I can't begin to tell you how depressing it can be to work here. We can't even leave camp until the end of the day. The gloom is a suitable backdrop for Kip's misery and mirrors my dim future and lack of prospects, working all day for less than eight pounds an hour in this grim, huge, lonely store on a charmless army base. Despite our very different lives, right now Kip Formby and I have more in common than either of us might think.

We're interrupted by another beep at the front door. Christ, Kip didn't lock it behind him. Another blast of litter and dust swirling into the store. Kip heads off, throwing a tennis ball for his dog. Around the corner slides Jim, one of the top men in the Regiment. He organises important things, they say. People like Jim have their own agenda and down tools for a break and change of scene whenever they feel like it – and that usually means turning up here.

'Hi, Monica.' Jim has a silvery, smooth, seedy New Zealand drawl and a slow, wide smile.

'Join the party,' I say, gesturing to the vacant, echoing store in a wide arc. 'We're closed, by the way.'

'Yeah. Sorry.' Jim is just-about good-looking, his sex appeal hanging on by a thread. He smells stale, like he's been sleeping on a park bench for six months. He smells like a man too busy doing important things to wreck his schedule by washing. He leans a shoulder against the wall and reaches into a pocket for a packet of chewing gum, pushing out a piece to me. I shake my head.

'Going somewhere special?' He looks at my outfit, grinning.

'Oh, ha-ha. Very funny,' I say. I'm wearing regulation steel-capped boots and heavy-duty gloves, and my dusty black trousers have orange blotches from splashed chemicals. I lean over and brush them down.

'No, you look good, Monica, honestly. Must be your healthy diet.' He winks. 'God knows what goes down that sweet throat of yours.'

I say nothing but give him a pleasant smile.

'Nah…' Jim uncrosses his arms and straightens, running a hand over his face and blinking as if he's trying to wake up. 'You're a good girl, Mon, you know that?'

'Yes, I know.'

'No, really. You're a lovely person.' He takes out another piece of gum and spits out the first piece into the dustbin nearby. He looks around. 'You've done wonders with this place. Never smelled so good, with you wafting that scent of yours around.'

'Thanks. Have to smell good – what with all you men coming in here straight from the range.'

'Testosterone, Mon. Tons of it,' he says.

Is he flirting with me? I need to call a halt to all this.

'Is there something I can get for you, Jim?'

'The missus fucked off, by the way.'

'What?' It takes a second to register. Then the news springs me into life. 'Jim, that's awful. Your wife's left you? Seriously? I'm so sorry. Are you OK?' I reach out and stroke his arm, like stroking a cat; a reflex action.

'No, it's all good. It's fine.' He smiles, looking at me intensely.

It's not fine. I can see that.

'No woman can tolerate my life,' he says. His eyes are clouded and red-rimmed.

'Do you just want to sit for a while? You can use the office, I've got things to do – if you're just wanting a bit of a break?'

'Nah. Thought there might be a brew going. We haven't any milk and the cookhouse isn't open for – ' he glances at his watch – 'fuck! Three hours!'

'You came in for a brew? I can't make you tea, Jim. I'm so sorry. I'd love one myself but there's no milk here either.'

'Oh, OK.' He looks around, considering his options.

'Sorry.'

For Jim, this is a lively conversation. When I first met him last year, when he was setting up his 'village' next door, he said yes and he said no and he nodded, but that was it.

'I'm off again on Friday,' he says.

I wish I could have offered him a cup of tea. And Kip too. Two bleeding hearts at Christmas, of all times. Two of the most elite soldiers in the world, and both are broken spirits about to spend Christmas in one sort of hellhole or another.

'Off anywhere nice, Jim?' I say. 'Christmas break?'

He lifts his arm limply and makes a gun shape with his fist and forefinger, simulating pulling a trigger.

'Nah. Out of the country. Eight months.' He finds the button for the roller door. 'And you wouldn't go there on your holiday.' And he's gone.

When the door rolls up it reveals two young guys, huddled against the wall outside. They straighten and stretch like cats who have waited at the front door all night, knowing that at some point, someone will open it and let them in. Jason and Chris are newly badged. They flash the dazzling smiles of men who haven't yet grasped the significance, and the burden, of their new regimental identity.

'Hello, boys,' I say. 'You know we're closed?'

'Any chance of a padlock?' asks Jason, jauntily.

'And for you?' I turn my palm towards Chris, as if taking his order in a restaurant.

'Batteries?' says Chris.

I make the 'ragdoll' pose, hanging my arms limply. 'Well, it'll have to be quick,' I warn them.

'Love you, Monica, you're brilliant,' says Jason.

'I know, so for God's sake, get in!' I reply, waving my arm as if I'm directing traffic. 'Too much charm.' I hold down the button to close the roller door. 'Doing much at Christmas?'

'Nah, on standby,' says Jason.

Chris shakes his head. 'Bloody hate Christmas. I'll be in the gym. You?'

'I take it as it comes,' I say.

Chatting helps us all through a dull afternoon on camp and this is why I love working here. I thought there would be a 'them and us' culture, but far from it. We're all working to the same end; they couldn't do their job without me; I wouldn't have a job without them, and we all put up with hell.

I point the boys towards the padlock aisle then go to help Kip find his bubble-wrap.

'You must miss your old days?' he says. 'The glamour? Bet you looked good in your heels.'

I grimace, impatient. 'Who told you it was glamorous, Kip? Where did you get that from? The same people who say the Regiment are all huge, hulking, handsome adrenaline-fuelled killers?'

'Fair play, Mon.'

'Anyway, I'm a has-been. Think yourself lucky.'

Kip heaves the huge pack into the back of his car, pushing it along the seat. His dog jumps up onto the front passenger seat.

'You must tell me all about it one day. Your, um ...' He reaches for the word.

'My backstory?'

'Yeah. Ha-ha. I suppose.' He puts the car into gear. 'And the thing is, you may be a has-been – but at least you've *been*.' He winds the window down. 'Thanks for unlocking.'

'It's OK.'

Poor Kip. He doesn't give a toss about me or anyone, and why should he? His wife has just sacked him. I fold my arms, shivering and look around. Up in the branches of the trees I can see plastic bags, discarded just like Kip and Jim, flapping in the wind.

'Doing much for the rest of the day?' I say. 'Joining the lads in town?'

He reaches for the dashboard and waves a slip of paper at me.

'Nah, got a coupon from Waitrose for a free coffee and a mince pie. I'm on the pager. Probably drive down there later.'

'Waitrose, eh?' I say. 'You know how to live big-time, Kip. For one awful minute I thought you were going to say Asda.'

'Nobody would want my shit life,' he says and drives off.

'Last of the Big Spenders,' I shout after him over the gusting wind.

II

I'm getting ahead of myself. My name is Monica and I worked on camp in Herefordshire with the world-famous 22 Special Air Service Regiment between 2015 and 2018. I was only going to stay a few months over that first summer but somehow I was still there three years later. I saw the men every day and was struck by how their secret, almost paranoid existence is essentially a burden that they bear with good humour and fortitude. My story is a 'first' – written by a woman who was also an outsider to all things military. I bring you a true inside story of the SAS and Hereford Garrison not written as a soldier who is part of the scenery there, and for whom many things are commonplace, but as a person with a completely different experience of life. As a friend in the Regiment texted to me one evening after a tough day 'We are indoctrinated against violence to a degree – we forget how foreign and terrifying it is.' I hope I can paint you an entertaining and colourful picture of their life on camp as I experienced it and tell the stories of the men who live and work there.

The soldiers in this regiment are the SAS, but they call themselves 'geezers', or at least some of them do. The older ones don't seem to like the name. Otherwise, mostly they are called 'two-two', which I will write simply as 2-2, or 'badged', which refers to the famous winged dagger emblem. We'd say, 'Is he badged?' meaning 'Is he SAS?' because, to be fair, there's no real way of telling unless they're wearing their blue Regimental belt. They're usually in their own clothes on camp.

I've developed a kind of instinct around the geezers. I know when to hang around and chat and when to leave them to themselves. Some days I think they're like spoilt teenagers and other times they come across as tired of it all, but I don't say anything either way. Sometimes I listen to everything they have to say, like I did with Kip and Jim at Christmas, or I laugh and tell them not to be silly, but that's it. I saw Kip Formby in the garrison coffee shop not long after, being the same overbearing, ego-laden character he ever was, so maybe he got over his gloom at his wife leaving. And forlorn Jim? Well, I saw his missus hanging onto a lanky young bloke, the type with no bum and his trousers hanging off, gazing at him adoringly, proving that one person's trash is another's treasure. So who knows? Did their husbands deserve to be stayed with? The geezers are elite and special, of course, but they're never here, and there's only so much pining a wife can do.

Anyway, I know that people would love to know more about what it's like inside the camp, but due to the threat faced by members of the UK's Specialist Military Units, and the secrecy this imposes, I can't talk too much about the place. However, I *can* answer the question, 'What are the SAS really like?'

14

I had a ringside seat on their lives and I've got to tell you, it's not James Bond here. An important lesson I learned when talking about the Regiment is to discard stereotypes, and by that I'm thinking of the huge, hulking, handsome heroes – confident, restrained, cool yet explosive. That's the image, isn't it? Well, immersed in the Regiment daily I experienced the reality as it happened, and while there are certainly some huge and hulking men, some are short, shy, loud, jaunty and hilariously funny; others are grim and taciturn. There are black geezers, white geezers, flame-haired and freckly geezers, bald, blond and anything else you can think of: there's certainly no 'look'.

Camp itself isn't exactly glamorous, either. In fact, its dullness and lack of facilities was the first thing to really surprise me. I'm writing this in a gloomy, cold corridor of the quartermaster's department while I wait for a meeting and I'll tell you what I can see. The only light comes from the two emergency Fire Exit signs and a small, dirty window high up. The window is partially obscured by a huge faded 'Help for Heroes' poster dated 2007, featuring a topless glamour model. She's wearing a Regiment beret at a jaunty angle, tight shorts, a blue Regiment belt with the winged dagger slotted into it and she's giving a cheeky salute. Outside is the gym and the camp jet wash – a great perk of my job – and a group of drivers huddled at a picnic table, cradling mugs of tea and holding cigarettes between thumbs and forefingers, lit ends turned inwards towards nicotine-stained palms so it won't go out in the bitter wind. However bad the weather is, the drivers are always out there first thing for tea and a smoke. I've never seen a badged guy smoke. I'm not saying they don't, but

I've never seen it. The sky is a solid, deep blue and the clouds are huge and billowy, moving fast with the biting wind. I get up and rock back and forth on my frozen toes, shifting about to keep some life in my feet. I'm dying for a pee, but the nearest ladies is three hangars away and the meeting might start any minute. I cross my arms tightly and sit down again, hugging myself in the chill and tucking my feet under the bench. They hit a rodent box and I kick it out of the way. Bloody rats.

The first few days on camp were like corresponding with an online date. There's a period where you're chatting away with someone about your mutual passion for travel and saving pandas. Their profile photos are taken in the gym or of them cuddling their dog. Then you meet in real life and discover that he's got a £20,000 overdraft, is six inches shorter than he claimed and isn't divorced yet. You're faced with a completely different person. The Regiment is like this. TV programmes like to peddle the image of the typical geezer as a tough nut, able for anything, getting the job done at any cost and adept at parking their emotions. Secrecy leads to conjecture, for who really knows? The internet is crammed with speculative claims about these men that make me laugh out loud, and a small number of ex-Special Forces soldiers appear to act as their representatives in the media, for who's going to contradict them? The truth is, when you see the geezers on camp it's like a football match in an empty stadium, or a war film with the sound turned off. When you watch the elite soldiers walk past or queue for their lunch you don't think anything. It's not exciting or mysterious. They look like a bunch of film extras, if I'm being honest.

I'm not trying to set myself up as an expert here. I didn't experience their world with a professional's point of view. I'm not a historian or a psychologist: this account is exactly as I experienced it and no more. I saw it all for real, and for the first time you can read a true account of the personal stories of individual men whose lives are played out in one of the world's most secret, elite fighting forces. These are my judgements – I'm a mature woman who's no stranger to everyday human problems. We all have our own story and our own backstory, but we move in and out of other people's lives as well. I entered into the worlds of all these different men at different moments, almost like a camera moving in for a close-up and then pulling back, so each individual disappears into the mass. This story won't be from the point of view of the huge, hulking, handsome heroes in an action movie – you'll see the disappointed ones, men who failed when they thought they would succeed or who now are weighed down with the years they've served.

This book tells you the bits that didn't make it into the fairy-tale.

III

The camp announced itself on a peeling, faded sign simply as 'Training Area'; the upper part of the sign obscured by overgrown bushes. I wanted to lift the branches to see what the rest of the sign said, but there was old barbed wire in front of it. Set deep in the glorious Herefordshire countryside along a rambling lane connecting several pretty villages, it was a place I'd cycled past many times when I first moved here without ever properly noticing it. With sheep grazing as far as the eye could see on the hillside behind, then woods beyond, these dilapidated bunkers surrounded by ancient high-wire fences looked completely abandoned. A tatty-looking chain fence ran the few miles of the perimeter in front of lines of tall, thick pine trees. Where the fence had fallen or had gaps, it was draped in hessian or black plastic sheeting. The whole structure seemed held together by the lovely mile-long verge of purple loosestrife and pink campion, and huge white convolvulus flowers wound their way up the fences like decorations for a wedding. It provided a lush bucolic frieze against the scene behind the fence, where mangled scrap cars were piled up and the outer shell of a large building looked like one of those ambitious self-build projects that had run out of money. I once stood there for so long, propping up my bike on the fence and trying to peer through the gaps in the thick foliage, that a police car glided to a halt soundlessly beside me and two friendly policemen asked if I needed any help. I said no, thank you, I was just resting but my heart was pounding. Had I done something wrong? They stayed until I went on my way. As I picked up my bike again, I looked up. A tiny camera, no wider than a small pencil torch was attached to a telephone pole high above me. It turned and tipped downwards to look at me. Whatever lay behind that fence, they didn't want anyone to see it, however innocent their stop on the side of the road.

I know now what's behind that fence, through those trees where it looks so tranquil. Out there sits a small brick building, surrounded by a group of half-cylindrical structures that look like old wartime Nissen huts. You definitely wouldn't think that inside the building is a small workforce of local women gowned in black aprons, long black gloves and steel-reinforced boots, many of whom have been there for decades, sweating, scrubbing and mopping. You certainly wouldn't believe that nearby men are fighting two against one on the floor, or large groups of them are punching one person in the face repeatedly. Those men have bruises and black eyes and sometimes they're hoarse because someone tried to strangle them. They hobble in flip-flops because the skin on their feet is in shreds. They sleep in spartan dormitories with threadbare sheets, use one manky shower, queue for their rushed meal break and then are off out for more of the same. This goes on for weeks on end. Well, I was one of those women working in the brick building and the men being punished were selection candidates for the SAS and SBS Regiments of UK Special Forces.

My interview for the job had been back in January 2015. I'd been searching the internet on New Year's Day for a plumber to fix the catastrophic leak from my bathroom, and as I did so the search engine also found civil service jobs in the Hereford area. Bored, I clicked on the link and carried on scrolling and the next thing I knew I was looking at a job description that stated in bold: Open to UK Nationals Only.

Well – that was me. I didn't pick up on it being a kitchen job. All I knew was that this position was out in the countryside, somewhere I could reasonably drive to. I didn't connect it to the big army camp in Hereford. So I applied, and they must have been desperate because I was called to an interview two days later. The interviewer, a kindly shabby uncle type, glanced briefly at my CV before pushing it aside and saying, 'Well, you're rather overqualified but we'd love to have you.' Before I could ask anything he said he couldn't tell me much about the job in case I didn't pass the security vetting, so I didn't learn anything except that it was a job in a canteen serving people on training courses. Nervous and desperate not to mess up, I didn't ask any more. I thought the security vetting might take about a week; two weeks later I'd accepted that they didn't want me after all. Then, as I was getting into my car at Tesco, my mobile rang.

'Monica? My name's Michael.' He had a cheeky-chappie, smiley tone to his voice.

'Michael?' I wasn't really taking anything in.

'Michael Reeves. I'm the Warrant Officer – er – mess hand job? I'm in charge of Catering.'

'Yes?' I said. 'Oh, I mean YES! Hello?'

'Monica, I just wondered what size uniform you are?'

'Oh.' My heart was racing. 'Size eight. Why?'

'Shoe size?'

'Four,' I said. 'Er, may I ask why?'

'Haven't you got the letter yet?' he said breezily. 'We'd like to offer you the job. Subject to security clearance, of course.'

I was so excited I drove out and straight through a red light.

I didn't start straight away, of course. Security clearance vetting took from January to July so I didn't tell anyone about the job. I suppose I was embarrassed. My friends and former colleagues wouldn't have understood how I could go from a high-powered career travelling the world to washing dishes on minimum wage, but really it's not so unusual. To tell you the truth, I was burned-out. Reaching for the sky in your career and staying there comes at a cost. For seventeen years in my last job I'd operated at full throttle with barely a break. Seventeen years of deadlines. Seventeen years of coming up with the goods, being better than the competition, seventeen years of breathtaking responsibility – seventeen years of working weekends and into the night and not even a full week's holiday and, if this sounds familiar, this is pretty well the life of elite soldiers. When my job ended, there was no ambition left in me, no drive or desire for responsibility. I felt so defeated, I didn't work for four years.

'But what about your education?' my friends said when I finally told them about my kitchen job. 'All those qualifications? How could you possibly work with that class of person?'

That's what they said.

I dropped those friends. Plenty of us have a change in fortunes and the elite soldiers here didn't think it strange at all. Yes, they're experts in tough mindsets and awesome skillsets but plenty of ex-Regiment men face difficulties in civilian life, don't they, and end up homeless, sleeping on park benches, or in debt or drinking; they know it can happen to anyone. A job's a job they say, someone's got to clean the kitchen. We're all human and their attitude of total equality is why I like working here. Of all the people in my life, these elite, awesome soldiers were the least judgemental.

IV

The bus stopped half a mile from the camp gates, and I'd allowed plenty of time to cut across two fields on a public bridleway. It was a typical July morning, hot and humid and not really the day for a walk, but with the skylarks ascending and the gentle rustle of the corn, for those moments I knew what happiness was. With no direction in my life, the last four years had sapped my spirit, but today I was starting a new job, and relief and happiness were mingling together. It was like a wedding that has taken an age to plan, with arguments and spiralling costs, frustration and anger, and now it was the Big Day. All my troubles were forgotten in an instant; things were starting to go right.

I strode towards the guardhouse feeling giddy with happiness, tense with anticipation. A pasty-faced, overweight girl in her thirties leaned on the counter, eating a doughnut out of a paper wrapper, engaging in banter with a policeman in a side room. She offered him some Monster Munch from a family-sized bag, which he took enthusiastically, tipping his head back to drop each crisp in before sucking his fingers appreciatively. He explained to me that he was on his break and the other policeman would be here any second.

It wasn't what I was expecting. I still didn't know what they did here, but six months of vetting must mean it was something a bit secret. I'd assumed there would be scanner gates, CCTV cameras and sniffer dogs. I thought it would be like the security lane at an airport and I'd have to take my shoes and belt off or something.

Another policeman appeared. I handed him my passport and he picked up the phone, punching a few keys.

'I have – er – Monica …' He flipped my passport several ways against the light, balancing the telephone on his other shoulder.

'Lavers,' I offered.

He ignored me, listening to the person at the other end. 'Yep, that's right. Starting in the kitchen.'

A young, thin man wearing skinny jeans and trainers appeared from nowhere and introduced himself shyly as Lance Corporal Knight. Police dogs in the back of a nearby van erupted in an ear-splitting cacophony of barking as I was swiped through the gate. I followed him through a car park and round the back of another nondescript brick building. The corridors stretched off darkly in all directions, lined with white tiles, their lino floors still wet, freshly mopped with a pungent mix of disinfectant and bleach. It reminded me of one of those videogames where you turn this way and that and, every now and again, a huge gunfight breaks out. We glided round bends, through swing doors, past a vegetable preparation area where a line of chefs with ramrod-straight backs and vacant faces silently cut and sliced and shredded, not looking at me. The young man in front of me politely held doors open while keeping his back to me, expertly, like an automaton, never losing his stride. Nobody was talking. For a mad moment it felt like Dante's Inferno, each of the nine circles of hell more deranged and punishing than the last.

Lance Corporal Knight took me outside again to a building with a stable door and no signs of life. 'The boss will be along soon,' he said. 'I think he's still in the gym.' He looked at the ground as he said this, not making eye contact, then turned on his heel and walked away.

I didn't know if I was supposed to go in or wait outside. There was a child safety gate across the doorway and a gigantic dog on its hind legs, straining to get to me. I looked around. Green buildings were lined up like Lego bricks in a row, with a couple of car park areas and a vehicle mechanic bay. In the distance there was an imposing building that I took to be the gym. A rustling sound somewhere behind me made me start: seven tall, almost identical men wearing jeans and T-shirts, with short haircuts, several days' stubble and extensive tattoos on their arms, were standing close to the corner of a Portakabin, each waving one arm in the air. I looked around. I wasn't sure what to do: I couldn't go into the office because of the gate and the dog, but I couldn't turn and walk off again to the guardhouse. There was a low wall, but I didn't sit on it because it was damp and crumbling. I pretended to fiddle with my watch. My excitement had evaporated completely. The breeze was messing up my hair and I wasn't sure how long I should wait.

'You look lost,' said one of the men with a bright smile and gleaming white teeth.

I felt a hundred miles from home. I'd been up since four o'clock in the morning due to the excitement of the day and it was beginning to catch up with me. I hadn't eaten or drunk anything for hours and felt suddenly drained of energy. This wasn't just another day, starting a new job: I had waited anxiously for six months to know if I would be cleared by security vetting. During those months I had scoured my house for documents, certificates, references, details of relatives long-dead, realising that I had no idea where my late parents had been born, and in between I had waited, wondering if something had gone wrong and the job was meant for someone else.

'Don't freak out,' he went on. 'It's just that the only mobile signal is right here.'

I came to, wrenching my thoughts back to engage with my surroundings. Ah yes, I was inside that long fence. Last time I'd been on the outside, wondering what it would be like. Now I knew.

He rapped a knuckle on the Portakabin wall. 'See?' He showed me his phone. 'Three bars.'

'I'm not lost,' I said. 'I start work here today and I'm waiting for someone to collect me.'

'Oh yeah?' said one of the others. 'You actually chose to come and work here?'

They all laughed, looking at me with identical smiles, identical white teeth, a friendly demeanour that I didn't trust; it was as if I were on a film set, with actors dressed for parts I didn't recognise. The whole thing was incongruous.

'Funny place to not get a signal,' I said, waving my arm towards a series of tall poles with red lights on top to warn aircraft.

'Yeah, great comms. Doesn't work on mobiles, though.'

As the seconds ticked on and I contemplated going back to the guardhouse to tell them I'd been forgotten, a tall, balding figure appeared across the grassed area, jogging towards me, beaming. He raised a hand.

'Sorry!' he panted from ten yards away. 'My rehab session. Ran late. I'm Michael.' He ran a sleeve across his damp face. 'Sorry. I'm a bit sweaty.'

He wiped his hand down his shorts before shaking mine. His other hand was holding his phone away from his face. He held up a finger – 'Hang on a minute,' – and walked away a few yards to maintain some privacy.

'Fuck, mate, I mean, what's the fucking point?' he said into the phone. 'You know what those wankers are like, mate, don't expect anything before next fucking Easter. Anyway, mate, I've got stuff to do, someone waiting, no honestly... yep... yep... No dramas, mate... yep... yep... get those tickets even if you have to sell your kids. Bye. Oh, me? Er, tonight. Yep, ha-ha, tonight!. OK. Bye... bye... bye...'

'Oh God!' he exclaimed, slumping his shoulders in mock exhaustion, and sticking the mobile into his trouser pocket. He took a deep sigh. 'Sorry. Sorry, sorry.' He turned to unlock the child gate and gripped his dog by its collar, shoving him into a kitchen and shutting the door decisively.

'Inexcusable. God, sorry. Come right on in. That whole rehab thing went on for too long. My ankle's been fucked – broken, sorry –' he smiled sheepishly and fiddled for a key. 'Sorry.'

He was wearing a madras checked shirt with sleeves rolled right up over impressive biceps, cargo shorts and open sandals. I'd never thought before about the significance of uniforms, but right now I could have done with a few stripes to tell me where this guy stood on the hierarchy scale. He could have been anyone. I suppose that was the point.

'So.' He bustled about with his bag, taking things out and shoving them quickly into the desk drawer as if they were pornographic. 'Sit wherever you can.' He waved an arm at the room. 'We haven't had cleaners here for months – short of staff.'

'I was going to say, are you preserving a crime scene?' I remarked in a weak shot at lightening the mood, which I instantly regretted.

He looked mystified for a second. 'Sorry. Um – coffee?'

'No, thanks.'

'Water? Bloody hot out there.'

'No, honestly, thanks, I'm fine.' I was consciously checking myself, making sure that my back was straight, my face alert and interested.

'Well, I'm Michael. Welcome to our little camp.'

The walls of his office had lots of charts on them, holidays and dates of meetings, colour-coded. There were military terms for things like CTC, SERE, CQB, Op this and Op that. Perhaps I didn't really recognise it all then. I don't really know what I thought that day when I was still suspended between two lives, not sure which road to take. I was still invisible. Nobody, except one friend, even knew where I would be working and spending my days. I did know that I had a new part to play and, after all, we're all playing a part of some kind, aren't we?

'So –' Michael spread his hands as if introducing a bridal couple at the altar. 'I thought it would be best if you came late morning as there's a natural break just before lunch.'

He was fiddling about on his desk, lifting piles of folders and letters and scraps of paper, and then let out a nervous laugh.

'Hate to be a dickhead,' he said, shuffling a bunch of papers around, 'but I can't remember your... oh, right! Here we are. Monica!' He held a sheet of paper aloft. 'Sorry. I know it was Monica. Just checking the – er... ' He was anxiously scanning my details then gave up. 'Well, we've been looking forward to meeting you.'

Michael looked up and gave that sweet smile again. 'It's been busy in here and we've been short-handed, so you're our saviour.'

'Oh, well, I hope so,' I said bashfully. I crossed and re-crossed my legs a couple of times and folded my arms, then thought better of it and left them meekly in my lap. My heart was beating heavily.

'So, yes, er, Monica, welcome. Do you know what we do here?'

Until then, I'd thought the camp was something like Outward Bound or Army Cadets, perhaps military reserves on weekend training. I hadn't thought too much about who the people on the camp were: it genuinely didn't occur to me during the interview process that it could be a special regiment because it all seemed a bit amateur and Heath-Robinson – held together with sticky tape. Now, my mind was going in several directions at once.

'This is where the SAS and other elite regiments train. You don't need to concern yourself with what they do,' Michael went on, 'but they volunteer from other parts of the army and navy, and they go through selection. Some soldiers will live here for six months. Others will come here for weeks at a time for further specialised training and exercises. Our job is to feed them. That means three meals a day plus packed meals, night trays and so on.'

He reached for two chocolate digestives from an open pack, holding them in his teeth as he offered the packet to me. I shook my head, no thank you.

'My blood sugar levels are a bit low,' he said. 'No breakfast.'

'Of course.'

'So, that's the Units,' he said through the crumbs. 'They live here for the six months. Others will come for weeks at a time for further specialised training and exercises.'

As I digested this staggering information about the camp, Michael rattled through a few things about health and safety training, fire safety and the number of inspections they had to undergo. I asked about shift patterns and weekend working. He pulled another biscuit from the packet and looked at me. 'The Master Chef and I – he's called T, by the way, long name – anyway, T and I draw up the shift rota for each month, but the girls – the other mess hands like you, I mean – they sort it all out between themselves.'

He straightened the papers on his desk and I sensed that he'd finished with me.

'So anyway, you'll get the hang of it, Monica. You'll have to work two weekends out of four, OK?'

Michael stood up, so I did too. I knew that face. He was desperate to get off.

'Look, I'm sorry it's all been a rush,' he said, 'but hopefully you'll love us, and you'll be here for years and years, so we can catch up properly soon.' Then he added, 'When I'm showered and better company!'

The young Lance Corporal must have been waiting behind the door in the outer office because he appeared instantly. 'Knighty will look after you. And here's a present.'

Michael reached behind to a pile of navy-blue garments. On top was a pair of serious-looking, black lace-up boots with steel toecaps.

'If you get changed into your safety gear around the corner in the toilet, Knighty will take you straight to the kitchen. There will be a locker room there for your stuff.' He paused to tuck his shirt in. 'You'll have a security briefing soon to get your permanent security pass. Oh, and by the way, we park our cars nose-out. It's just a thing here, OK?'

Uniforms take away our identity, which can be good or bad depending on what you want to achieve, and a few minutes later I was wearing the uniform of a civil service member of an elite unit. Five minutes after that, my status was reinforced when I was introduced to two of the army chefs, in the vast place they called the Meat Room.

'Heyyyyy – everyone!' called out Knighty, arm outstretched to introduce me. 'Say helloooo to Mon-eee-ka! She's the new mess hand!'

Everybody stopped and looked over to me, then, uninterested, carried on with what they were doing. A grey-haired woman was sweeping the floor and a short guy in chef's whites and a small red bellboy-style cap was standing by a sink, sharpening a carving knife. He gave a smile and tipped his head back a little, asking me to come closer as it was noisy.

'Hey, Monicaaaaa,' he purred. 'I'm Devnand. I'm Corporal here. Mind if I ask you a question?'

'Course not,' I replied.

'Are your tits real?'

A loud shriek came from a side room and a large lady in her fifties poked her face out. She had frizzled, damp, dyed black hair, with two inches of white roots showing, a gash of red lipstick on her red face and was wearing a black voluminous apron. She grinned maniacally, eyes blazing, then came into the room and struck a crude pose against the white-tiled walls, patting her hair like a stripper.

'You want anal, Moe?' laughed the short chef guy, thrusting his crotch at her.

Knighty glanced at the guy. 'Give it a rest, Dev,' he said, winking. 'It's Monica's first day.'

'Yay! Monica!' Moe yelled at me. 'Welcome to hell!'

V

My first weeks in the kitchen were a nightmare. I felt as if I had been jerked out of civilisation and thrown into a primordial world where there was no peace, no rest, just constant, ever-present anxiety. I felt anxious going to work and anxious when I got home, knowing I would have to go back. Days off were meaningless because I counted the hours until I was back in that hellhole.

The kitchen was a wall of noise and all the equipment looked medieval; particularly the thing called a bratt pan, which we had to tip up to clean using a hand-cranked wheel (sixty-two turns each way, I counted them). 'Pan bash' was a small, dim, grimy room where we mess hands waded through scraps of food and blood from meat preparation. Hot water would fly everywhere as scrubbed pans were thrown sideways into a rinsing and draining area. The three sinks were so deep that I felt I was being lowered into them with only my armpits hanging over the top. You could switch on the taps, leave them running while you took off your coat and had a coffee and they would still be only half full when you came back. Plates section was where the men scraped their leftovers into binbags and stacked up their dirty plates, putting their cutlery into a washing-up bowl of soapy water. For two hours straight I would wash dishes with my fringe stuck to my forehead, dripping sweat into the sinks. I'd look out through the plate room serving hatch and see the men sitting there, hair sweaty like mine, combats wet with rain or covered in mud. There was nothing elite about this process, not for us and not for the soldiers.

I'll never forget my first contact with one of the men, dressed all in black with his gun holster strapped to his thigh, body armour covering his torso. He dipped his head under the hatch with an imploring look on his face.

'Have you got any of the creamy yogurts?' he asked. 'Because there's only the low-fat ones out there today.'

'I'm sorry,' I told him, 'but it's one each, and some of you have been taking two so we ran out. Sorry.'

There were nine mess hands working in rotas across two eight-and-a-half-hour shifts each day. Usually there were three of us on each shift, and three chefs with different responsibilities for the day, like desserts or soups. At lunchtime the two shifts amalgamated for a couple of hours before the early shift went home at two o'clock, and that was when the worst of the sniping and bitching would start. The kitchen was small, divided into separate sections for washing plates, scrubbing pans and managing the dining room. The mess hands worked on a rota system which we agreed between us, but whatever area we were on that day, it was dominated by sweeping and mopping between mealtimes and emptying the huge, heavy binbags, which needed doing every hour. The only word I could think of to describe it was drudgery. We lumbered about in a weird waltz around one another, up and down the kitchen, carrying plates, fetching fruit for the dining room, filling bowls of this and that, replenishing tomato sauce or teabags or paper napkins. Even scrubbing the pans, which were massive, became a job one could settle into like a robot; swinging pans between sinks was almost hypnotic. It went on for hours. If there was a lull, you simply took off your long black gloves and stood outside pan bash, maybe watching a chef make soup or rice pudding. There were no set break times in our shifts, but I enjoyed these times and learned a lot about making proper stock or a decent omelette. These military chefs were generally quiet and stony-faced, moving almost mechanically, stiffly uniform in their starched whites and little red hats. They appeared from one side of the upper end of the kitchen and disappeared through the arch on the opposite side, gliding like figures in a cuckoo clock, in and out all day at the same pace.

The kitchen opened out into the dining room, which seated about ninety, and out there the men ate gratefully, enjoying every morsel. I saw the SAS cold and I saw them wrung out with sweat from arduous, backbreaking training but they were always polite. It was as if the morning had been a game and was now all forgotten as they talked about their children or their beekeeping hobby. Mostly they gossiped about each other, though, and that was funny to overhear. I was in the perfect position to observe.

What sort of person does nobody pay any attention to? Someone who can go about their business without anybody noticing because what they do is not interesting. Someone like me. We are not important. We're the kind of person you look at every day and never see. When I arrived in a navy polo top and trousers I would take the place of someone else who had been here wearing a navy polo top and trousers for twelve years, and nobody had noticed her either. These men train for a long time to be grey and unnoticeable, shadowy, but I had got it down to a fine art all by myself!

In those first weeks in the kitchen, the other staff mocked my 'posh' accent, asked if I'd been privately educated, suggested I'd never mopped a floor before. When I said no, I wasn't privately educated they asked where my accent came from. They laughed about me as I approached, said things like 'Stop swearing, Monica's coming' even though I'd never said a word about the constant swearing. I became mute. Expressionless. Nervy. I worked hard and made sure they couldn't complain about me.

If you have ever seen the acclaimed 1972 film *Deliverance*, you'll know that it sets out to portray a familiar, calm, safe world in a remote wilderness in America, populated by everyday country folk who are slowly revealed to be capable of brutality beyond belief. The film's four city-boy heroes, away for a weekend of fishing, are sodomised and subjected to feral, merciless and inbred behaviour for no apparent reason. It felt a bit like that in the kitchen on camp. Everybody looked normal but what they seemed capable of made me fearful of what bomb might be set off at any time. The 'banter' between some of the chefs and the younger mess hands felt intimidating to me and I worried that I might be grabbed, but they seemed to enjoy it. It could be quiet then somebody would throw down her rubber gloves and erupt into great jags of sobbing and shouting. The women were in their fifties and sixties and it upset me to see them breaking down, but it happened a lot.

There was also the general background noise of it all. The richer you are, the quieter your world becomes. The wealthy can live deep in the countryside, far from main roads or neighbours, or in a world of triple glazing and people who bring coffee to your desk so you don't need to stand in a kitchen and wait for the kettle. The rich drive quiet cars and travel first-class. That is a world away from the atmosphere on camp. Here, everyone does their own thing. They turn the radio up loud on some godforsaken channel without asking if anybody minds. They shout instead of talk, yell across a room rather than walk a few steps towards the person they're speaking to. Outside, the men on selection are being treated like animals, sworn at, pulled along, worked beyond what seems physically possible. I felt like an anthropologist studying a forgotten tribe.

God, it was tedious. Every morning I'd wake and wonder, what day is it? My alarm went off at four-thirty and by eleven-thirty, in that doldrums time before lunch service, we'd sit down at one of the dinner tables because a 'break' here just means not standing up. There's nothing we could do except wait for events to pick up and get us going again.

Sat at a chair, the long window facing the front gives us our only view of life outside. I feel limp. Not tired and not sleepy. I can't identify the feeling. We can't go outside – nobody says we can't, but we just *know*. I look at the thick pine woods stretching as far as I can see and listen to the gunfire and watch the helicopters landing. It's like watching television. Barbara nurses a cup of tea, hunched over. She's worked here for twenty-two years. Outside it's been drizzling for an hour and seems set in for the day.

'They didn't say anything about rain,' I say.

The clock on the wall ticks another minute away.

Barbara sighs. 'That poor lad's getting drenched,' she says.

We both fix our gaze on a figure a few yards from the window, with a black hood over his head, manacled, moving gingerly while being steered by two gnarl-faced men in black, the sort who are probably forty but have the faces of old men. The hooded guy stumbles, but they pull him up roughly by the scruff of his jacket. 'Get fucking up!' one shouts, then shouts again, louder, snarling into the guy's faceless head. *'GET THE FUCK UP!'* It's so loud, we can hear it in here.

'I put my washing out this morning, too,' says Barbara, looking at them in the rain. I sigh and re-cross my legs, which are aching.

'Yeah, so did I.'

Barbara looks at her cup of tea and takes a final swig, grimacing. 'Don't know what's wrong with these bloody teabags these days,' she says.

These men, they want to be here, the instructors told me when I first voiced dismay at their treatment. They can leave any time they like, they said. All the beasting and interrogation – they know it's going to happen.

Outside the door in the dark, narrow corridor, there's a tall blond guy who is always first in the queue. He never speaks and he looks away when he pays for his meal. Maybe he's anxious too? He has a baleful expression and today his black eye has turned purple and the weals on his neck are really coming out. It's some choking thing they do.

It's just fighting. We've all been through it, the chief instructor told me, but even so, poor guy. His face carries no hope of being let in and he's probably dying for something to eat. I shift my position in the chair so I can't see him.

I look up five minutes later and the blond guy's still there, staring at the noticeboard. There's nothing on it except the fire drill stuff. He is beginning to look like a dog nobody wants to adopt. He turns his blank gaze on me bleakly for a second with no hope left in his eyes, so I raise my left arm and tap the imaginary watch on my wrist, then raise both hands, fingers splayed. *Ten minutes.* He doesn't respond, but he disappears with the lumbering, dragging gait of a recalcitrant teenager who has been told he is damned well going to spend the day visiting churches with his parents, whether he likes it or not.

We always unlock bang on twelve. It's three minutes to, we're ready and the whole line of elite, fabled warriors stand out there in the rain, wet, cold and hungry. The queue snakes round as far as the gym, but Shelley looks at the clock and says, 'Make 'em fucking wait.' I once took pity on them and unlocked a few minutes early; I've been called 'arse-licker' ever since. 'Those fucking two-two bastards,' says Dev. 'Pampered cunts – who the hell do they think they are?'

What a load of nutters there are in here. I couldn't believe it the first day I started. I'm sitting here with the corners of my mouth fashioning a sort-of smile, the effort from holding this pleasant face wearing me out in a strange way, but if I don't fix this expression I look bewildered, fearful. I checked in the locker-room mirror. The other mess hands have no idea of the uncharitable thoughts swilling around in my mind. The older ladies are respectful in a resentful way, but the younger ones despise any concessions to the Regiment's status. To me they seem like parasites, sucking the blood out of the place, despising every atom of it yet clinging on, year after year, taking the pay, helping themselves to chocolate bars from the rations store, stuffing their faces all day long because they feel it's their right. I'd no idea it was going to be like this. We're out in the countryside, the sun is shining and it's so beautiful here, far from the main HQ. Yet all I can see is people being dragged about or sworn at. When they come into lunch all beaten up with bloody feet I used to flinch, but not now. I've only been here four weeks and it doesn't even bother me anymore.

From the back of a van marked POLICE DOGS deafening barking erupts and I see a poor guy nearby cowering at the noise. He's got his hands tied and he reaches out for help, but all he gets is a shove in the back. Shelley comes back from her fag-break and collapses onto a chair next to us.

'Jeez, do I have a headache,' she says, pressing her fists into her eyes. 'I was slaughtered last night. My bum in that dress looked like a fucking Bulgarian meat-packer, Barb.' She straightens up, tearing open a family pack of Penguin biscuits and shaking her shoulders as if to stay awake. She's massive. She reaches into her top to hoist up her bra strap and asks Barbara if her boobs are even, moving them around like she's guessing their weight, and inspecting her reflection in the coffee machine.

Outside a car that's had its engine running for over an hour is keeping some equipment charged-up. Next to it, two men wearing identical shirts and shorts, full-sleeve tattoos and sunglasses are leaning in the doorway of one of the huts, mirroring one another's stance, chatting in a languorous kind of way like strangers in a bus queue. They're Directing Staff (DS) on one of the specialist surveillance courses but they look like they could be anyone, which I suppose is what they want people to think.

Some soldiers from the green army were in for breakfast this morning – we don't see them here very often. They eat like it's going to be taken away from them, crouching over their plates and leaving a mess on the floor. If they don't want the burger bun they take it anyway and chuck it into the bin later. Their language is different from the badged men too. 'We've been told to get a brew kit,' says one, or 'We're not allowed to go in there,' from another, passing responsibility for their request to a higher authority. Badged men don't talk like that. It would be wrong to suggest that elite soldiers draw an immediate profit from their elevation to this regiment, but from the moment they take on the sand-coloured beret and blue belt it seems as if a process of refinement occurs and they behave just the right side of courtesy. They'll ask the chefs to kindly remove the burger bun so that it might be usefully used elsewhere. I wonder if they are taught these things? Maybe it's like a servant in a royal household developing a taste for caviar and fine wines because they eat the leftovers on their employer's plates and drink the dregs of the finest the cellar has to offer? I don't know what it is, but they behave like a different class of soldier, which of course they are.

Two minutes to twelve. God, I ache. There's a low hubbub out in the corridor from the queue. Devnand slides around the corner.

'Am I missing something, ladies? Any chance of a lesbian mud fight?' He shoves an arm round my shoulders. 'Still need a good seeing-to, Mon? Hey, why aren't you calling me Dev? All my favourite friends call me Dev. Nepal's cream of the crop, that's me. I'll give you one of our hard-boiled eggs from the sandwiches, shall I?' He thrusts his hips several times and the others laugh. 'You like things *hard,* don't you, Mon? Don't you? Hard as a rock? I'll give you hard!' He waves a hand with a grasping gesture near to his genitals.

I stand there silently with that plastered-on smile. What else can I do?

Andy comes around the corner with a pudding bowl of roast potatoes he's just taken from the hotplate, stuffing them into his mouth whole. Honestly, you wouldn't believe it, he's a Staff Sergeant and the Master Chef but he looks a total disgrace. He shuffles about in baggy prison-style jogging bottoms and is as coarse and disgusting as Dev.

'Hellooah! Laydeez!' he leers, in his thick Geordie accent. He reaches round the back of his pants, spreads his legs menacingly, then scratches.

'Woo-hoo, Andy,' Shelley says. 'How's the arsehole today?'

'Fucking ring of fucking fire, mate. Hey, M, you haven't seen my operation have you? On my arsehole? It is ulcerated to *fuck*!'

The queue is getting longer, the rain heavier. Shelley is at the window, hands on the glass, breath steaming it up.

'Go on, Marcus! Fucking kick the bastards in the balls!' she shouts. Nobody can hear her. Marcus is one of the chief interrogators, retired from the Regiment but still filling those blindfolded men with terror.

'They're off to the gym next,' Kayleigh says, gloating. 'For interrogation.'

VI

I went to see the boss. I gave Michael advance warning that it might amuse him and that was okay, then I mentioned the tits comment. He didn't smile. I added the hardboiled egg jibes and a couple more. I said I was genuinely trying my best and the job wasn't difficult, but being called posh all the time and the sexual remarks made me uncomfortable and I wasn't sure what he thought. Was I being too sensitive for this place?

Michael leaned forwards and clasped his hands. His steely blue eyes were hard, and for once I could see that he was genuinely concerned. He held up both hands.

'I'd like to keep this within this unit, Monica,' he said. 'But I will go and speak to Devnand and the others. It's unacceptable, they know that.' He leaned back again.

'I'd rather we just moved on and I promise you, this won't happen again. Dev won't want this against his record. It makes him look bad, and to be honest, Monica, it makes me look bad too. I'm afraid that with Dev what you see is what you get.'

Which isn't saying much, I thought.

'I will sort this, Monica, you have my promise.'

The next day I was on lates, starting at twelve, and today it was me and Kayleigh. We usually went straight to sweep out the veg and meat rooms and change the bursting binbags while the morning staff sat down for ten minutes. Kayleigh was just twenty, tall and vaguely Scandinavian-looking but not someone I was particularly friendly with. To make matters worse, she was close with Shelley, the coarse one.

The pastry room was its usual mess. Kayleigh and I mopped in wide sideways sweeps from opposite ends of the room, pushing the mop under the worktops, pulling out the gigantic fridges.

'Monica?' Kayleigh said in a sing-song voice, glancing over briefly at the long line of soldiers shuffling into the dining room silently.

'Yep?' I was concentrating hard on getting into a tight corner under one of the work surfaces.

'Did you know what working on an army camp would be like?'

'What d'you mean?' I carried on mopping, pulling the huge fridge back into place.

'Like ...' There was a long pause. I kept mopping. 'Like ... well, do you know that soldiers do a lot of, like, *banter*, Monica? I mean, it's part of life here and like ... I heard you were like, well ... you complained?'

I straightened up, red-faced. I finger-combed my fringe back to where it should be and pulled down my polo top. My chat to Michael had obviously done the rounds.

'I'd like to be able to say no,' I said in a low voice, 'but yes, I did. I'm sick of all the sex talk. It's not appropriate in a workplace, is it?' I kept my gaze on Kayleigh, leaning on my mop.

'Yeah, but this place is, like, *different*?' she said, with that irritating upward, final inflection they all use these days, as if trying to explain to a small child. She gazed out of the window momentarily again, as if searching for examples of how it was different from anywhere else.

'You couldn't do it in Marks and Spencer,' I went on. 'If we worked in any shop, any doctor's surgery, any hairdresser, we couldn't spend all day swearing and talking about tits.'

Kayleigh chuckled. 'Oh, Monica, you don't know *anything*,' she said, smugly. 'Course they do. Anyway, you went running to Michael.'

'*Running to Michael?*'

She started fiddling with her topknot, pulling out a few hairgrips and the band, letting it fall to her waist, then starting to twist it back up again.

'Yes, you ran to Michael to complain, Monica,' she said, studying her split ends.

'He's the boss,' I replied.

'No, I mean, you shouldn't have spoken about it to anyone,' she said, getting shrill.

She was having another go at twisting her hair up, moving to look at her reflection in the metallic fridge door. Two young guys wearing jeans and trainers popped their heads uncertainly around the door holding several large green canisters called Norwegians.

'Er – we've been told to get a brew kit,' said one. He had a cheeky face and floppy hair but he looked hesitant, unsure. He must be from the green army, I thought. I straightened up.

'Brew kit?' I said. 'Have you just come all the way through the kitchen? Who let you through?'

'Woman on the till. She said to ask one of you cos she's busy.'

'Hmm.' I could hear plates rattling, and a draught through to our end told me that someone had wedged the dining room door open, which could only mean one thing: the queue was long.

'OK,' I said. 'Who's it for?'

'We're on SERE.'

That was Survival, Evasion, Resistance and Escape.

'Oh, right,' I said. 'See that big round thing between the ovens?'

I stepped to the archway between sections and pointed to the middle of the kitchen. The chefs were standing meekly by the hotplate in their immaculate, freshly starched whites looking a mile away from the coarse loudmouths they'd been all morning.

'That's a water boiler. Fill up from that. And see those chefs? Ask one of them for teabags and some milk and sugar. They'll help. Oh, and be careful when you open that lid, the water is actually boiling inside it, right to the top. Best use a pan to scoop it out.'

Looking down to the hotplate, I saw a long queue of dirty-faced, greasy-haired men from the specialist units eagerly forking chicken breasts onto their plates. I felt sorry for the selection lot, or the vehicle mechanics or even these lads on SERE, come to think of it – there'd be nothing left, and this wasn't a running buffet. We locked up again bang on one o'clock.

I turned to resume my task.

'Thing is, Monica,' said Kayleigh, coming back to the subject with a mouthful of hair grips, 'I came to this job because there'd be some banter. You know, like ... it'd be fun? Not deadly serious all the time.'

I started changing the binbags.

'Not serious? I take my job seriously, Kayleigh.'

She turned around. We were squared up to one another now, several yards away across the wet floor. I felt the yawning gap of aspirations, experience, hopes and fears. My fear that the place was a brawling bear-pit of inappropriate sexual connotations, and Kayleigh's fear that it wasn't.

I could hear boots coming down the passageway. A combat-clad figure with gun holster strapped to his thigh stood in the archway between this room and the cooking area. He struck his usual pose, hands on hips and for a second it was an almost surreal image, the gleaming white tiles as far as you could see, the shining steel ovens in the background, the white-clad chefs standing to attention in a pristine row and this huge, camouflaged figure in the foreground, dirt across his chest, legs planted, face lifted to the light, like a Soviet propaganda, Neo-Romantic image, 'Triumph of the Will' promoting values of duty and devotion, bound to blood and soil.

It was Kip Formby.

'Where's the gaffer?'

'You can't come in here like that, Kip,' I told him, moving at pace, flapping my arms as if a bunch of chickens had escaped into the kitchen.

'Why not?' he snapped. 'I've got a blue belt – I can do what I like.' He smiled at that, knowing it was ridiculous, but he went on irritably, 'I've been asked to pay £1.94 for my fucking lunch, Mon, and I should be on the list.'

My heart sank.

'For God's sake, Kip,' I said, 'there's always a complaint with you. And there's no reason for filthy language – a man of your calibre. I don't write the list, sorry. There's been a bit of a thing about it and the boss has decided no exceptions. Take it up with him.'

'Yeah, yeah – so where is he?'

'And you can't just go adding your name to the bottom of the list either.' This was something a lot of geezers did – added themselves to the list of free meals until there was a long line of names right round to another side of A4. Michael had cracked down.

'OK, Hitler,' he said. 'I'm going to sort this.'

'Office just behind you, down the corridor on your right.'

'Oh and by the way –' he swung round – 'what's his fucking name?'

'Are you going to stop swearing?'

The fire doors behind me clanked open and Steve, another senior instructor, one of the nice ones, relentlessly handsome and boyish with his dark colouring and infectious smile, despite the generous spattering of mud flecks, came so timidly around the door that without the camouflage outfit he could have been a priest. Steve was retiring by nature, never one to make a fuss; in truth, never wanting to be seen at all. Had he stayed in Jamaica he would have studied music and philosophy: Kip would have wrestled bears. Yet both were equals, elite soldiers with special skills, which just went to show that an important part of understanding the Regiment was to discard stereotypes.

'Steve?'

'Sorry, M,' he said. 'I didn't want to come in through the kitchen, thought it would be better this way – ' he looked down at his chest – 'as I'm a bit dirty, sorry.'

Behind me, Kayleigh was huddled with another chef, heads together, roaring with laughter at a video series of epic fails he'd brought up on his phone.

'Steve, mate!' Kip raised a hand.

'Kip!' said Steve, calling across me and smiling broadly. 'What are you doing here?'

'Trying to get my fucking lunch sorted... you on duty?'

This was ridiculous. Kayleigh was ignoring her work and the low hubbub beyond in the dining room had reached a crescendo. I stuck out my arms like a boxing referee holding the two opponents apart.

'Kip! Steve!' I said. 'You have to get out of this kitchen. Steve, I'll sort you out in a sec. Kip – his name's T.'

'Who?'

'The gaffer!'

Kip marched off. I swivelled round to Steve.

'It's OK, Steve. Can I help?'

'Yeah, well, sorry. It's about breakfast today.'

'Breakfast? I've only just come on, Steve – I wasn't here. And by the way, could you just use the hand sanitiser?'

'Oh. Oh yeah, course,' he said, springing to the sanitiser. 'I'm not touching anything.'

'Even so.'

Steve pumped the gel onto a palm, wrung his hands together, then wiped them across his chest absent-mindedly.

'Steve!'

'Sorry!' He held up his hands like a surgeon, trying not to touch anything, and launched into a story about

Weetabix. Seriously, *Weetabix*. I remember now, thinking back, how loud the place suddenly seemed. I had one eye on Kip, who was shuffling about irritably in the corridor as T was pointing out things on a clipboard. Another part of me was listening to Steve, who had an imploring look on his face. In the distance Dev looked anxious. Kayleigh was laughing as the pastry chef flicked through his phone. Out in the dining room I could see a line of camouflaged figures, heads bent to view the range of food. Some of them clutched paper plates. Oh my God, I thought, they've broken open the boxes of paper plates now.

'Thanks, Mon. You're genius.' I must have said something to Steve, but the low noise was making me anxious. He gave me a wide, winning smile.

I shook my head.

'Please, just go now and get your lunch. There'll be nothing left.'

'Thanks, so, so much.' He almost backed out of the kitchen holding his hands out, still sanitised.

I turned to Kayleigh, who was sliding down from her perch, cackling. The young chef was fiddling around now putting jam onto two Victoria sponges for the evening meal. She was poking a finger into the jam and licking it off. Out in the dining room it was still hectic. I picked up my mop and bucket.

'As I say, Kayleigh, I take the job seriously. There's no place here for sexual banter, I don't care what anyone says. And Michael agrees, by the way.'

Kayleigh looked at me, blank.

'I don't understand a word you're fucking saying, Monica.' She shook her head gently with a pitying smile, though I wondered if this said more about her than about me. There was no animosity between us: this wasn't a deep conversation and I knew we'd forget about it by tomorrow.

'Thing is, Monica... like ... thing is, I *like* being told to get my tits out,' she said. 'It's why I like working here.'

I've thought about this a lot in the five years since it happened. Was she wrong to have her opinion? We live in a thoroughly PC world now where saying the wrong thing on social media can see you branded a bigot. Yet the respectable and the right-on love nothing more than mocking 'chavs' and 'toffs.' They slate the working class for getting drunk and ridicule rich society for eating *foie gras*; mock both the 'Croydon facelift' hairstyle of the council-estate poor and the 'Get me the manager' attitude of entitled middle-class types. These opposing sectors of society are buried in an avalanche of media abuse, and yet in that military kitchen both the elite soldiers and the kitchen staff were a true amalgamation of every area of society, working together regardless of accent, education or lifestyles, both needing one another. When I think about it now, it was a storm in a teacup and indeed, when I got back to my section a few minutes later, I didn't talk about what had happened. I didn't need to – a hush had descended on the place and I could see it tied in with my conversation with Kayleigh. Mark said something about getting me a brew, breaking the silence, but I just shrugged. I wasn't embarrassed exactly, far from it. But what I wished more than anything was that the whole thing hadn't happened. I thought that by keeping quiet and getting on with my work, I'd be doing everyone a favour.

VII

Don't get me wrong, it wasn't bad all the time. I soon got used to the fact that the people here were just like that, and my horror and discomfort were no different from moving to another country with customs they think quite normal but are upsetting to outside eyes, like wet markets and slaughtering rituals. The bullying from the younger mess hands was quite horrible but I don't think they saw it like that. They called it 'telling it like it is'. Yes, I thought, but didn't say, telling it like *you* think it is. But they were decent people on the whole, they were all devoted mothers and wives and while I often wondered if their husbands knew about the messing about with chefs thing, I decided it was nothing to do with me. They had ways of speaking that I hadn't come across before; to be fair, they thought that about me too.

'You don't exactly look the typical person for pan bash,' said one of the DS. Directing Staff ran things on the courses and during selection, assessing performance and so on. I like to be judged on my work not the sound of my voice, so when they said I didn't look or sound like a typical kitchen hand, I thought it was strange coming from people like them, but what did they know? I wasn't going to get into a discussion about it because we'd just started a really good, productive few months.

In September that first year, things had sped up. Life had been busy but steady in the summer; little did I know how the workload was going to escalate. This selection was still running at breakneck speed but soon they would be moving to a different location for another phase and we wouldn't see them again. Throughout August there were other short courses visiting, such as a police counter-terrorism course for five days, but by the start of September a new intake had arrived, this time on selection for the specialist surveillance regiment, and there was no more sitting around for the kitchen staff, bitching about each other.

Whereas the men on the earlier selection, the one that had looked so brutal to me, had stayed up at HQ so we might not see them for days or weeks, the new students would live on camp here in a rather shabby accommodation block just yards from the kitchen. They'd also have access to a rest room right next door to the dining room with basic supplies of tea, coffee and milk. Anything else they wanted, they had to buy themselves. A briefing week earlier in the year had given them a taste of what to expect, and those selected then were now here for the monster that is United Kingdom Special Forces selection. Selection for each unit was slightly different because different regiments specialise in different areas. Some courses stayed more often, living on camp for six months. It was like a new term at a top boarding school, without any frills. The UKSF selection included experienced men from other elite units, put forward for the course to add a valuable extra skill to their accomplishments. Whatever the reason for their being here, I was about to see a whole new slice of life for these soldiers.

Michael sat at the head of the dining table, looking smart. I was keen and eager to find out what he had to say, but the other mess hands and a couple of the chefs had heard it all before and made a great play of dragging themselves to the meeting with bad grace, smirking the whole way through.

'OK,' Michael began, straightening his bundle of notes and addressing the group. 'No radios anywhere – no radios at any time of the day or evening. No TV, no phones – nothing that might have the news.' He nodded at the chefs, who usually had their radios on at full volume.

'If anybody asks you when mealtimes might be,' he went on, 'just say you don't know. OK? And they *will* ask. These guys will be hungry. They don't know if they're going to get food, any food at all, or when. All mealtime notices are coming down and you must speak as little as possible to them. You can say thank you at the till when they pay, but even then, try not to.'

Shelley leaned heavily on the table, stretching out her arms and laying her head on them briefly, signalling her boredom and exhaustion. Barb and Moe gave one another dark looks and raised their eyebrows.

Michael continued. 'You mustn't engage in any kind of conversation. You are their main contact with the world outside. These guys will be staying here and they won't have their mobile phones or any other devices. They might want to know something as innocent as a football score, you'd be surprised. Boxing matches, the two-thirty at Doncaster, you name it, they'll ask. You must give nothing away, no engagement whatsoever. Poker faces. OK everyone?'

The mess hands rotated duties through different sections every shift: pans one day, plates another and then dining room. I was on the dining room that first day, which meant the students' rest room was my responsibility. I went in to check that there were enough teabags and cartons of milk for them, and that the place was basically clean, though threadbare. It was the most depressing room imaginable. There had once been a bar next door to it but this had been abandoned and turned into a store, and a rough dividing wall had been assembled from a length of plywood. A sink area was clumsily boarded up and the old counter used for the students' tea and coffee trays. The entire room was thrown together with a handful of old leather easy chairs that looked like utility furniture from the 1950s. Given the large intake of student hopefuls at the start of the course, and only about twelve chairs in their room, it was going to look suspiciously like a game of musical chairs with quite a few people left standing, but I hadn't yet caught on to the fact that they were rarely relaxing and, by the end of the first day, half of them would have been binned and on their way home already. There was one small fridge, and any attempt by the new super-health-conscious intake to stock it with almond milk, vegan cheese or gluten-free yogurt would, I suspected, be abandoned when selection got into full swing. I'm not saying that the catering department didn't welcome all dietary requirements, because they did, but the chefs wanted notice of any special request. As the students didn't know where they'd be half the time, they sometimes had to make do with a plate of rice and vegetables and be glad of it. These men were desperate to pass the course: I knew of two strict vegetarians who, when told that the only food left was chilli con carne looked panicked but insisted it wasn't a problem and ate the lot just to prove it. Standing out as different wasn't going to get them kicked out, but life on this course felt like it was hanging by a thread. Drawing attention to yourself as having special dietary needs could be a precarious position to be in.

On popular TV programmes about selection for elite soldiers, participants are either ordinary members of the public who want to be put through their paces or well-known people testing their limits of fame or endurance. They can be any age, even into their sixties. That isn't the case for the real thing, where volunteers must have prior regular or reserve military experience and be no older than thirty-five. The assumption with these criteria is that participants will be fit already and have an understanding of the military way of life. Even so, these guys were settling in as if they had just arrived for a lads' stag-do in Ibiza. The thrill of not wearing a uniform and calling the instructors by their first names must have been intoxicating.

'Hi, who are you?' A tall, gangly red-haired lad with a small, boyish face flung himself by way of a backwards leap like a high jump over the arms of one of the easy chairs and grinned widely. 'Are you sorting us out with supplies?'

He was like a bouncy puppy, excited and keen. The others scattered themselves around the room in chairs and one tried to put the TV on. It was incredible, seeing not one or two but a room full of young men, whose bodies and minds were not yet accustomed to the entire range of emotions that the middle-aged and older soldiers were familiar with; all of them telling themselves that from this point, the whole course of their lives would be smooth sailing and they would be different from others who could not hope to make the grade, as they could. On that day it was clear that they thought their lives would always be like this; on the up. Right now, the room was tidy, maybe not comfortable, but adequate. Looking at them, ecstatic and overjoyed at their newfound release from uniforms, deference and certain rules, there was something touching about the mutual energy of these men, destined to be worked like pit ponies.

'You'll be fine,' I said. 'There's everything you need in here. The TV is broken, though. Sorry.' It wasn't broken, but it had been disabled. Mindful of Michael's warning about keeping communication to a minimum, I smiled and checked the fridge.

'When's dinner?' said another of the students. 'I haven't got my watch, and they took our mobiles off us.'

I addressed the whole group. 'I'm Monica. I'm afraid I don't know when the meals are today, sorry. They vary. I can't help, sorry. Please excuse me.' And I left, going through the door that led straight into the dining room and bolting it firmly behind me. They couldn't unlock the door from their side.

They vary! How did I think up such a stupid thing to say? I burst out laughing and had to rush down the corridor in case they heard me.

VIII

'Didn't hear you hiding in here, Mark. Ooh – someone getting married?'

I was shuffling around the kitchen putting spatulas away in their colour-coded trays – green for veg, red for meat – when I found the nicest of the chefs decorating a huge fancy cake, concentrating on piping beautifully around the outside.

'Nah,' he told me, refilling the piping bag and twisting it. 'It's for evening meal.' He surveyed his cake. 'It started as a few Victoria sponges, but I got carried away and stacked them up.'

'Looks fantastic.' I hitched one hip onto the work surface, side-saddle, and swung my leg. 'Mind if I watch the genius?'

'Course not,' he said, not taking his eyes off his piping, placing wiggly lines in blue across the centre, to depict waves, I think. Mark stopped to survey his work, then started to ice the other half of the cake differently. His skill was mesmerising. He stood back, holding a long knife to judge the exact centre, hardly breathing, with the concentration of a martial arts master about to slam his hand through a pile of bricks.

'Tell me something,' I said, 'if you don't mind?'

'What?'

'You've been in the army now for – what – ten years?'

'Thirteen.'

'Oh, right. And how long here?'

'Four.'

He placed the cake on a high shelf above the workstation so it was at eye level. He splayed his legs for balance, leaning forward and concentrating, a few inches from his work.

'So is it vastly different, being a chef in the green army?'

'God, yes,' he replied without thinking about it. 'For a start, these days they're all contracted staff in the green army, civilian. It's all outsourced. The chefs aren't military.'

'And you were specially selected?' I said, interested. I liked Mark. He was the calmest, funniest guy out of all the chefs. Mark was short and pale, with blond hair, dazzling blue eyes and a stocky, muscular bearing from playing rugby.

'Yes, we were selected. We don't stay here forever, but it's a privilege. It's a different kind of cooking, and they tell us all about that.'

'Tell you what?'

He started wiping his hands down his white apron and fetched a fresh glass bowl.

'Well, it's a higher standard and they pay once. There's no extra charges for sauce or a dessert or coffee like there are in the green army.'

Catering here all depended on budgeting. This wasn't a place with anybody just turning up to eat. Courses were booked, student numbers were calculated and permanent staff like the police or mechanics were estimated based on probability of numbers, with an allowance made for visiting military, but that was it. Michael would know how full we were likely to be, and numbers would be booked months in advance. The bottom line was that nobody, however elite or senior they might be, could have second helpings, unless there was some left at the end of the mealtime. 'Is anyone having that steak?' became a common question from a badged guy approaching the hotplate five minutes before closing, plate in hand like Oliver Twist holding his bowl.

I watched Mark concentrate on a clean line of piping on his cake. A tap dripped. Outside a helicopter, one of those huge *thwack-thwack* types, was approaching low over the trees, heading for The Area.

'Any plans for the weekend?' Mark asked as we finally cleared up and switched off the lights, ready for a sit-down.

I shrugged. 'Working.'

Mark grimaced. 'You'll have the CQB lot in then. Bloody hell.'

'Glasgow muesli,' I said.

'What's Glasgow muesli?'

I grinned. 'Bacon, black pudding, eggs, fried potatoes, mushrooms, baked beans ...'

What do the SAS eat? It's quite a popular source of speculation and according to some news outlets, at one stage commanders on our camp were concerned about elite soldiers failing fitness tests because there were too many chips being served and so, it was claimed, they'd ordered that chips were taken off the menus.

What nonsense! I was working and eating there every day and it wasn't like that at all.

Of course nutrition plays a huge part in an elite soldier's life, and for eighteen months I was behind the scenes in the kitchen at the training camp, and for another year and a half I ate all my meals with them at the main HQ, so I can tell you exactly what the geezers eat at work. The Regiment doesn't have its own separate dining room or cookhouse. 22 Regiment, 18 Signals, the logistics people, firefighters, dog handlers, civilians like me and just about anybody can eat together on camp – that's the spirit of equality there. There's the Officers' Mess and the Sergeants' Mess, which are open to people of those ranks from other units, including visiting military from all over the world, but in general the cookhouse was thought to be the most sociable place to eat. Even the Commanding Officer used the bustling cookhouse once a week, queuing like everyone else and squeezing himself a place with the rest of us. He was a nice guy and his dog was usually waiting for him outside. There were soldiers from all over the world eating there, and the food was inclusive of all varied dietary requirements: as a woman who has always been focused on a healthy diet, I had no complaints whatever. I never ate the chips that were on offer and I observed that not many of the badged men ate them either, preferring baked sweet potatoes. Nothing was banned, they just did what any reasonable person does and exercised their own judgement and discipline. I noticed that when chicken wraps or steak burgers were on display, most of the badged men politely asked for the bread to be removed by the chefs, leaving just chicken and vegetables or the steak. They often cut a baked sweet potato in half and left the other half for someone else. Nothing was ever taken and then discarded thoughtlessly into the bin.

This wasn't a running buffet, though. The men had exactly an hour to eat each meal. When they're away they eat at amazing field kitchens staffed by army chefs from Hereford. There are 'night trays' for those who have to work all night and packed meals when they're out training for the day. I prepared both types of meal for them and although I would groan when I looked in the kitchen diary at six o'clock on a freezing morning to see 'Packed Meals x 80', I was deeply committed to the task – we all were. Those lads were *our* lads, and we couldn't bear to think of them slogging away all day only to open a below-standard packed meal. Apart from the obvious sandwiches or rolls which I would make for them, I put in little bags of pumpkin and sunflower seeds with nuts and sultanas and fruit portions too.

Another myth is that these soldiers are training hard the whole time and need to cram in as many calories as possible. Of course, that's true in certain circumstances but badged men are human beings too; deployments come and go, there are periods in the classroom on a course maybe, or special projects where they might be in a bunker or behind a desk in an office for months or even a year or two. They have children, they have home lives and relationship breakdowns. They get injured and need to rest. There are lots of training weeks away, and situations where the infamous ration packs are needed, but on the whole, I'd say the fable of elite soldiers eating roadkill or butchering wild rabbits is wide of the mark. They spend a lot more time in the camp cookhouse eating good, wholesome food.

That's my opinion of the food but not necessarily theirs, however. I brought up this subject very recently while chatting to some of the fittest men in 2-2 and they disagreed with my view of the great food on offer. They thought it was repetitive and terrible. When I was there the men paid around £2 a meal for three courses, and the food was always freshly cooked by the best military chefs, but they still complained about the quality. Some elite soldiers are on special diets that are usually quite extreme, so if they don't see exactly what they want on offer – meaning steak, chicken and broccoli at every meal – they think the food is rubbish. Some soldiers will moan about anything. I felt that these men let the side down and came across as spoilt and entitled, completely opposed to the Regiment ethos of humility, humour and classlessness.

In their own homes, my badged neighbours were keen on protein smoothies, whey protein shakes and cooking everything from scratch but they were realists too. Quite opposite to gym and bodybuilding fanatics, I think the Regiment understood that their fitness levels were part of their job, like professional athletes. Their bodies had to see them through many years of hammering, so weird or unrealistic regimes wouldn't stand the test of time. I will admit that some of the newer geezers' theories about diet were a bit skewed, however. When I was there, the actor Hugh Jackman was the big name on all their lips. Even if the best diet experts in the country had stood there giving them facts about nutrition, they would still have done whatever Hugh Jackman was doing. Playing the Marvel character Wolverine in the X-Men franchise for seventeen years, with his ripped, muscly physique, Jackman followed a sixteen-hour-a-day fasting regime that had everyone on camp talking. Well, the newer badged men anyway. The more senior men lost their edge on diet. Hugh Jackman isn't a hardcore bloke at all, I pointed out once, he's an actor. He's paid to look like that, I said, and if he were cast as an overweight, unfit slob in his next movie role and was paid enough, he'd gladly pack on the pounds. But still they trusted him.

Not all the badged men ate on camp. Many of them prepared their own meals back home in the evenings, and over time I got to see these guys' kitchens, usually during someone's leaving function when we might all pile round to their place and I could have a sneak inside their cupboards. One young man, Ben, just twenty-four, in the Regiment for a year and keen as mustard, drank beetroot juice and had only two items in his food cupboard: a mountain of tinned sweetcorn and dozens of tinned pilchards in olive oil, stacked up like a motorcycle display team. Ben was a wiry, tough, nervy-looking cycling supremo who spent every evening and weekend engaged in some sort of punishing hundred-mile time-trial. When he ran out of time-trials he turned to virtual time-trials, taking over the shared front room in his vast Victorian house by installing a second bike attached to a Turbo-Trainer. By contrast, his housemate Scott, an older guy of forty-four, in the Regiment for fourteen years and now very senior, had completely empty cupboard shelves but several fridge compartments stashed with wine, multi-packs of beer, a multi-pack of individually packed cheese portions, a large wedge of Stilton and a huge mature Welsh Caerphilly wrapped in a cloth. In the cookhouse Scott rather ostentatiously ate white sliced bread filled with butter, cheese and Marmite, adding half a dozen grapes as an unconscious concession to his guts.

Scott was not untypical of some of the older, senior badged guys, who seem to lose all sense of reason when it came to their elite status, almost kicking against the traces and looking as shabby as possible to prove that they could. Scott had a robust reputation as a drunk and a brothel-creeper to get a reaction, having reached a certain stage as a fabled soldier and thought, fuck it. He certainly wasn't the only one in the Regiment's higher echelons to embrace the worn-out action man character, but I daresay he had his reasons – and his demons too. If every picture told a story, these two elite soldiers were bookends, twenty years between them, marked 'before' and 'after'.

New ideas were coming in about the psychology of choice, an example of a libertarian paternalistic approach, making it easy for people to do the right thing by suggestion. Small nudges in good nutrition came from the knowledge that most people fill their dinner plates with whatever are the first three items on offer, so salad was switched to the first item after the till instead of the last. Guess what, ravenous soldiers with an empty plate shovelled salad onto it so the place resembled a harvest festival! What was it about the hotplate, though? It seemed to destroy the entire judgement aspect of a straightforward meal and some of them made it look like a death row meal. When they couldn't decide if they were finished, they would start pacing around the semi-circle of the hotplate, accosting others, asking 'Where did you get that?' when they spotted some freshly griddled chicken. On a particularly fraught day, men might be shuffling around trying to find a space on their plate after the meat, potatoes and vegetables had been stacked in a sort of leaning-tower-of-Pisa arrangement, a bowl of soup in their other hand with a bread roll tucked under their chin. During times when the men were on a special task for months and confined to a bunker, they might bring their own food, often just multiple bananas and some cold chicken. Bananas always went fast. Sometimes I had to stop someone because he'd taken three when one each was the rule. James Devon, an unfeasibly tall, slender and almost graceful elite soldier, was almost always the thief.

Joking aside, I can't emphasise enough how decisions on their nutrition were left to the individual. There were no 'orders' in the cookhouse. The men knew that being fit and nutritionally sound was expected of them, that good and poor decisions and taking responsibility for their choices was a key part of being in one of the most famous regiments in the world. So if you want my advice on how to eat like the SAS I can only tell you what was the most popular: an omelette filled with peppers, mushrooms and spinach, or a flame-griddled, flattened chicken breast. Steak, obviously. Baked sweet potatoes, broccoli and salad. Large platters of whole fruits like plums, or wedges of melon to get their faces into. Apple or peach crumble and custard is hard for anyone to resist. But to any hardcore body fanatics out there wanting to eat like the 2-2s, or maybe just trying to lose a bit of weight, I can tell you these elite soldiers nearly always cut a jacket potato in half and ate the burger without the bun.

IX

During the first few months I rarely stepped outside the cookhouse building; in fact, I didn't walk further than the narrow path that led from the big turnstile gate to the kitchen. I wasn't afraid, exactly. I knew that nobody would stop me if I wandered off in a quiet moment after lunch, but there was this unspoken understanding that 'out there' was nothing to do with us. It seemed a tremendous injustice to me that industrial staff weren't considered to need psychological refreshment, fresh air and a change of scene during an eight-hour shift, rather as Victorian gentry didn't allow their gardens and grounds to be open to view from the servants, but it was just one of the things accepted by everyone there.

Occasionally I had to go up to the main HQ, which was on a different camp, and I was just amazed at the freedom there. I saw people walking about with their dogs, sitting on benches underneath beautiful bronze statues or popping in and out of the coffee shop or swimming pool. That didn't seem possible down here. I glanced in the book every week to see which courses would be on, and watched the men

GEEZERS

arrive in their groups, decked out in serious training kit and body armour, looking like they were off on a secret mission blowing things up and kicking doors in. Off they'd go to The Area and come in to be fed, and that might go on for a week. Then I'd see them pack their things and leave dressed in jeans and T-shirts with a strange, carefree attitude, driving back in their own cars to HQ with its shiny insignia and flags, where what to do was all worked out for them. I watched with astonishment. If you'd told me then that a year later I'd be doing the same thing, driving gaily in and out of the main gate, waving at the policemen and reception staff and eating my meals with the most famed and admired elite soldiers in the world, I'd have thought you were mad. But by the time I'd been there for six months I was like a different person. I don't know how different, exactly, but Michael had commented several times on my good timekeeping and the fact that I was always there first, and that my social skills were great. 'You have great front-of-house skills', he said. So I knew they were more or less pleased with me. I was even beginning to look forward to my day's work.

In autumn 2015, what with the 'aptitude' taster weeks for the surveillance course, the SERE course and everything else, we were packed, but in a nice way. It was good to be busy. Steve, the camp's general factotum, who had been here for more than twenty years, was talking about sprucing up the Memorial Garden ready for Remembrance Day and I realised I'd never seen it.

It's funny now, recalling my apprehension on that day as I set off to find the garden, but it also shows how the atmosphere of the place fed into my spirit. It reminded me of when I was a child and my father told me that a boggy bit of field had a bogeyman in it who would grab my ankles and pull me under, and somehow that area became so terrifying I had nightmares about it. It turned out to be nothing more than a big puddle, but fear is a great motivator and I would walk home the long way round rather than think about that puddle. The sinister atmosphere I sometimes encountered in this place ensured I didn't tempt fate, although, as it happened, I tempted fate a couple of months later, and fate took the challenge.

The garden lay behind the mess facility but I'd never seen it because we had no windows facing that direction. I wasn't sure how to get there but I worked it out, going through a maze of rooms and corridors, snaking this way and that, past some rather nice washrooms for visitors, the oak-panelled conference room, the musty-smelling lounge bar that I had never seen used and out past female accommodation blocks, which were pretty much mothballed.

The autumn sunshine was stunning and soothing. For once there was no sound from The Area; no long line of vehicles clattering their way over the cattle grids, a sound I will always now associate with the camp. *Rattle, rattle, rattle,* it went all day every day as Land Rovers, ordinary cars, lorries and vans were swiped in, changing gear and rattling the cattle grid as they accelerated up onto The Area then, muddily, up through the woods. But today there was no sound of car engines idling as they sometimes did for hours, or helicopters, or the patter-pat of rapid gunfire. It was completely silent, save for the odd buzz of an insect in the overgrown brambles. I longed to lie in the tall grass and drink in the atmosphere.

Ducking under low branches and crunching on conkers and acorns, I rounded a corner past the remains of a fallen-down wall. For a second I got nervous that I'd be in trouble for going out, but there was no point thinking like that. I was a mess hand, for heaven's sake, nobody important. But still... the niggle that had been growing in my mind since I came here was taking root. I was new. I might be the very person they might want to keep an eye on. And then there it was: the Memorial Garden.

It felt like the garden had come to meet me, rather than the other way around. It was small and circular, another place where the legend of the entire camp probably lent more to the scene than it deserved. There were no graves, just a neat semi-circle of wreaths around a memorial cross. I turned, and there was a convenient parting of the wild bushes and branches and a clear sight of a criss-cross of paths surrounded by neatly clipped low box hedge.

I went through the gate and stood, transfixed. For a moment it seemed impossible that I could be in this place that I associated with brutality and anger and pain and suddenly feel overwhelming peace. The attention to detail was unsurpassed; there was not a single leaf on the ground, the grass was lush and cared-for. I was just taking all this in when I heard a very slight click. Had it been one of the usual days on camp, with noise coming from The Area, I wouldn't have heard it, but that click and the slight whirring sound made me look up. I saw a tiny camera high on the side of a wall. I looked at it, though I didn't know what I was hoping to see because I knew perfectly well that it was a CCTV camera. Suddenly, instead of it just being a motionless thing, it seemed to come to life. Its face dipped down slowly and almost soundlessly to look at me directly, like a parent looking down at a toddler to warn them to behave. I felt like a prisoner caught on the run.

In the next moment I heard the slight crack of a twig and a rustling; I was aware almost of the temperature changing. I turned and saw a couple of badged men sitting on a bench. I couldn't tell if they were looking at me because they were wearing sunglasses and the sun was too bright in any case, but they must have been there all the time. I felt stupid, as if I had been caught rifling through someone's private drawers. I tried to work out why I felt like this – it was only a memorial garden, after all, and I had my security pass around my neck. I was keen to give the impression that I had every right to be there, so I made my walking posture very casual and turned to read the words on the memorial. I couldn't see them without my glasses but I stood and pretended, which was absurd. I think I also made a point of bending to re-do the laces on my shoes, then thought better of it and pulled myself up sharp. Eventually I set off in a deliberately nonchalant way, not really sure which path to take. Going back was different from coming to find the garden, and I crashed along the path, tripping once on a low bramble and hurting my knee. I wanted to get away but trying to be unnoticeable was impossible.

'How're you getting on here, then?' asked one of the guys. He was a squat, powerful man with a flaming red beard, short hair and a broad Lancashire accent. He took off his sunglasses and gave me a nice smile.

'Settled in?' asked the other, a very tall, dark and almost spectral bent-over type of guy, the sort who is just too tall and gangly to fit in anywhere. I recognised them – I'd seen them both in the dining room.

'Well,' I said, deciding to keep it light, 'um... yes. Thank you. You're the DS, aren't you?'

'Tough work, I bet, yours?' said the first.

'Oh, it's OK,' I said nervously. 'I enjoy it. My name's Monica.'

'Charlie,' said the first guy. He got up and came to shake my hand.

I knew perfectly well who he was – Charlie Rossall, known as the Blackpool Bruiser, was infamous. For what, I had no idea, but he was almost in the 'legend' category on camp.

'Jos,' said the other man.

The course members had been given a task, the DSs told me, and they had another half hour before they needed to head back to The Area to see how they'd got on. We talked about the younger, newer Regiment intake, and to my surprise, they asked if I'd been hassled by any of them.

'Hassled?' I said, puzzled. 'You're joking? Nobody in their right mind would come on to me, kitchen cleaner and all that.' I was looking at the ground, beginning to blush.

'I think if they had the bottle they would,' Charlie said. 'It's not the coming on to you. It's more the rejection.'

Charlie was ursine, short-limbed, massive-bodied, legs and feet looking fused as he lumbered heavily but his running ability took everybody by surprise. You should see him go, they said, especially on hills. He leaves everyone in the weeds, they said.

'Thing is, Monica,' said Jos, looking at Charlie for confirmation, 'we all think we're the dog's bollocks, don't we, mate? When alpha males are all thrown together in one organisation, it's carnage. We're all like that.'

'You need to look at us like dogs,' agreed Charlie. 'Take a German Shepherd, for example. When it's a young dog all it wants to do is fight and fuck, then as it gets older it calms down and starts to become sociable as it understands the game.'

'True,' Jos said. 'Then a dog gets to my age and all it wants to do is sleep and be stroked.' They both chuckled.

It was nearly three o'clock and the sun was quite fierce now. It was beautiful. Both guys kept running their fingers round under the necks of their base layers, and their faces were glistening.

'Aren't you uncomfortable, sitting in all that body armour?' I asked.

They shook their heads and shrugged.

'See, this is where I'm strange,' said Charlie. He leaned forwards, elbows on his knees, making a steeple with his fingers as if he were about to launch into a long tale of battle. 'I have a real thing about my uniform and my armour. I hold it quite sacred, in that it's meant for my protection in battle and all that. I'm a romantic at heart with all that knight stuff. In the dark sense, not the rescuing a damsel thing. Does that make sense?'

It didn't – how could it? But I nodded.

'To me that's why I would think of it as sexy,' he went on. 'A tool of war, and all that.'

They both stood up and looked at their watches. The way Charlie and Jos looked right then was deeply impressive, forceful and intimidating, but these top dogs who could take control of any war situation were simply chatting and enjoying the sunshine on a quiet afternoon like I was, something we all can do.

'Can I ask you a question?' Charlie Rossall made a strange stance, which seemed to suggest that he wasn't comfortable with what he was going to ask.

'Of course.'

'You're not exactly the typical mess hand. What made you come here?'

I took a deep breath, not sure how to put this, but the memorial garden and its atmosphere of spiritual contemplation had inspired me.

'You've heard the saying "Cast your nets on the other side"?' I asked them. 'It's a parable from the Bible which says, basically, that if you don't go fishing, you can't catch any fish. So you have to make an effort. In the parable the fishermen have been out all night and caught nothing but then they're told to cast their nets on the other side.'

'I remember now,' said Jos.

'Well, if you follow the prompting in your head to try something new, that's the moment when a miracle can happen,' I said. 'Cast your net on the other side and you might find your net bursting with fish.'

'And you think this job was your best catch?' Jos asked.

I looked at them, caught in the autumn sunlight, handsome men, the cream of the crop, that was for sure, men who hadn't yet experienced work drying up, people turning their backs on them. They had only known the security of the army.

'I think you have to be open to finding out what else there is,' I said. 'It might be washing dishes today, but who knows which fertile fishing grounds I've uncovered just by looking somewhere I hadn't considered before?'

As the two men left, I secretly hoped they would be back later for evening meal although I guessed they wouldn't. They had homes to go to. They probably had wives, complaining about them working weekends, and children needing to be taken to ballet or football.

I have rarely felt more conspicuous than I did that afternoon in a beautiful, sunlit, peaceful place dedicated to the fallen heroes of one of the most famous regiments in the world. It was strange: once back in the mess building I felt relief, like a rabbit being chased finding its way back to the burrow. I decided not to venture out there again. For now, my life was inside that kitchen. Everything out there that we saw, we saw through glass. There never was much to see, no people walking about, but I think we all still gazed to take our minds elsewhere, like when the doctor takes your blood pressure and tells you to think of a nice holiday scene to relax you. I sat there until it was time to get up and start mopping the floors.

X

People often ask me how I can possibly remember, in the detail I have given, all the things that happened during my three years on camp, especially as I couldn't take photographs or tell other people about it. The answer is, it was simple. It's like learning a piano piece or a poem as a child and finding you can recall it precisely many years later. I bet you can remember the number plate of your family car from your childhood, but probably not one you had five years ago. My private life, such as it was, was so uneventful that my mind emptied when I left work and remained completely blank until I returned. A lot of us know how this feels. I bet you do too. Without much meaningful happening in my life, there was plenty of empty space in my memory.

Somebody else will be working in that kitchen now in my place, but it isn't like a house you've sold where you wouldn't recognise it if you went back: I can almost guarantee that the dining room on camp will be exactly the same as it was when I was last there, in 2017. I want to go back, but I never can. With a house you've lived in you could knock on the door and say 'I used to live here' or drive past it and see what they've done to the garden or look it up on a property website. None of that's possible with camp. Once you've left, that's it. I understand perfectly why some ex-forces men feel so bereft when they leave here. It's not just a place to work, it's a community and family home.

As autumn came on I began to get more used to the place, and I noticed things I hadn't seen earlier. The two special forces regiments and the different specialist units attracted different personalities. For example, the British Army's newest regiment, the surveillance specialists, were on the whole more individual, more sociable and more well-rounded than their illustrious forebears. There was intense rivalry between the two forces. The fighting force – soldiers as you would imagine them to be – were there to train and to eat, and in fact they were the ones I got on with better. The surveillance people were extremely nice and personable, very chatty and smiley, but somehow I felt I couldn't trust them.

I met one of them during my first few days in the training camp kitchen. He was very senior, aged forty-six, and he more or less ran things. I suppose I engaged with him because I was very new, the atmosphere was horrible and I was dreading coming to work. This guy had an open, friendly face and was interested in the backroom operations of the kitchen, so back then I was quite pleased when I saw him. He was good-looking in an obvious way, which I didn't find attractive. His wide, confident smile was a little too wide; his massive shoulders and chest and his hands were a trifle too big and his mouth was full of rather too many gleaming teeth. Even his voice was direct and commanding. Possibly he was too far removed now from the world of social pleasantries or more probably he thought me a class of person not worthy of courtesy, because one of his first comments to me was, 'Have you made use yet of any of the young men for entertainment?' I remember I smiled despite his rudeness and decided to make it my business to be sure he'd be a bit of entertainment for me, but not in the way he'd implied.

It was a typical Saturday. The students had been allowed home for a rare weekend so the camp was very quiet and only two of us were on duty. A small brunch had been laid on and I only needed to pop my head around the corner now and again to see if I was needed. The good-looking geezer had a plate of breakfast and we started some sort of conversation as he went through the usual rigmarole – asking where my accent was from (Cheshire), him telling me where his was from (Lake District) and then, after a while, I said, 'What's your name, by the way?'

He looked at me with that wide smile and spread his legs slightly, as if steadying himself on a rolling ship in rough waters.

'OK, so what can I call you then?' I said, folding my arms. I knew the drill.

'Hmm.' He put his bacon and eggs down and stuck his hands into the pockets of his neat fawn chinos, leaning his head back just a little as if challenging me. 'What's yours?'

Before I could tell him, he reached across the counter and grabbed my pass, which was stuck into the breast pocket of my polo top. His hand lingered.

'Ah, Monica. Monica Lavers. Great.'

'And yours?' I persisted.

He picked up his plate and started walking away to a table.

'You'll have to find out!'

I ignored him and carried on with my tasks. I had tables to wipe. He came to the plates section a few minutes later and ducked his head through the serving hatch.

'Nobody will tell you,' he said. 'Asking questions around here will set bells ringing, but good luck anyway.' He winked.

'Oh. OK.' I shrugged. 'I doubt I'll find out who you are, you're too clever for me, but thanks!' I was aiming to be nonchalant, but I thought he must be joking if he thought this little game would be hard for me.

As soon as I got home that evening, I heard a ping on my laptop. A message on Facebook. It wasn't something I normally looked at because ever since working on camp I'd had nothing to post anyway.

Hey! You're far too easy to find!

The message was from an account in the name of Jack Daw, and no details except a rather pornographic pose of a male in silhouette. I messaged back.

Who are you, please?

We spoke today in the kitchen.

Ah! It must be him.

Well done. You searched my name on Facebook. You should be in MI5.

I waited for the reply.

Ha-ha. You'll never find my real name. This is the name I give to girls. You could offer the lads blow jobs and they still wouldn't tell you my name.

How unpleasant, I thought. Talking about blow jobs. I hardly know him and for all he knows, my mother has just died. Or I have a child at home with cancer. That'd shut him up. Instead, I tapped back:

When are you next in?

Dunno. Next week sometime. I'm having a long weekend away.

And he shut down Facebook messaging.
This charmer gives a fake name to girls, huh? Too much to resist.

The next time I saw him, he came in bang on five o'clock on the Tuesday, for evening meal. He had rolled back the cuffs of his shirt so they rested directly on his biceps and I noticed he kept his arms bent to enhance their size. I wasn't trying to embarrass him or anything so I waited until everyone on his table had gone and then just happened to say, as I was replenishing the sauce bottles, 'How's your day been, Dave Bingley?'

He looked up.

'Well, missy, who's a clever girl then?'

'You're *far* too easy to find,' I said, swishing my cloth about, pushing the empty chairs in. 'It is Dave Bingley, right? Just back from a long weekend in Amsterdam? Happy birthday for Sunday, by the way.'

He shrugged, nonplussed. 'Well done. But who did you ask? People talk, you know.'

'Best not to give them anything to talk about then,' I said, walking away, back to the kitchen. He followed me.

'I told people not to tell you anything,' he said under his breath as he stacked his plate. He was smiling and appeared not to care.

'You obviously didn't tell the right people.'

I had done the simple thing – picking an older instructor and throwing myself on his mercy. 'Please help, Fred, I'm so embarrassed,' I'd said in a hushed tone, clapping my hand to my mouth. 'You know that guy over there – don't look, but the one in a blue top – well, he told me his name the other day and I've forgotten it! I feel stupid, please, *please* can you help?'

Fred looked across. 'In the blue and white checked shirt, you mean? Dave Bingley?'

I grasped his arm. 'You're a lifesaver!' I said.

Perhaps it's stretching it to claim that I had outwitted Dave Bingley, but the whole thing pleased me. A week later another message came through on Facebook from his alter ego, Jack Daw.

Hey Monica. Saw you outside the kitchen today. Couldn't mistake your assets. Any time you're alone at

work on a weekend, shout me in. And when am I going to have your tight pussy in my mouth?

Truthfully. That was his message, I've still got it. I mean, I didn't *keep* it for any reason, it's just there somewhere in Messenger. I thought of checking to see if he had a true Facebook page in his own name; I didn't need to look far. I laughed out loud. Dave, you moron. His main picture was his wife, head to toe in her white wedding dress, plus his two young children. I looked at the date. The old devil had sent me that saucy message – and then got married the very next day. His weekend in Amsterdam had been a brief honeymoon.

It didn't end there. A month or so later I was mopping the dining room floor and Himself drifted in, out of hours, expecting coffee. It was easier to say yes than to get into some point of order on opening times, but while he was helping himself, I disappeared into the walk-in fridge where we kept fresh veg and fruit and loitered behind the parsnips to avoid him.

'Weeeell, Mon.' He slimed around the corner like a slug, antennae searching. It was a tiny place, room for one person only with high shelves on either side and it was very cold. Dave was so big, he filled the doorway.

'How's married life, then?' I said, trying to sound bright. Behind him one chef went by, another chef passed the other way. Both darted looks at him and then at me, then eyes to the floor. Dave was pretty high up the pecking order, everyone knew that, despite this being a 'no ranks' camp. A few others drifted by, and it felt like a scene in a film where the servants pretend they can't see the abuse happening right in front of them.

'Good, actually. Very, very good. When I'm home.'

'I'm so pleased to hear it,' I said. 'Do you miss home?'

He shrugged and shifted his weight to the other foot, glancing behind to see who was about.

'I miss the kids. They're up north. You live near me in Hereford, I think?'

'Do I?'

He gave a slow smile and a very direct stare.

'Yes, Mon. You do.' He folded his arms. 'I'm – ooh – five hundred metres from your house.'

This was boring.

'You're a nice man, Dave,' I said, 'but, well –'

He interrupted, sizing me up. 'Which makes you even more attractive. And a challenge.' He fixed me with his eyes again. I turned and pretended to carry on counting the bananas.

'I'm not put off,' he said. 'How do you feel about a man like me? I could lift you above my head with one arm. And you can tell me how wet your –'

I was saved by Barbara.

'Oi! What you doing here?' she said in a piercing voice. 'Out you go, lad, bothering people. You shouldn't be in this kitchen. Go on, back to your hut!'

Barbara had worked here for over twenty years. She remembered Dave as a newcomer – and knew his reputation. She flapped a tea towel at him. Then she pointed at me.

'Monica, pass me those radishes, love. Chef's in a bait.'

I remember things like this happening to me at work when I was younger, and at the time the first woman to hold a senior position in a job previously only ever held by a man. Harassment was almost a normal part of working life for women, except we didn't call it harassment back then. They were simply blokes – usually older ones – 'trying it on'. Nowadays it was me who was the older person. On that camp we were all struggling to adjust to our new lives: me being a kitchen worker, the men who had gone from being normal soldiers to elite, badged soldiers and as all this happened five years ago and it's pointless trying to judge Dave Bingley now. Maybe Kayleigh was spot-on when she said, 'This place is different.' She liked being told to get her tits out, she said, and the others were as bad. So how could a man like Dave Bingley know where the boundaries were? He'd been trying it on with girls here for years: mostly they enjoyed his banter and encouraged it.

I could have told him where to go. I could have made a formal complaint about him. I could have done a lot of things. But 'could have' is meaningless – because I simply carried on with my work and forgot all about him. And the real tragedy of all this is that men like Dave Bingley, who masquerade as decent people, have loving wives at home who are, I assume, unaware that their husbands make some pretty bad decisions and behave like morons.

XI

I can clearly remember that Tuesday morning in January. It was freezing, a day of raw cold and likely to stay that way. I was first to arrive at ten to six and I went around the kitchen flicking switches and turning taps on as usual, but something didn't feel right in the dark dining room. Sure enough, there was a figure hunched in the corner, curled over in a C-shape. I moved nearer. It was Sam, one of the badged guys they called Surfer Dude.

'God, it's you. Morning, Sam,' I said, walking towards him slowly, as if approaching somebody high on a parapet, about to jump off. I couldn't imagine how he had got in. We bolted all the doors before we went home after late shift.

Sam was holding a paper napkin, folding it this way and that, then rolling it up as if to distract himself from the thoughts swilling around in his head. He couldn't have been to bed yet. I'd been on lates yesterday and I'd seen them all in the computer room as I passed by at eight o'clock last night; most of them were still there now, ten hours later. It wasn't unusual. They'd been on the course now for several months, and things were starting to get tough for them.

'You OK?' I said gently.

He didn't look up. He usually looked fresh, like he was going to grab a board and hit the waves, but his fine red mane had become long and greasy, and I could smell his breath several paces away.

'Yeah, fine.'

I pulled out a chair and sat down opposite him. Sam was the bouncy, boyish-looking guy I'd met on his first day here. He'd already done selection a few years ago as part of the Royal Navy and had been put forward by his specialist regiment for the surveillance course, to gain new skills. He knew what he'd have to go through this time, or at least that's what I assumed.

I reached a hand to feel the radiator under the window. It was cold.

'It's freezing in here, Sam. Wouldn't you be better in bed? You can still get a quick hour and a half before breakfast. Freshen up a bit?'

He didn't reply. I thought of just leaving him to sit there in peace, but he looked like he needed help.

'They're taking the piss now,' he mumbled.

'What's happened? This isn't like you, Sam.'

He took a deep breath, then let it out quickly and said nothing.

'Too much?' I prompted.

He nodded and kept staring at the table, pushing around a couple of crumbs, rolling them under his fingers then brushing them onto the floor. Eventually he spoke.

'There's no respect, Mon. Yeah, I know it's a hard course, I get that. But I'm already badged. I've been in five years. It's not the course –' he shrugged and paused.

'The DS treat us like shit.' He looked straight at me, as if pleading for me to believe him.

I knew it was hard for the guys already badged to go through it all again and be spoken to like they were idiots. I'd heard it from one of the longest served DS, Declan, who told me that some of the badged guys either left of their own accord or were failed on their attitude.

'There's no respect, Mon,' Sam repeated.

I reached a hand out to comfort him but thought better of it. 'It's OK,' I said quietly.

Something else must have happened. Or maybe he just reached the wall when sleep deprivation stops you thinking straight. That's why they kept them up all night, bending their circadian rhythms to the point of madness, testing their ability to concentrate when exhausted: Sam should know this. He hadn't been out of this place for weeks. The weather was awful, and it was dark at four-thirty in the afternoon. But that couldn't have been the only problem, surely?

We sat there quietly for a couple more minutes, looking out at the dawn light slowly illuminating the stark landscape. It was that time of year when Christmas seemed long ago, but spring and summer were out of reach. We all felt it.

He'd lost weight. His skin was greyish-white and grubby. He had stopped taking care of himself and I'd noticed him moving as if he were in an invalid's body, aching and stiff.

'Let me get you a tea? Or coffee?' I kept my voice low, partly because he looked unwell and partly because I didn't want anybody hearing me. We weren't supposed to serve this lot coffee, full-stop – and certainly not out of hours.

'Coffee'd be fantastic.'

The other two mess hands on early would be here any minute. I went back to the kitchen and turned off the taps, checking if anybody else had arrived yet, hurrying slightly, afraid that when I returned, Sam would be gone. I couldn't bear to think of him like that. I quickly grabbed two milk cartons from the fridge in the beverage room.

Time is elastic. Time is what you need it to be and what is six months on a course when you are twenty-something? To the young men who come here for the first time, the enthusiastic ones flipping over the chairs in the students' room a few months ago, excited about the course, six months will soon be gone. Then they find out how unpleasant it can be, watching a clock all night long, overturning their sleep patterns, missing mealtimes, sent out on the road on an exercise for which there is no given finish time – and it feels like the course will never end.

Television programmes about selection show the course in a scaled-down version of eight days – but anyone can survive eight days. This course had much more than hill walks and falling off cliffs into water – there was classroom work and dull surveillance skills and working all night in front of computers. There are a hundred and sixty-eight hours in a week for all of us, but to these men the grim reality now ground down to chunks of time where every minute was unpleasant. For some, sheer determination to succeed against the odds will get them through. To someone in the green army it's a huge step up to succeed here, but to a person already badged – I don't know why some of them they failed *this* course, but they did.

'Here you are, number nine.' I put two cups of strong coffee down on the table, dropping a few packets of sugar, in case. 'The second cup is for when you've finished the first.'

'Ha! Number nine.' He shook his head limply. 'I'll show you.'

This was a joke, started in the lunch queue. You didn't get to know the students at first because there were so many of them, but they thinned out pretty quickly. They began to be familiar to us; we could see them change and grow throughout the course. They would tell us about their families and, after a rare weekend off, we would ask how the children had liked the theme park or how their parents' anniversary had gone. Some students were intense and never looked at us, but most became like friends; they liked that, in a world where they would eventually become anonymous, we engaged with them as real people. Outside those gates, they had to make up a story about their lives, but not here.

Anyway, Sam always looked different from the others. He was chatty and interested and, if it was particularly quiet, he talked about Devon and what made him try out for an elite regiment coming from the Marines. For reason of making conversation one morning, I'd said something like 'Nice to see a clean-shaven guy here' and his reply was along the lines of 'Yeah, I know' and I don't know what made me say it, but I replied, 'Yes, but you're not a ten, Sam. Let's say I give you nine out of ten.' He gave me a cocky look and came straight back at me with 'Nah. I'm a ten.'

Ever since, I had called him number 9.

Nothing much changed during the next week. Sam and the others came and went as usual, each day looking more defeated than the previous one. But all it had taken was one chance remark and it was like passing a mirror you've passed for years when you suddenly notice you've got bags under your eyes. My short encounter with Sam that morning had changed our roles in some weird way, and instead of seeing him as this handsome, capable, elite soldier, he'd been vulnerable. He looked ill and frail. I delayed week by week, then I scribbled on a piece of paper: 'I'd quite like to see *The Revenant*. It's on at the Odeon this week and next. Would you like to come with me?' I added my mobile number. Then I carefully folded the note, so it became no bigger than an inch square and kept it in the palm of my hand.

I'd had this picture of myself, standing there working up the courage to give him a note, but the fact was, I had nothing to lose. I even went to *The Revenant* on my own to see if it were the sort of thing Sam would like, deciding that it was spot-on. My hopes rose and my luck might be in. With the picture of poor, thin-looking, deathly white Sam in my head, I waited until it was my turn to be on the dining room and hung back until his mates had left. He always sat right at the back, by the windows. I moved towards him purposefully, taking a cloth and bucket with me just in case, and said nothing as I let my palm open so the note slipped onto the table. Using my cloth, I pushed it under his plate. 'That's for you.' I didn't want him thinking I'd dropped something by mistake, leaving it there to be cleared away.

He didn't look at me, just placed his left palm over the note and carried on eating with his right fork.

What was I doing?

I knew very well what I was doing. I was playing with fire. I was aware Sam might think I was coming on to him and expect something else, but I really just wanted a night out and I wasn't going to let coyness stand in my way. I'd never asked a man out in my entire life, but anyhow, he might not have thought anything of the sort. I thought it was worth asking.

I didn't have to wait too long for his answer. He cornered me as I was filling the juice machines in the dining room next morning. He pretended to get himself a coffee and glared at me as if to say, 'Act like you hardly know me.'

'Hey, Monica, just read your message,' he said, barely moving his lips. 'Yeah, I'd love to see *The Revenant* with you, when were you thinking?'

I didn't look at him but carried on hoisting the big containers of juice high above my head to fill the machines.

'Good. I finish early Tuesday and Thursday this week, or of course tonight. It's on at five or eight-thirty.'

'Can't do tonight as I'm out working,' he said. 'Thursday sounds like an option. It'll have to be a later showing because we finish at five most days.' He came closer to me. 'Monica, we are going to have to keep this to ourselves, just in case.'

'I don't want people knowing either,' I said. 'Don't worry. I understand you might be nervy. It's just a film and we bumped into one another, right? Let's say Thursday then, half eight.'

He smiled. 'Ha-ha, I know how to play it. Don't book in case they drop a fast ball on us, and we end up working Thursday night. If it's a go, do you want me to drive?'

'We can either meet at the Odeon or you can call at my house.'

'Yeah, OK, I'll pick you up. It's no problem. I'm looking forward to it. You in work tomorrow morning?'

'Yes – why?'

'I was just going to say, poker face.'

I finished filling the machines and switched them back on. They resumed their slow, hypnotic paddle-stirring of the fruit juices, and I picked up all the empty containers.

'Of course. I'm just worried about being seen with a nine.'

'Ha-ha, no you're not.'

I didn't want him getting any ideas. It was a hard thing to judge, but the opportunity for a night out was all I wanted and Sam was such an easy guy to get on with. I pictured a coffee beforehand, maybe at the Costa upstairs in the cinema, then a few terrified moments with the bear scene and stuff like that, then he could drop me back home, thanks very much. We could become buddies.

At ten o'clock the next evening I got a text.

Sam: Good poker face today, I'm impressed

Me: Thanks.

Sam: I have literally just finished. Well, we're still looking good for tomorrow night. Just so you're aware, I have a lesson on after the evening meal. I don't think it should take too long.

Sam borrowed a van and picked me up promptly at eight. As we were driving into the Odeon car park he said, 'Just wondering, M – is this a date? Or a friends' night out?'

'What d'you mean?'

'Is it a date?'

I chuckled, embarrassed. I didn't want him to get the wrong idea. 'We're just going to see *The Revenant*, I think.'

He was silent for a second as he grabbed the ticket from the machine and the barriers lifted. We found a parking spot.

'OK, I know what I'm doing now,' he said, pulling on the handbrake, suddenly brisk. 'Come on, missy, mustn't be late.'

We enjoyed the film, although if you know it, you'll know there aren't any laughs. Later, as we climbed back into the van, and just as I reached around to grab the seatbelt, he lunged across the front bench seat and made to kiss me. I sort of turned sideways as if my seatbelt was twisted and acted as if I hadn't noticed. Blimey. I wasn't sure what to do, to be honest. I liked Sam, but he was just a bored guy on camp and I knew this road all too well. It led nowhere.

He drove me home.

'Can I come in, Mon, just for a minute? I'm desperate for a pee.'

Obviously I said yes. I didn't feel awkward or embarrassed. I didn't feel anything except refreshed from a night out, so I made two mugs of tea and took in some biscuits. The film had been long and he hadn't eaten since five o'clock.

'This is nice,' he said when he came down from the loo. 'Your house is very calming. It's so fucking fantastic to have some time away from camp, I can't tell you.'

'Will you get into trouble?'

He gave a hollow laugh.

'Right now, I don't care, M. But no.' He took his tea and glanced at his watch. 'The DS won't know I wasn't there; they go home at night.'

We lapsed into silence. The TV was on, but muted. We stared at the news for a moment, not really looking.

'What's your actual name?' I laughed. 'Is it really Sam?'

'At work, yes. But it's James.'

'Blimey, *James*?'

The clock on my iPad announced midnight. I think I knew why he was hanging around.

'Tell me,' I said quietly, 'have you ever regretted what you went into?'

'Me? No, not really. It's hard, though.'

'Which bit?'

He smiled and shook his head. 'Dunno. I just wanted to be the best. I had the skills, but looking at it now, I didn't have the temperament. When you're sixteen you don't think about it, but it's years and years ahead of the same thing. I got badged, got a house and all that, and now I miss my quiet life more than ever. I didn't have much when I joined the Royal Marines, I came straight from my parents, but now it's all changed. I didn't know until I bought my own house that I want that life – do the garden, maybe build an extension. I'd be better off being a builder – that's what I'd like to do. Or a tree surgeon. Right now I want some time off to spend the day cutting back all the brambles and stuff.'

'Looking through seed catalogues, planting some daffodils?' I suggested gaily.

'Yeah, all that.'

He should be having a family, I thought. Move life on a bit.

'Do you worry about when you leave, Sam?' I asked. 'I mean, it's a long way off, I know, but it'll still happen, and you'll have a lot of life left.'

He snapped a look at me.

'God no. I've got all sorts of ideas of things I want to do. Like I said, I'd start my own building company. Property renovation. I could be given three days' notice right now, and I'd be fine. Some of the people down there, back at the Regiment, I mean, they're sheep. Sheep, following orders and not thinking for themselves. Fucking hate them.'

'How could you possibly have known what you wanted, at sixteen? You were still just a boy.'

'I got to see a lot as a boy,' he said, looking away. 'A boy Marine, anyway.'

'Yes, but you wouldn't know, would you? You had no other life to judge it against. Don't most people just want to get away from home and school at that age and long to do whatever they want? I know I did.'

For a moment we were both gazing across the room, not really looking, remembering our younger days. There are people and places, whole scenes – lifetimes really – that can flash through our minds in a moment.

'I was a pretty decent Marine,' he said. 'But five years felt enough and I was pretty much ready to try for an elite regiment. It felt right.' He had shuffled up closer to me now, his wiry, taut body really just a skeleton with its prominent muscles and a coating of pale white skin stretched over it. When I looked at him again his eyes were almost closed. Poor Sam, he'd been up since dawn, working hard all day and it was gone midnight.

I suggested another tea for the road. He followed me to the kitchen where I brewed two more mugs of tea.

'I'm sorry it's been such a short evening,' he said. 'But it's been a lovely change.' He looked at me and allowed a brief silence for me to fill with an invitation to stay. I bustled about with the milk.

'I'm going to head back,' he said when I didn't reply.

'Yes.' I wasn't looking at him, stirring the tea gently. The tension engulfed us and for a moment there was just the sound of the fridge juddering quietly to a halt and, outside, a car door being pushed to and people saying goodnight. 'You should.'

Sam sighed. 'Well, I've been to a film with a lovely lady. I'm not greedy.'

'Was it one sugar?' I said, holding up the teaspoon.

Next morning I opened my eyes to this text:

I really enjoyed my evening with you Monica. I want to come back. You are an amazing woman.

A couple of weeks passed, with no sight of the students. Then one morning I saw Sam coming into the dining room for breakfast with all the others. He ducked his head under the serving hatch to leave his dirty plate on the pile.

'I wasn't ignoring you all week. There was no signal where we were. It was a long week.'

'It's OK. I didn't expect to hear from you at all.'

'We're going away again this evening, but I should be back next week if you want to do something? Nothing weird. I'd like to take you to dinner, book that steak place in the Old Market?'

Someone came into the room and put a lot of dirty knives and serving spoons down. Someone else dumped a dirty food mixer for me to wash. Time was ticking on. Sam was hovering. I looked up at him, a good foot taller than me, slightly more healthy-looking now, fresher and wired-up.

He came closer.

'I think you know what I want, Mon.'

I was switching taps on, making a fresh sink of soapy water. 'No, I don't.'

'I want you.'

When the inevitable calm fell just before evening meal, Kayleigh sashayed over to me with her wheedling look.

'You all right?' she lilted in her little-girl way. 'You're smiling like you won the Lottery.'

'Really?'

'Yeah. C'mon, what's floating your boat then?'

I thought for a second.

'Just had a good day,' I said. 'Is that allowed?'

Just before our shift ended, Dev came into pan bash.

'Michael wants a meeting later with everyone. As soon as we're finished, in, say...' he looked at his watch, 'fifteen minutes?'

For once, Michael looked vaguely business-like. He sat at the head of the table and adopted a serious air.

'Some of you know the routine, but I'm just going to run through tonight. The course is going abroad at 03:00 hrs. They won't know until they are woken at 02:00. Tonight we're putting extra food on for the students and you needn't worry about them having second helpings.'

Seconds weren't usually allowed.

'In fact, Dev and all you girls, don't hassle them to leave at seven-thirty like you usually would. Say you're staying for something, cleaning or whatever, and say the boss isn't here so they can stay and enjoy a few more coffees, finish the desserts and so on. OK?'

'Well, they'd rather sit in here where it's warm than their students room anyway,' said Barb.

'Precisely,' Michael agreed. 'Speak as little as possible to them. You can say thank you at the till, but you mustn't engage in any kind of conversation. Any questions?' He looked around the table. 'If you can stay, we'll make up the extra by giving time off in lieu.'

Maureen fretted about getting back for her dog, and Barbara said she had her elderly father to see to. I said I'd stay, and so did Kayleigh and Tracy.

Michael picked up his notes and tapped them into shape. 'You must give nothing away, no unnecessary engagement. OK everyone?'

I went down to our tiny locker room and hid among the coats, texting Sam. If he were going away, I'd better accept his dinner invitation.

Me: Next Thursday? Say 7.30?
Sam: 7.30, perfect. Can't wait.

They were away for five days. The following Thursday came around and I hadn't had confirmation of our date, though I'd seen the students back on camp. They looked bouncy and bright: refreshed. I didn't contact Sam, but he looked fine and even gave me a quick smile as he left lunch to start the afternoon's lessons.

I'd expressly made sure of an early shift so I could get home early because, after all, I hadn't been out socially for over a year and it was probably taking on more significance than it deserved. A couple of hours later, I was looking out of the dining room window before I went off duty when I spotted Sam and two others loading items into cars. They were way across the car park, partly obscured by other vehicles. Taking something up the top, I thought, or just loading kit. The three of them drove away in separate cars. Must be a surveillance exercise, I thought. Ten minutes later, the senior DS came in to ask for some milk.

'Um, Declan... you know that lot, three of the guys on the course – can I ask if they've gone somewhere?'

He flashed his usual smile. 'Yeah – well, they've gone, I think,' he said, helping himself to a coffee while he was here.

'For the day?'

'Maybe more than a day,' he said over his shoulder as he studied some photographs on the dining room wall.

'But I've just seen all the others on the course going to the gym. Declan?'

'OK, look, actually they were free to go home, Monica,' he said, turning to look at me properly. 'Those three.'

Sam couldn't have gone home to Devon, surely? Maybe they just went for a drink? He probably had a lot of sorting-out to do, after being away. I didn't hassle him with a message and instead went home and looked at my clothes. It meant one of my dresses being retrieved from my wardrobe and tried on, for fear of finding it too loose, too tight, too low or too high. Time went by, three hours, four hours. Seven-thirty came and went. There was no sign of Sam and no text. I could have sent him a text myself, but he might have been working somewhere secret. You never knew with this lot. Then, at eight-thirty, I had this message:

Sam: Hey Mon, I'm not going to be able to make it tonight. I've been pulled back somewhere to sort some stuff out.

I was stunned. He was supposed to pick me up at seven-thirty and I'd been waiting for an hour. He wasn't detained, he was in Dorset. I didn't mind things being cancelled, but he'd left at three o'clock and knew then that he couldn't make it.

Me: That's a shame. I'm disappointed. But I was even more disappointed when Declan told me you were free to go at three this afternoon.

I waited half an hour for a text back.

S: Monica, I might be off the course. Well, as it stands I'm off the course. Me and three others got kicked off yesterday for getting on the piss. I'm genuinely in Poole

Me: You left at 3 and didn't bother with a quick message to cancel. What happened?

S: Like I said. The three of us, and we decided it was OK to have some drinks.

I didn't reply. I didn't know what to say.

S: If it's any consolation I passed the course, they just don't want me to deploy on a particular job. But I've got two weeks leave so not all bad, need to get my head back in the game for when I get back as it's all changed now.

Me: So it's true? You're gone?'

S: Not gone exactly: I mean, I'm still in - here. I'll have
to go and explain myself. But at least I'll get some time
alone in my cottage. I think I've had enough. I'm ready
to go, well, maybe a year, no more. I want my life
back. Nice meeting you Mon, you're great and kept
me going when it was grim. Good luck.

It didn't really matter. Failing this enormously important
course in the most famous, specialised military unit in the
UK for a simple lack of control; three of the top men in
their regiments egging one another on to *have a drink* while
still on selection? What were they thinking?

It was still an achievement to have got this far, I
understood that. There was no apology for leaving me
waiting, though, and how long does it take to text 'I'm
sorry'? For all his elite status, he had no fortitude to stick
it out and I think that those three, already badged, were
maybe consoled by the fact that they were already in. Sam,
though, it was almost as if he'd wanted to fail; he needed a
reason to get off the roundabout and start something new.
He'd been inspired, he told me, by my decision to go for
the job with no responsibility. Well, I thought, he's right.
He'd done it – and now it was maybe time to see what else
the world had to offer.

By chance, later that year, another guy already badged
in the same elite regiment as Sam was thrown off the course
on the last hour of the last day too, just before Christmas.

Amazingly, he used the same words as Sam had, months
before.

'There's no respect, Monica,' he said, looking at the floor. 'I've been badged for twelve years.'

'What happened?' I asked, as he was packing up his car, just like Sam had done.

He drew a slash mark across his throat. 'I kept questioning them.'

I think that was another way of saying he'd outgrown his place, like we all do. Orders I would have easily taken years ago, I wasn't too happy to accept these days, from people younger than myself. That's a weak point. It could also be a sign to move on to something else.

XII

To everyone's astonishment, and by some miracle of the military system, Michael was promoted and sent to a new post up the top. His replacement George had a pinched face, a sharp delivery and could only be fairly described as 'brisk'. He was humourless and taut, totally unsuited to the relaxed atmosphere of this particular camp. I had a feeling as soon as I met him that he and I weren't going to get along, and indeed this particular incident, which stuck in my mind for a long while after the event, was an example of how, in my opinion, the military have no idea how to work with civilians.

'George would like a word with you, Monica,' mouthed T, sidling up to me through the throng one lunchtime. It had been pandemonium, with 120 men coming in within fifteen minutes, geezers politely asking for more blackcurrant juice, the bread rolls running out, nobody having change for a fiver and only two of us to do everything.

'What? Now?'

He shook his head then tapped his wristwatch. 'George's office. Two o'clock.'

It was now June 2016, I'd worked on camp for nearly a year, the harassment issue had died down and I was really settling in. I didn't love my job but I could think of worse – until George arrived on the scene, that is.

'Monica. Have a seat,' he said briskly when I went over an hour later. He had transformed Michael's scrappy Nissen hut into his 'Field Office'; it was like something out of a glossy magazine, with pots of geraniums outside, of all things. It'd be hanging baskets next.

'I'll get straight to the point. Security Cell have been in touch about something that happened about...' he looked down at my file in front of him on the desk to check his dates, 'three weeks ago.'

My brain was raking through the days.

'Three weeks ago? Why, what's happened?'

He spread his hands. 'I need to ask you why you ate in the dining facility up the top on Sunday?'

'*Need* to ask me?'

'OK, I would *like* to ask you,' he conceded, taking a deep breath.

'I'm cleared for working on both sites,' I told him, frowning. 'I'm allowed to use the gym and the swimming pool up there ...'

'Yes, but you didn't go to the gym or pool.' He fixed me with a steady look.

I gave a short laugh. 'I went to eat. My boiler had broken down, if you must know, and I cook with gas so rather than go and sit in town... well, I was told they did brunch up there like they do here.'

George leaned forwards.

'Who told you that?' he said. 'Told you there was brunch on, I mean?'

'Mark.'

'Mark?'

'Mark – Mark the chef. Here. We were chatting.'

George folded his arms tightly and seemed to be choosing his words, looking down at my file almost rocking himself as if in an effort to hold his emotions together. I sat, rigid.

'It's clear to me what happened, Monica,' he said in a stifled voice, 'and it's not appropriate. Yes, you are employed to go to both camps if needed. Popping in for a cheap brunch at weekends doesn't come under that privilege. You and Mark are friends?'

'We're *friendly*,' I corrected, tartly, 'not friends. I ran into him in town and told him about my boiler emergency and he suggested I go up there to eat.'

George glanced at the report from Security.

'The police on the gate didn't just let me in with a wave,' I went on, 'but they suggested what was good on the menu! And the cost of the meal was nothing to do with anything.'

'Cost of the meal?'

'You said I popped in for a cheap brunch. You could have said "popped in for brunch". I may be a mess hand but I can pay for a meal.'

George kept his gaze on my file.

'You started a conversation with someone there and were asking questions, apparently, about where he spent Easter and all sorts of other things.'

'*Asking questions?*' I was incredulous.

'The Security Cell brought this to my notice.'

'Brought *what* to your notice?'

I lifted my hands, then took a deep breath and started again.

'Tell me something, George,' I said, mustering my self-control. 'Why bring me in here? I should be on my way home. I've been up since four-thirty this morning and I've had a hard shift. You could come to me in the kitchen and say all this, a friendly word about being careful or something, yet I'm in here while you read from notes written by other people who have nothing better to do, it seems.'

'Yes, but Monica –'

'What a colossal waste of time.' I looked at him, seething, as I went through in my mind what had happened.

It had been Easter weekend and we had four days off. My boiler had packed up and I couldn't get anyone to look at it over the holiday so I had no hot water and couldn't cook. I could have easily gone into town to eat but who really wants to sit at a table for one? George had no idea how excruciating it was for me to sit among couples gazing at one another, families with balloons and party hats and glasses being raised. I'd spent years eating alone. I thought I might as well go and join a bunch of other unfortunates on military standby, who had no choice about eating in a gloomy canteen. I'd be among friends. The kitchen staff knew me, so I'd get a friendly smile and a damned good meal. I wouldn't get any of that in Frankie & bloody-Benny's.

So I'd driven to camp, waved my pass and all the other things and up went the barriers. I got a cheery wave from the policemen on duty, Jim and Pete, who knew me by now.

'Nice seeing you up here,' said Jim.

'Boiler broken!' I shouted out of my car window. 'I'm coming for a bite to eat.'

He put his thumbs up.

'Bad luck! The cottage pie is good, and the smoked haddock kedgeree is excellent!'

I headed for the cookhouse. Only a few men were there, finishing up their meals. In the cookhouse, the custom was to sit at a table with others. It was contrary to the theme of the camp to separate yourself, to sit on your own. That's how I found myself sharing a table with the only other person left in the building, a middle-aged, distinguished-looking man wearing a green 'Visitor' lanyard. We both gazed absentmindedly at the news on TV. I can't remember what it was now, but some item came up that made me clap a hand to my mouth in amazement.

'I never knew the Scilly Isles had all that going on,' I said.

He laughed. 'Neither did I.'

We carried on looking at the TV, commenting on the odd news item. How was your bank holiday generally, I asked, and he said he'd spent it in Didcot with his sister and family. I'd piped up, 'Oh, I know Didcot well, my sister lives there too!' And off we went, talking about bloody Didcot house prices being exorbitant. As you know, a conversation about house prices is a good one for two strangers and can keep you going for ages. He asked me how long I'd lived in Hereford and why did I choose it, and on we went, and the conversation moved from house prices to stolen bikes.

He was a nice man. He spoke with a soft, commanding voice, and I guessed he must be military with that sure gaze and economy of speech and the green visitor status. My pass was clearly on show around my neck, saying 'Permanent Staff'. I didn't know who he was any more than he knew me, but we chatted away as if we were two people sitting in adjacent seats in A&E having just been told the wait would be four hours.

He fetched me a coffee from the machine and one for himself. It was a great conversation. I ended by saying, 'Are you in Hereford all week?'

'Only for another day or so,' he said. 'Then back to London.' We shook hands and wished one another goodbye.

I didn't tell George any of this. I hadn't the energy and it would be a waste of time. He'd brought me in here to reprimand me on behalf of some busybodies for a reason I couldn't begin to work out. I couldn't believe that conversation could be the cause of this fuss.

'So what's the problem?' I said.

George looked at me. He closed my folder. 'It's OK, Monica.'

'He reported me to Security? Seriously?'

'No. Someone else did. You need to be careful, Monica.'

'Someone else? We were the only two in the whole cookhouse!'

'Being excessively inquisitive,' George went on, ignoring me. 'It can be taken the wrong way.'

'OK.' I held both my palms towards him in a 'halt' gesture. 'I'd love someone to tell me how "Have you had a good bank holiday?" can be taken the wrong way. There's a difference between asking questions for information and engaging in conversation.' I leaned forwards. 'We were two strangers passing the time, George, in a place that we were both fully allowed to be in.'

The long hours in that kitchen, the early mornings, travelling, the lack of sleep had all crept inside me, become part of me. I could see it in everybody else's posture too, the way everybody moved and talked here, the total tedium of dead-end life. I longed for a proper conversation with somebody. Don't tell me I was going to be muzzled as well as confined to that stifling kitchen my entire working life? I got up. It was time I went home.

George leaned back in his chair and adopted a completely different, casual pose as if relaxing after dinner had been cleared away. He went on to say there wasn't really a problem – he was only the messenger. He repeated I ought to be careful. Then he got to his feet.

'Look, I know you live alone, it can't be easy and I'm sorry about your boiler etcetera but I'm just telling you to be careful. With your ... erm, chatting,' he said. 'The girls tell me that you often have long conversations with one or two of the men on weekends.'

'Oh *really*?' I turned around. 'And?'

'OK. Let's leave it,' said George. 'You don't have to stay, it's the end of your shift, I know. We'll come back to this.'

'I don't want to come back to it,' I retorted. 'I don't tie those guys to a chair, George. They're willing participants, if you can believe it, and maybe they chat happily because their job is so bloody stressful it makes a break for them? Maybe they like it that I'm interested in them, not like this lot who hate their guts for some reason? Are you going to ask them in here too? The DS? Tell them not to talk to me? Thought not.'

I was calm, but inside, I was seething. I haven't raised my voice my entire life and don't need to. I know how to say something and leave nobody in any doubt about how I feel.

'This is me. As it happens, I didn't spend Easter on my own, the Padre invited me. And I'm not lonely. I don't have a social life because I don't want one and I like my own company but it's nice to chat to people in the same workplace, over lunch. That's what people do, isn't it?'

'Yes,' George went on, ignoring that comment, 'but it's also because you have worked in London and you may not know it, but your intellect can be very intimidating to some of the people here, Monica.'

'I see.' I folded my arms and leaned against the office door. 'When the hell am I supposed to have demonstrated intimidating intellect? When I suggested freezing all those surplus bread loaves?'

'Monica.' He went back to his chair.

'When I suggested using the third sink in pan bash for long-term soaking? Was that my intimidating intellect? How about moving the tables around to make more space? I keep hearing about this so-called intellect but all I'm doing is using language I'm used to. Did you know that Shelley complained the other day that I was using long words? I said tepid!'

He held up a hand to halt me. I stopped and dropped my arms to my sides. There was something vaguely offensive about being paid the lowest wage they could get away with for gruelling physical work that I had never complained about, that made this whole encounter even worse. I took home just over £1,036 a month, £1,180 with weekend shifts.

'Please sit down again. I know I'm keeping you beyond your hours, but you can come in an hour later tomorrow.'

I sat down.

Being on camp is like being in hospital, in a sealed world with its own food and its own strange routines. I still hadn't told anybody that I was working here; I knew it would set off a whole barrage of questions about the men, the place, why the hell was I washing dishes for a living but, more importantly, I knew there would have been ravenous curiosity about the Regiment. Telling people we worked here was as tricky for civilians as it was for the badged men themselves but I would never have broken the bonds of trust between the Regiment and me. I abided by the terms of confidentiality I had signed.

'There was a time, Monica, around September I think, when you asked Barbara questions about the course and the students. And Shelley, I believe?' He ran a finger down a column. 'You were asking questions about what she thought of the job? And you were – er – seeing one of the badged guys who got thrown off the course.'

That was it.

'Seeing?' I said. *'Seeing one of the students?'*

He held up a hand to stop me. 'Well, he was disciplined for leaving camp.'

'I know perfectly what "seeing" someone means,' I said, 'and I resent the suggestion. What I do in my own time is nothing to do with this place but if you're referring to "social informalities", that's disgraceful. Sam was fed up and struggling. I can ask a young man round to my house, surely, without it being seen as something sinister?'

George let out a sigh. We paused, like two boxers in mid-fight, suddenly falling apart limply when the bell goes. He lifted a hand as if waving a fly away and shook his head.

'Look, I agree, but –'

'Not that it would matter if we'd just decided to get married, George!' I interrupted him. 'Nobody can interfere in my private life. And as for asking Barbara,' I said, 'we were cleaning the silver, a mundane enough job at the best of times, I was still new and I'm interested in my job. What's wrong with that? Have they been compiling some sort of dossier on my innocent conversations?'

'OK, yes –'

'And as for Shelley –' I was on a roll – 'we were standing by the till waiting for lunch to start, I asked if she was happy working here and I asked because she's always so damned miserable and spiteful and bitter about her life!'

'OK –'

'It's not as if I was actually interested in whether Shelley was happy, by the way, it's called making conversation.'

George waved a hand.

'Can't do right for doing wrong!'

We paused. I took a deep breath. I'm laughing about it now, writing this, because I remember how ludicrous it all seemed even then, arguing about having conversations. None of this actually bothered me but I was exhausted and I thought it was a stupid time of day to bring it all up.

'Although it may not look like it, I am actually on your side, Monica,' George said eventually, arms on his desk, leaning towards me. Now he looked like a psychiatrist, making me feel loved and appreciated. 'The 2-2 guys like talking to you. You're a hit with the Regiment, as far as I have been told. Your customer-facing skills, front of-house and so on, are exceptional.'

'Yes, I know,' I said. 'That's why I'm annoyed. The civil service go on about leadership skills and assess us on "making a difference, being objective, growing and changing" for God's sake – oh, and while having our innocent conversations reported!' I crossed my arms again, feeling suddenly unable to stay awake.

'Well, look,' said George, standing up and looking at his watch, 'I'm going to make a note that I've spoken to you, and that there was a misunderstanding. But I don't think you should go up the top again. Let's leave it that you stay on this camp.'

I was stunned. The bastard.

'George, the terms of my civil service contract say that we can use the gym and swimming pool.'

He shook his head and held up a hand, gathering up his bags.

'Best stay on this camp, Monica. Just to satisfy Security. Your pass will be revoked for up there.'

This was getting worse.

'What? Seriously? I'm a civil servant. I'm not employed by the MOD.'

'I know, but it's the best way. Just for now. You don't need to go up there. I'll have a word with the Security Cell.'

He bustled about with papers on his desk, straightening everything. Beyond George, through his window, I could see the distant hills and the fields and sheep, and in the foreground a knot of visitors trying to find the mobile signal. They had been here several days and were charming, polite and engaging. I didn't want to leave this place, but I would if I had to.

'Please take this as my verbal month's notice. I'll complete the necessary forms tomorrow.'

George hung his head in exhaustion and put his hands in the pockets of his immaculate, razor-sharp-creased trousers. His hair looked stuck down and his parting judged with a spirit level.

'Don't do this, Monica. It'll leave us in a real pickle. We can't replace you in under six months. All the vetting. Please reconsider.'

'Why? Because it'll make you look bad?'

He didn't say anything.

'George...' I took a breath. 'George, how can I explain this to you?' I said. 'The world is not run as you think it is. It's run on goodwill. People who can't keep their staff get a reputation and poor reputations precede us. "Can't keep his staff", that's what people say out in the world. That's why in civvy life a boss would have a quiet word. Not all this ... ' I waved my arm at my file on his desk, '... this drama. Drama over a conversation. In your world, you can haul someone in, say what you like and they're stuck with it. Soldiers can't walk out if they don't like it, but I can. That's how the world works, George, and that's why you're going to be left in a mess. You, or rather the security people, didn't take the diplomatic route first; a quiet word, keep me on side. Maybe a bit of an explanation, how about that? Explain that asking another mess hand if she likes her job is pure dynamite.'

I told you that I'd tempted fate and fate took the challenge. But, I thought, on the other hand, maybe George would think twice about challenging me again if he knew he'd get an argument. I could but hope.

'People don't have to put up with bad working conditions, and right now, this isn't looking like a great job.'

'This is your world too, now, Monica,' he said limply. 'You're under different conditions here.'

'No, I'm under different terms of employment. Thirty days' notice. That's the contract.'

I'm making it all sound pretty bad, but the whole thing lasted maybe twenty minutes and, looking back now, I'm glad I didn't in the end do what I threatened in that hot-headed moment. George seemed to me to be a weak man in many ways, going through a nightmare divorce, struggling for money, arguing about access to his children and catering for weddings on the side. I suspected that the crackdown here on any perks had been his attempt to gain control in his own life, not ours. Make him look good.

Poor bugger.

'Thanks for coming in,' he said, shaking off his professional exterior and attempting an unaccustomed chilly smile. 'Anything exciting planned for the weekend?'

I tried to look pleasant in return. We were back on common ground.

'Defrosting the fridge.'

Even now, when I'm on a long train journey and my thoughts have nowhere special to go, I close my eyes and find myself going over everything again. Why did I make such a stand against the 'questions' thing? Could I not just have kept it all to myself, gone home quietly and resigned anyway? I didn't do anything wrong; I wasn't criticising anybody or even talking about camp, but they had to shut me up. Keep me in my place. The whole thing really did affect me.

I left George's office and went out into the sunshine. I stopped by the bench. I was exhausted, upset and downcast. I wanted to weep, but instead I put my forehead into my hand and let tears trickle down my cheeks silently. My chest felt crushed by the effort. I longed to lie down and sob, but I could just picture those cameras whirring round to capture my distress on CCTV. I pulled myself together, stood up and held my head high. I had some pride left.

I swiped my pass and headed out, waving cheerily to whoever was in the guardhouse. Across the road, I yielded to my tears again as I reached my car and sat in the front seat, upset beyond belief. Why couldn't I fit in? Would I really have to start swearing and shouting in order to be accepted? Should I resign after all? I didn't know what to do.

At that very moment, the Padre's car turned from the lane into the car park and she saw me in distress.

XIII

If I'd gone home when I should have that day and not been detained by the whole 'questions' thing with George, I wouldn't have run into Zero Johnstone. As he loved to remind people, Zero rhymed with hero but the most impressive thing was that it didn't matter who you spoke to, everybody liked Zed.

Zero was a badged superhero down here on a long project and was always in for two meals a day. You didn't need to notice Zero – he was in your face the minute the dining room doors opened, wise-cracking, plunging his hands deep into his trouser pockets, shifting from foot to foot with a barrage of jokes and questions and challenges, which were fine if you'd just come on duty and were feeling fresh but tedious if you'd been there since dawn. Some of us actually hid if we heard his voice. I'm not joking.

If I tell you that Zero's birth name was Oliver you'll see where I'm going. Zero, or Zed, was a one-off, born when his Norwegian mother was working in England and gave birth prematurely to her son in London. Oliver got a British passport, his siblings back on Scandinavian soil didn't, and he made the most of it, moving back to the land of his birth aged sixteen, settling in Torquay with a relative and later joining the army. 'Norway's gain was the British Army's loss' went the grim joke in Zed's squadron but, true to his Viking identity, which Zed adopted when it suited him, he cut a swathe through the army's ranks, sailed through Special Forces Selection and landed in Hereford. I only learned some time later that his name was Oliver when something in the boss's office was labelled for a Sergeant O. Johnstone.

'Hey, Monica, going back to town?'

I was by my car, trying to fix my face, when who should be tiptoeing carefully over The Area cattle grid but the unmistakeable Zed. I'd shed a few more tears after my chat with Padre Jill, who, understanding that I was desperate to get home for a rest, suggested I come for a proper chat in the garrison church up the top as soon as I had a day off. Zed raised a hand, and for once his easy-going, knowing smile cheered me instantly. Dressed in a checked shirt and jeans, daysack slung over one shoulder, his compact, glossy, muscular frame appeared fashioned from marble. With his crew-cut hair, wide grin and quick-fire banter, he seemed more like a stand-up comedian than an elite soldier. Yes, Zed could be tiresome sometimes, but he embraced whatever the world had to offer and I admired that. Elite soldiers aren't all about guns and blowing things up: Zed was unusual in the Regiment, having worked professionally for several years before joining the military. To be fair to him, he brought with him a range of useful specialist skills.

'Any chance I can bum a lift to town?' Zed said. 'You live that way, don't you? Or have you got plans?'

He squeezed himself between my car and the one parked next to it. The car park was a small area which used to be a tennis court, surrounded by a dilapidated chain fence. He crouched down very slightly to check his face in the wing mirror, rubbing away the sweat.

'Well, no, no plans, not really.' I smiled. 'I've just finished. I just want to sleep. How do you know which way I live anyway? Stalking me?'

'No, I've got mates near you. I've seen your car.'

I pressed the key fob to unlock.

'You'll have to forgive me,' I said, 'I smell terribly of cooking.' I was embarrassed. 'My shoes...' My voice trailed away as I looked down at my feet. I usually climbed out of my uniform the second I walked through my front door and headed straight for the shower after throwing my clothes into the washing machine.

He waved it away. 'No problem,' he said. 'Look at me! My mate was going to take me back but I finished early. So if you're going that way...?' His ice-blue eyes were twinkling, tempting me.

'To town?'

'I'm going to camp, but you can drop me at Asda.'

'No probs,' I said. 'Get in.'

For action-oriented people, inaction can be extremely stressful. I'd found out that much since I came here, and some of the elite soldiers were particularly bad at relaxing. There was something kaleidoscopic about Zed, as if one twist of the lens would shift random pieces of his personality around and a completely different aspect would fall into place. To me, he was mostly a pestering, capricious man who didn't appear prone to bouts of introspection. Zed may have lacked social graces, emotional intelligence and certain manners, but he lacked nothing else. His badged mates envied his astonishing physique, saying that he did almost nothing to stay so buff (allow me to add that I saw him once straight from a shower, stark naked, and the effect was not unadjacent to a masterpiece.) Sunny and optimistic, contrary to the usual stereotypes of a Nordic temperament, he laughed easily and acted spontaneously. On the downside, everything had to be his way. If you didn't want to do something, go somewhere or try some food, Zed pestered until you caved in. He could be exhausting, his mercurial, agile mind thinking up ever grander plans, most of which were ridiculously out of the question. Zed wasn't a man to countenance obstacles. Later in our acquaintance, he texted fourteen times at midnight to tell me which route he wanted to take on a walk that I didn't want to do anyway, but he'd pressured me into it, saying I'd love it. My heart sank when I heard that his new shared accommodation was in a house a minute's walk from mine, news which he announced with glee. 'I'm living right behind you! I can come over any time! What are your plans on your day off?' he'd say, one of the most irritating phrases I never want to hear, and when I took to saying, 'Oh, I'll be relaxing, doing nothing special,' he'd reply, 'Right! you're coming on a walk with me!' as if doing nothing wasn't a valid way to pass one's time.

Like me, Zed didn't have many relatives. Mine were mostly dead and he hadn't seen his mother or sister for five years, something we talked about at length once. 'We don't get on,' he said simply. I know that he didn't receive any cards or wishes from family on his birthday, so perhaps something went badly wrong. Maybe he was the black sheep of the family? Getting into the SAS is a glittering achievement, but without the support of loved ones, he was like a lonely boarding-school boy having to stay at school on his own during the summer holidays because his parents decided they had better things to do than spend time with him.

'Hey, I'll drive,' Zed said, more as a statement than a question. 'Put the top down?'

'Er, OK,' I said. 'That'll be nice, thanks.' Actually I wasn't sure about this. I quickly pulled and locked the boot separator and leaned in to hold down the button that operated the roof. It folded down expertly in fourteen seconds, like origami.

'Neat,' he said. He was almost skipping about now like a boxer in training, jigging from foot to foot, keen to get going.

I moved to the passenger side of my car and slid down into the low, blue leather seat. It was taut from lack of use, almost like new. I messed around with the switches for a moment, adjusting things to make it easy for Zed. The car keeled to one side dramatically then there was a gentle thump and a slight creaking noise, like bedsprings, as the seat was manipulated backwards as far as it would go. I felt the tight press of his enormous thighs overflowing the seat next me, previously only occupied by my small frame. Zed was in the driving seat.

The roads from camp to camp are a dream for boy racers. At one point, a notorious black-spot for speeding, Zed coolly announced that he was just 'topping the ton' – 100 miles per hour. I was gripping the seat. 'Please don't,' I said, 'I'll get a ticket.'

'She's going well,' he shouted back, adjusting something so the car roared forwards even faster. 'Bet you don't get her out much. Did you know that's an overdrive setting?'

I'd owned the car for eleven years at this point and no, I didn't know it had an overdrive.

Zed was blue-light trained, as they all were, but it was still nerve-wracking. He pulled into the Asda car park, half a mile from town. I didn't know how he intended travelling the remaining four miles to camp, but we were going in different directions and I wasn't going to devote too much time to thinking about his onward travel plans. I wanted to get home, out of these horrible stinking work clothes, have a shower and a nap.

'Tell you what,' he said, gaily. 'Take me to camp to drop off my stuff, drop me back in town and I'll give you a driving lesson?' He pinned me with his bright, blazing eyes and raised eyebrows. Oh God, he'd hit my weak spot. I can't bear to disappoint anyone.

'Go on then,' I said, shaking my head. 'Cheeky. I passed my driving test years ago.'

'Hey, yes, but this is a special lesson!' He released the handbrake, checked his mirrors and drew back into the supermarket traffic.

'You were going super-fast on that stretch, Zed. You could have got banned.'

He shrugged.

'Seriously,' I persisted. 'Do you get, say, parking or speeding tickets? I've seen a woman in MT who seems to be paying off tickets every week.'

'Only if we're working,' he said.

'Well, what would happen if you lost your licence, like if you got caught over the limit and were banned for a year? Could the Regiment get you off then?'

He laughed maniacally.

'I'd be *fucked*!'

Badged men must adhere to the same laws as the rest of us and I think a lot of people would be surprised at that. Over the next few weeks my car and Zero Johnstone became inseparable. Mine wasn't a special car, it was a 2005 model I'd bought new and saw no reason to change, but he began running over to my house now and again and driving me anywhere and everywhere. It was a great summer for this, especially when I had a day off and Zed came round after work to take me for a late spin. Anyway, it was a drive out, and like some poor old lady who doesn't go to many places, I felt grateful for the change of scene.

Calculated risk-taking is part of the Regiment mentality. If a light were red, Zed would try to drive through it; if it were amber he would speed up. He changed lanes expertly, but it still left me clinging to my seat. We would park, go for coffee, then off again.

One sunny Saturday he was again treading water for something to do. Staying afloat but going nowhere, badged guys could often be at a loose end if they were living on camp or in accommodation provided for them and didn't have the sort of house and garden maintenance that homeowners like me had piling up every weekend. Going places in my car to give him a bit of an adrenaline boost was his idea of a day well spent. Unfortunately, he insisted on providing a running commentary on how to anticipate a tricky bend, reading white lines in the middle of the road and other things I would have been interested in if he hadn't gone on about them for the entire journey. Eventually he settled into a rambling commentary about the car in front, who we followed for a good twenty miles. Despite my trying to change the subject, he was enthralled with it, eagerly anticipating when she would hit the brake as she answered her mobile, a gentle smile never leaving his face. 'See! She's just answered her phone!' he'd cry, pleased with his powers of deduction.

Whether I was getting bored of his story or maybe I just wanted to get home, I interrupted him.

'Yeah, fine, I don't have to hear every last detail about the car in front. Can you talk about something else?'

Yet I would never have done any of these things without Zed needling away at me to come out and play. His mates had wives and children and chores at the weekends and would go home, miles away. Hereford at the weekend could be a deathly place if they were single, and even single housemates might go and stay with their parents sometimes, leaving Zed to amuse himself, which was never a good thing. I was cycling down a route that follows an old railway line in Hereford one Saturday morning when ahead of me I saw Zed, running. He kept stopping and twisting about like you do in a warm-up and then he'd start off again, but he kept stopping to walk. He wasn't injured: I knew Zed, and his heart wasn't in it. I got off my bike and walked behind him at a distance but then I decided not to catch up with him and instead I turned around and cycled home. Zed was a nice guy, but you wouldn't want to get stuck with him for too long.

Anyway, one day I was giving him directions to Bristol via a country route to avoid a bottleneck.

'It's easier this way and we'll go through a gorgeous little chocolate-box village, you'll see,' I said, hoping he'd take my suggestion on board, which was never guaranteed. I rather fancied stopping in lovely Frome or Bradford upon Avon, but he kept driving and said nothing in reply, which was unusual for him. Then suddenly he said, 'Why chocolate box?'

I started to explain how nice the village was that I had in mind, but he interrupted, 'Yes, I get that, but why did you call it a "chocolate-box" village?'

'Well, I suppose that's just the way it's always been,' I said, puzzled. 'It's just a phrase. A tradition.'

He was still driving on the M4, not taking the diversion.

'But why? Why is a pretty house on a box of chocolates?'

I realised I was in a corner.

'Well... you know at Christmas those tins of biscuits, say, sometimes have pictures of cottages with snow all over them to look Christmassy?'

'Obviously.'

'So, I suppose a thatched cottage with a pretty garden –'

'Yeah, but why's it on biscuit tins?'

I held up my hands in surrender.

'Look, forget about the chocolates and the biscuits, Zed.'

'But the village?'

His driving was beginning to worry me as much as the conversation was annoying me. With one hand on the top of the steering-wheel and the other somewhere on the back of my seat, he kept darting puzzled glances at me.

'Zed, *forget the bloody chocolate box*!'

Badged men could be persistent. It's in their nature. These brave men are good at what they do precisely because they're willing to take risks, push their luck and tempt fate. I guess it's part of the mentality and traits many criminals possess, except geezers are trained to rein it in.

I remember Zed telling me on one of our long journeys in the car that they would always have a go. It might be seeing if they could get us to unlock the door so they could get a coffee or ask if there were any sandwiches going when it was out of hours for food.

'Geezers will always try,' he said, 'but if it doesn't work out, they don't mind. They'll just go quite happily and try somewhere else.'

I was glad he told me that. I decided to say no a bit more often and let him go and nag someone else for his entertainment. I admired his nerve, though.

Eventually Zed's special project came to an end, he went back up the top to HQ and was away doing the tough stuff for many months. I went into a totally different job too. Then, lo and behold, I heard that he'd got married and was now the father of twins, for heaven's sake! Good for him. Maybe now he would go on adventures with his family.

Some of the men thought Zero was a nice sort of psychopath. Others just described him as lonely. True, he lacked a certain empathy for my life and its exigencies, he was impulsive and, despite the hundreds of hours we spent in one another's company, I doubt that he really knew much about me. But now we were back to the 'questions' thing. People here didn't ask questions. I might have told Zed in passing that I came from up north, but he would never have asked. That's what it was like here. Like all of them, Zed was brave and steadfast and if anything got him down, he didn't show it. While most men moaned, I never heard Zed complain about anything. When he was fed up, he laughed at the absurdity of all those crazy people, issuing impossible orders. 'You can tell him to fuck off,' said one of his mates one day, 'but he just bounces back.'

Everyone agreed that it was impossible to offend Zed; he simply laughed it all off and I think that was why he was so popular. I also heard amazing tales of just how brave he was, and of his awesome capabilities, and I think that his single-mindedness, that ability to see to the end of a problem and to get the right result was what also resulted in him being such a selfish companion and yet one of the most compulsively lovely men on the camp. He knew what he wanted out of life and, despite the crushing hold the organisation had over all its people, Zed knew which side his bread was buttered. There's nobody quite like Zero Johnstone, and I'm privileged to count him as a friend.

Quite a few of the men on camp were bordering on the 'good psychopath' spectrum – some former elite soldiers even boast proudly that a touch of psychopathic traits is essential in the Regiment. I personally don't think there's such a thing as a 'good' psychopath; I believe all this talk is just a way of grabbing attention. There are plenty of military fanatics out there who are inspired by characters like Travis Bickle in *Taxi Driver*, played by Robert De Niro, who practises an intimidating, thuggish persona in the mirror of his bedsit. We all know the type. Some are inspired to think of themselves as possessing special military skills like De Niro's character again in the gruesome 1991 psychological thriller *Cape Fear*. That type of character, the soldier with a grudge who has dieted to four per cent body fat while in prison, and honed his muscles for revenge, appeals to some rather dangerous people, and this obsession is only fuelled further by former elite soldiers who peddle stuff about ruthlessness, impulsivity, fearlessness and lack of conscience being the essential components of an elite soldier's toolbox. How do you answer people like that? It's bullshit. They've never done anything except be in the military. I'd love to put them into a PR company for three years and see how their famed resilience holds up then.

Some people who are fans of this stuff admire a soldier who has the 'guts' to leave a marriage – running off never to face their wife again because he's 'feeling trapped' – as a true hard man. Yet it's moral cowardice, isn't it, not heroic single-mindedness? Where's the famed resilience in a man who runs away and can't face his responsibilities? The reality is slightly less awesome when it lands back in their laps as they cope with financial ruin, divorce and lots of other mundane matters which have no respect for anybody's elite or fabled status. It sounds good to say these geezers lack emotions and 'get the job done' but I can tell you that when I worked there, a lot of the time they were on their phones to divorce lawyers, sweating in panic as their lives crumbled ahead of them.

On a more positive note, I didn't ever meet more than a handful of psychopathic types. They're mostly good people who'd help anybody. Their fearlessness was admirable, but the ruthlessness... how far might they take that?

XIV

I came to work on early shift at six o'clock on the morning after the UK had voted in the EU referendum, Friday 24th June 2016, and at 7.20am, during breakfast, the result was announced. Well, you should have witnessed the uproar and excitement. I'm not suggesting that the Regiment were all in favour of Brexit, I'm just reporting that there was a huge amount of whooping and clapping. I'll leave it at that. The same thing happened when Donald Trump became President-elect of the USA that November: the dining room was agog at the news coming through on the cookhouse television, and the geezers' analysis of Trump went on for weeks. That year there was also an extraordinarily high number of unexpected celebrity deaths, including George Michael, Victoria Wood, Prince, David Bowie and many more, but the only time I saw real shock and the absolute undivided attention of the Regiment was during the terrible Grenfell Tower tragedy in 2017. It seemed to me that every single soldier in the garrison was watching as the horror unfolded in that tower block. It was the UK's worst residential fire since World War Two, and the sight of the tower on the skyline was one we were all familiar with on the approach to London, a city we all knew well. I think that was part of the horror. It was something that could happen to any of us.

I'd decided to stick it out in the job. Padre Jill had become a friend and we spent many hours sitting in St. Christopher's, the garrison church, talking about how I might deal with the different life I was experiencing. At home, I cried a lot. They were usually tears of frustration at being singled out and discriminated against because I was educated. Padre Jill said I had nothing to be ashamed of: I should continue being true to myself, working hard and 'soldiering on' and maybe it would set an example.

So I did.

Each regiment on camp had its own chaplain, called a padre. They ministered to the military personnel, their families and the civilians in that regiment. Much later, the principal padre, Adrian, would ask if I'd like to apply for the job of verger of the garrison church. It was a job I would have loved, but it wasn't coming vacant for another year and whilst it was all very well making grand gestures of resignation, I didn't have the courage of my convictions, I suppose: I needed a job and they weren't plentiful. So I stuck it out and ended up spending the rest of 2016 in the kitchen taking Jill's advice. I began to enjoy my time at work a lot more. Eventually I was tipped off about a job as a storekeeper at the main HQ. It didn't sound remotely like my sort of thing but nevertheless it appealed to me in a strange way, especially being taught to drive a forklift, so I applied.

My interview for the storekeeper job was an entirely different occasion from that for the kitchen job. Based in the quartermaster department, it was a routine but very important job supplying the SAS with things they would need anywhere they happened to be. The clincher for me was the level of responsibility: I would work with just one other civilian on a day-to-day basis, and a corporal would oversee us.

The conference room where the interview was held was big and polished and smelled musty. A massive square table dominated the otherwise bare room, and there were no windows. I've never been to a court martial, but with a couple of the badged soldiers sitting opposite me in uniform, and a senior civil service representative chairing the whole thing, it felt like I was being reprimanded for something. I steeled myself.

The Regiment men said very little but sat still, looking at me the whole time. Knowing the job was a dirty one, with lots of lifting and pulling boxes around, I'd put on a carefully thought-out ensemble of practical walking shoes and jeans to show that I was at ease with a tough job, topped by a crisp white blouse and tweed jacket to demonstrate both that I could pull off some style when required and that I was no stranger to the outdoor life. I cut right back on the make-up too, in case it suggested I'd spend my time stressing about smudged mascara and, of course, I pulled my hair back. I knew even if I wore a boiler suit, my general bearing wouldn't scream 'forklift truck driver' but I wanted to make as much effort as I could – without looking like I had.

The older man, who turned out to be the quartermaster, only asked one question. The QM had a soft voice and an endearing manner, smiling whenever my eyes caught his during the rest of the interview. He had once been an adrenaline-fuelled soldier, for heaven's sake, but I couldn't imagine it.

'How are you with – um –' he wiggled his fingers as if using a keyboard – 'you know, computers and so on? Because there's a bit of that involved.'

'Oh, well, I'm not brilliant,' I admitted – might as well be honest – 'but I'm a very quick learner.'

He sat back and smiled kindly. Was that a good answer, or not? Why didn't I just say it was no problem? My future was in his hands. The civil service man, another kind uncle-type, was asking the questions, but the real clincher was, could the QM see me as one of his staff?

The other guy from the Regiment was the RQ1, a temporary line manager of the civilian employees in the stores, the line manager proper being away on a three-month course. There would be eight of us, he told me – storekeepers, a carpenter and a tailoress. He was fair, stocky and animated with a strong Cockney accent. He wore the combats and blue belt ensemble, and he had just one question: 'Are you OK with being trained on the forklift?'

I completely overdid the enthusiasm. 'Oh, of course! I absolutely can't *wait* to learn something new. It's exciting,' I added for good measure, recalling my previous interview for the kitchen job when I'd been shaking with nerves and didn't know if I should cross my legs. No wonder Michael hadn't remembered my name when he interviewed me then. I shot the men my best full-beam smile of confidence and remembered not to fidget.

Well, it must have worked, because within days I was notified that the civil service had approved my application.

I was over the moon. Whatever notes had gone onto my personal record about 'asking questions', they can't have been that bad. The storekeeper job was straight Mondays to Fridays so I lost the shift allowance payment, and it would be the end of free meals too, but even so, I eagerly signed on the dotted line. I was getting away from the kitchen and this time I didn't even have to wait months for security clearance. I secretly decided that whatever the job was like, I was going to damn well make the best of it.

On checking the interview feedback on the civil service jobs portal, I noted with pride the QM's comment: WILL MAKE A GOOD MEMBER OF THE TEAM.

Working at the Regiment HQ felt like living on the set of the 1998 film *The Truman Show*. If you don't know the film, it's a comedy-drama about an adopted baby who grows into a man without knowing that his whole life is a TV show, watched by millions. State-of-the-art technology and 5,000 cameras record Truman's every move from baby to adult, while all the other people in his life are actors. The perfect homes behind white picket fences where his neighbours live with well-behaved, obedient children, and the cheery shopkeepers in his home town all paint an image of Utopia, yet all the while the whole thing is completely rehearsed and scripted.

On the face of it, HQ was similar. People moved out of the way if you drove past, with a friendly lift of the hand in acknowledgement; nobody looked at you with suspicion or unease or annoyance as they sometimes do in that other world outside the gates, the world without the razor wire and sniffer dogs. Nondescript vehicles would glide by almost soundlessly on the rigid grid system, observing the 20mph speed limit, which added to the sense of unreality. After the confines of the training camp, my eyes could rest, looking out across the huge expanses of green, taking in the distant buildings. People walked their dogs at lunchtime, played rugby or football, went for a run or a swim. There was little sense of the military here, no saluting or sharp uniforms, except on special occasions, and everyone was called by their first name only. The little church was always open for quiet contemplation and they held christenings, worship every Sunday and even regiment funerals. Having spent a year and a half feeling locked up down at the training camp, working at HQ was like being let out of Guantanamo Bay into an open prison.

There were problems, of course there were. Here, the geezers walked across the grass wherever they chose and parking was chaotic, with vehicles pulled up over kerbs, two wheels dug into muddy channels forged by more and more vehicles. This wasn't careless behaviour, it was necessity. The camp was big, but not big enough. The men here were all of a similar build and seemed alike. When training down the road, the men would be aggressive, fearless and bold; here, they moved without purpose, as if at a holiday resort.

If your only knowledge of this elite regiment's camp comes from books written twenty-five years ago, I can tell you that place doesn't exist anymore. In *Married to the SAS* published in 1997 by Frances Nicholson, who was the third wife of Andy McNab, she writes about life on the camp in the 1990s:

> Driving into the home of the SAS, Britain's elite regiment of troops was, on most occasions, easier than walking into a children's playground. The security on the gates was so lax no-one bothered to ask for a pass or seek a name or identification from a total stranger. When men from the Regiment couldn't be bothered walking the extra few hundred yards around to the main gate they would simply climb the gate and drop into the base.

That description is simply astonishing to me. The old camp is now a housing estate, and whilst I can't give out any further details of the tight security procedures, I can assure you that girlfriends definitely aren't sitting at the camp bar or coffee shop, and you will need much more than a pass to gain entry, for certain.

In the 2015 James Bond film *Spectre*, a young geeky man meets Bond in an art gallery to tell him, 'I am your new quartermaster,' whereupon he dishes out a range of fancy gadgets. Well, I'm afraid our quartermaster department was nothing like that. We were based at the furthest perimeter of the camp, almost sliding off the map and into the weeds, despite the fact that, as any military person knows, the QM is a very senior and important person, holding a substantial budget and responsible for everything the garrison needs in the way of kit, furniture – anything you can think of.

Gradually, as you walked or drove down to the quartermaster buildings, the gardeners and statue polishers faded away, to be replaced by weeds and litter. Not that it was pristine in the centre of camp, but it was tidy and clean with spectacular lines of daffodils in the spring. Down here was like a large industrial estate, with trucks, Land Rovers and forklifts here and there, in and out, delivering, collecting, loading and unloading, reversing and clattering. People shouted instructions over the din, gigantic telescopic handlers and rough-terrain vehicles manoeuvred in and out of the shipping containers ready to be filled with kit that were left right outside the store's front door. We were housed in a line of identical huge green hangars with plain name boards above the doors. Ours was the biggest of the stores and, I soon discovered, the busiest. Other stores were staffed usually by one person, maybe two at the most, but nobody mingled. We met when we collected our keys in the morning from the quartermaster building and met again when we handed them back, but apart from that, I didn't see the others. 'Where is there to go anyway?' the tailoress, a jolly, contented-looking woman called Pam said, genuinely puzzled. She parked her car right outside her little cabin, stayed in there all day with her two dogs, walked them a couple of times and then went home. She had been in the job twenty-three years, and thank goodness she signed her keys in every night, otherwise nobody would have known she existed.

The main quartermaster building was twenty-five yards away from the stores. Once you'd swiped your pass to get inside (nobody could get in anywhere on camp without a security pass), there was no reception, just stone floors, lots of noticeboards with instructions and dates for procedures or tests or briefings, and chalk blackboards with immediate instructions for the day, or reminders of classes. Absolutely nothing on camp, as far as I could see, had any softness or personality. It was like a prison; practical and serviceable.

The store I was to be working in was in a pretty desolate place. Either side of the door were two gigantic rubbish bins that filled up several times a day with discarded packaging from the numerous deliveries. Every time someone opened the bin to put more rubbish in, the same amount flew out, especially Styrofoam, which wedged itself into every nook and cranny, hanging off bushes and branches. There were also cages outside, lots of them, for hazardous equipment or batteries that couldn't be stored indoors; Portakabins that groaned in the wind as if crying for attention and housed stuff nobody wanted but might need one day; and shipping containers, mostly with nothing inside, there for years sinking into the ground as if they had put down roots, listing to one side with weeds growing a foot high around them. We sometimes had to search for something desperately needed and Craig and I would grab handfuls of keys with cage or container numbers on them, having decided to take the lot and see what worked. In the unlikely event that something did, we prised open the rusty doors and were greeted by the hot, pent-up smell of old chairs piled in long ago and left to gently stew for several hot summers, or, on one occasion, knocked back by pungent gases from chemicals stored for eight years. When I gained the confidence to ask Craig why 200 boxes containing chemical cleaning compound had ended up in an ISO container since 2011, he told me it had been a simple accounting mistake. A couple of extra noughts had been added to an order and when the stock arrived they had to hide it away quickly and cook the books accordingly. Everybody seemed in on it too. It didn't matter how far up the chain of command you went, nobody seemed bothered. I slipped an innocent word about what to do with this mountain of forgotten stock to the sergeant and staff sergeant who would be moving on soon to other jobs, and to the RQ1, but nothing happened. I even mentioned it to the QM, who shrugged and smiled and said, 'These things happen.' So we locked it all up again.

It was the wind that did it for me. Whatever the true weather, you only had to get out of your car or come out of the building and it was like being caught in the vortex of a cyclone. It drowned out all thoughts, challenged dignity and vanity; hair was clutched and hats held on tightly, and unbuttoned jackets flew open. Rubbish from the bins would whip about wildly like a thousand feeding pigeons suddenly airborne as a flock, causing you to duck. Still, set against my memories of the kitchen, at least I could be free here, I thought.

I came in on my first day to the sound of telephones that nobody was answering being amplified and echoing around the store. There was no welcome for me; indeed I wasn't noticed as I arrived. The corporal in charge was busy, but I soon understood that I would be one of just two people working there full-time, with a sergeant and the corporal overseeing things in between managing other stores. I wasn't given any instruction about what I should wear, apart from safety boots – and these had to be a special order because nobody had considered that a woman with size 4 feet would ever be in this sort of job. The rest was up to me. I had some Barbour black trousers at the back of a cupboard and a light zip-up black jacket for mountain climbing, so I put those on. I asked the corporal, when he arrived, if I was wearing the right sort of outfit but he looked at me puzzled, shrugged and said, 'Whatever.' Nobody cared what the hell I wore.

It was completely dizzying, the amount of everyday stock the store held for anything you can think of, from storm candles to fencing wire to rolls of muslin to sandbags, fridges and ironing boards. Whole aisles were devoted to equipment for field kitchens, there were padlocks – oh, the range of padlocks! – and safety goggles, sun lotion, insect repellent ... on and on the shelves went, and we supplied the entire garrison. Funnily enough, while it was a huge amount to take in, I felt calm and strangely excited to face a job with so many intricacies and unknowns. Unlike a civilian store, these items were in colourless rows of green crates, labelled with a name and stock number. This wasn't a shop. The majority of our job was fulfilling long orders from each squadron, which had its own storekeeper, and these orders had to be put in six weeks in advance, that's how big they were. Some orders were built up over a couple of months, filling shipping containers gradually because the job was too great to do at the last moment. The kitchens placed orders for field kitchens, mountains of supplies that might take me a week to forklift to a despatch bay. These weren't shopping lists, either. Official forms were used, with something called NSN (NATO Stock Number) and other abbreviations I had to learn quickly, and this was a huge responsibility, especially packing hazard items which needed all kinds of special paperwork, and the potential for disaster if we got anything wrong.

Most days, a few men wearing the blue lanyard of 2-2 Regiment came in for an item they might need. It could be a pair of pliers, a bale of rags or a Stanley knife. These were opportunities to have a chat and also, as I got to know the job, stop them taking everything they might also want for a spot of home decorating or bike maintenance! It was easy to see how these men lost all sense of reality around the question of cost, especially as Craig and Adie would often just give them what they wanted to save the paperwork.

Craig was the forty-two-year-old senior storekeeper. Loud, ebullient and dynamic, he was a Yorkshire family man, ex-army and powerful as an ox. Craig did all the really tough outdoor jobs; although I was supposed to do the same work and no allowances were made for my being female, he wouldn't have it. 'I wouldn't want my wife hauling around piles of scaffolding all day,' he said, insisting that I could be most useful if I stayed and minded the store, otherwise we'd have to lock up. It wasn't until many months later that I wondered if he'd wanted me to mind the store because I was too small and useless to do anything else, but to be honest, it suited me to run things my way.

'You'll find it all if you look around,' Craig said, and smiled. 'Pick it, put it on a few pallets and I'll pack it later. We'll be the picker and the packer team!' He slapped me on the shoulder, which almost knocked me over. 'Oh and watch out for Adie. He'll be in soon. He's a cunt.'

Adie was the corporal from the Royal Logistics Corps and indeed another c-word – corrupt. Corrupt to the bone. The military presence – or rather, absence – in our store, he was free from the shackles of honesty, decency and plain good manners, fancying himself as some sort of Mafia Godfather. He drifted in about three o'clock every day, switched on the computer, propped up his mobile phone and commenced a series of calls to different women, smooching them in a language which, mercifully, I couldn't understand, all the while banging the keyboard with his fingers to process invoices. Once completed, the paperwork would be dropped straight onto the floor, where it remained for months. When Adie left, we found paperwork stuffed everywhere: hundreds of dockets and demands and receipts crammed, not filed, into what the new corporal called the 'drawer of death'. How he had got away without the sergeant in charge noticing was another question altogether, but I was learning how this place worked. It was chaos. I'm baffled as to how the chain of command in the logistics department was allowed to fail so badly, but my conclusion was that some people were left alone for fear of offending certain sensibilities, and admitting that somebody had failed so badly meant that those above him would 'look bad' for not taking steps, and so it went on, with blind eyes turned all round.

Every week, Sergeant Jules would come into the store and snap at me to be sure my paperwork was signed and yet she was several months behind countersigning anything. She never looked around or went upstairs, where she'd have seen the blatant health and safety failures. Fire exits were blocked with towers of boxes, aisles were impeded by pallets so we had to tiptoe across them and actually climb over boxes. In my second week, my size-four foot slipped between the pallet struts and got caught, resulting in nerve damage to my leg which was still painful two months later, but being new, I didn't say anything: I didn't want to be seen moaning the minute I got here.

Adie was one of the most deeply unpleasant people I've ever met, and that's saying something. He picked up some paperwork one day and glanced at it with narrowed eyes, then thrust it my way with a straight arm while looking determinedly in the other direction, as if he were trying to avoid seeing some exam results.

'Do something with this,' he said in a quiet, lisping voice. 'You'll pick up the destination details from the top line. File them.' He beckoned me to follow him down the row of furniture. 'That sofa goes to HQ. That sofa is for the QM's office – and that one's for me.'

'For you?'

He stopped and turned, coming closer. He towered over me and glared into my eyes so that I had to look up at him. I felt like a young altar-boy waiting for the sign that I should swing the incense burner and waft the prayers of the faithful towards him. He loved to see me looking up at him with wide, obedient eyes, taking his orders. There were tyrannical dictators in the world who were nicer than Adie.

'I'll bring a van at four o'clock,' he said. 'A friend gave me a lift to Heathrow airport. The sofa is a gift in return.' He gave his thin smile. 'Keep him sweet.'

I didn't know then that Adie had all the administrative means at his disposal to write it off.

I wish I could describe the myriad sensations that washed over me in that first week, but that still wouldn't be enough: you'd need to smell it. The store smelled of coffee, urine from dirty toilets with unclean floors, dust and oil. You'd need to be in there when the wind blows hard and you think you're onboard a huge container ship, its creaking and groaning sounding perilously like it was about to collapse. Hear their men's chat and the endless beeping of dozens of passes being held to the pad outside the door. My brain was on fire with thousands of new things to see and make sense of and remember. It was hard telling one person from the other; even the sergeant barely displayed a gender, dressed in those camouflage clothes with her hair invisible in its tight bun and wearing no make-up. It was confusing.

Although Craig was away a lot, we started the day together, catching up with the jobs schedule, and during those times I got to know him quite well. He made me laugh with tales of his five children, all girls, and he'd had an interesting life in the army before becoming a civil servant like me. One afternoon I was alone in the store and I'd decided to get the shelves and stock into some sort of shape, a job that would take me weeks. I was trying to learn the system of NSNs, and something called the D of Q, which was all about denomination of quantities.

The fire door between us and the store next door clanged open and Sergeant Jules bustled in. She strode across the vast flooring area, threading between the boxes as though she were slalom skiing down a mountain.

'Monica, hi. Come into the office, will you?' she said, not even looking at me or breaking her step.

I felt mildly annoyed that my train of thought had been shattered while counting tins of foot powder for the troops. I'd just got to 258.

'I've come to see if you're settling in OK?'

Jules was a severe, humourless-looking woman with a high, shrill Scottish accent and she was already sitting at Craig's desk, hands clasped, looking at her watch as if irritated that I'd taken thirty seconds to reach her. The two desks faced one another with another table we used for paperwork in between them. I sat opposite her. She spoke quickly, eyes darting around, constantly twiddling her watch and shuffling her feet. God, I thought, I hope I don't have to put up with that voice too often.

'Oh, hi, yes – I'm fine. A lot to get through but I'm really enjoying learning –'

'OK, Monica, I'll just go through things,' she rattled on, clearly not expecting an answer to her question. 'You know your hours?'

I nodded.

Off she went, reinforcing the terms of employment I already knew, and the tight control of our lunch hour (for which we weren't paid). She was counting things off on her fingers. As she was talking, a badged guy came in and, while he was waiting his turn, used the toilet located one pace away from the office. It was one of those moments when you need to rattle a drawer noisily or clank some keys to cover up the sound. I felt hot and bothered.

'Anyway, Monica, in the meantime, welcome. Any questions?'

Jules drummed her fingers on the desk then beat her palms as if playing the bongos. I'd already learned that 'Any questions?' meant nothing of the sort.

'Okey-dokey then, I need to go. Oh – except you'll need a health and safety clearance. And … ask Craig to explain the laundry.'

And she disappeared.

I finished laminating the new signs and watched the clock hands crawl round to four o'clock. It didn't seem as if Craig would be back to ask about the laundry and I thought maybe it was a good time to check it out myself.

The laundry room seemed to be a place where things were kept rather than laundered. There were rails and rails of weird kit I didn't recognise and lots of rugby shirts in huge piles. The floor was covered with heaps of dirty tea towels simply dumped there. It was a dark, narrow, long room with a massive industrial washing machine and dryer. A small, dirty opaque window at one end allowed a view of a cardboard recycling area in a skip at the top of a set of metal steps. The peeling linoleum was repaired here and there with shiny gaffer tape and the floor was sloped slightly towards drains that ran the length of the room. A cracked mirror, mottled brown like you see in junk shops, was somewhat carelessly hung with string high up on a wall behind a shelf of duvet covers. For a state-of-the-art training camp for elite soldiers, it seemed they'd reached the perimeter of the estate and run out of ideas.

I stood on the bottom of some racking to gain the height needed to look into the mirror. I pulled my cuff over my hand to rub a clear spot, not really because I wanted to look into the mirror, but because it pained me to see it looking so dirty and neglected. Behind my reflection, a face was looking straight at me, shrouded in murk from the mirror, a wraith, an apparition.

'Oh my God!'

My heart raced. I swung around, clapping my crossed hands to my chest. I expected it to be nothing, my imagination running wild. But there was the big face I had seen in the mirror with its all-encompassing bushy black beard. It belonged to a hairy, naked man and I could see from his

146

blue lanyard and security pass that he was all too real. He was one of the geezers. He must have been here all the time.

'I didn't see you,' I said. Aside from the lanyard, he was completely naked, his pumped-up biceps and mass of chest hair adding to the strong, musty smell from his armpits and wiry, tightly knit hair extending down over his abdomen, covering his genitals and legs. He didn't attempt to cover himself but reached an arm to the shelf next to him to retrieve some sports kit. In the gloom, and disturbed by his movement, a small glistening little pink knot pointed straight at me from his mass of black pubic hair. He looked at me, a steady gaze that had a touch of contempt about it. It felt as if I'd ventured into a private garden to have a nose around and the homeowner had suddenly appeared behind a hedge.

What was he thinking? Was he thinking at all?

'I'm getting changed.' he said. 'For rugby.' He lifted the shirt over his head, finding the sleeves. Shorts were next, stepping into them and pulling them up, and in that moment, the elasticated waistband left his mister hanging over briefly. He tucked it into his shorts, looking straight at me the whole time. I didn't move.

'OK if I bring these back tomorrow morning? To wash?'

'Sorry. We don't do individual kit.'

He plunged a hand down the front of his shorts and ferreted about, rearranging everything rather extravagantly, I thought, as if to make a point, then held me with his eyes.

'May I ask a tricky personal question?' I said.

'Go for it.'

'Who are you?'

He didn't flinch. And he didn't answer.

'I'm Monica, to get you started. How did you get in?'

'Pete. Through the fire exit from next door. So you work here?' He gave one last shake to the stuff inside his shorts, withdrew his hand and held it out to me to shake. He was trying to embarrass me. I ignored him. He fiddled about with the drawstrings on his shorts and once again adjusted himself, squeezing and moving things around, shaking his legs, all the while looking straight at me. He wouldn't have done that if I had been the Commanding Officer's wife. He wouldn't have done it if I'd been one of his mates' wives or if I'd been dressed top to toe in Dior. Something about me and the job and the clothes I was wearing ruled out, for him, the need to show me any courtesy or respect. I wondered if he had a daughter? I wondered if he might have something to say if, one day, someone treated his daughter this way?

I was somebody's daughter.

'Well, Pete, you can't change in here, I'm afraid,' I said, calmly. 'Can you go into the loo down the corridor, for your own privacy? I have things to do in here.'

I was a Samaritan volunteer in the era before the internet and mobile phones, and people would often come to our building rather than use the telephone service. We offered tea, biscuits and a quiet room to chat for as long as they liked. We rarely encountered anyone who was actually contemplating suicide, but quite a few men with domestic problems and depression and despair preferred to call in. One of out every three men would expose themselves, having 'got it out' while I was in the kitchen fetching the tea. It was not unexpected; we were trained for it.

Never walk away. That says they have upset you. Let them know that the deed isn't wrong, but the place is.

Never ask them to leave but tell them to put it away.

'You can't be naked in here, Pete. I'm sorry, but this place isn't private.'

'Just sorting myself out.' A slight smirk flickered around his eyes. 'It's what big boys do.' He shifted his shoulders about and moved his head to crack his neck.

'That's OK,' I said with a thin smile. 'But another time, if you need to change, go to the gents, or your room if you have one on camp. Or there's a rugby pavilion, isn't there?'

I got to know Pete quite well over the next year and he wasn't what I'd call an 'accidental' man. Nothing in his life happened by chance. He was the type of man who adopts an air of insouciance to hide his immaculate rehearsal of events. I believe that he knew I was in the store alone that day, and he waited to hear my footsteps coming down the corridor to commence stripping off. It was a game in his mind, a prank with an element of risk. There was a real chance that I could have reported him and I guess the idea excited him during a period on standby where nothing much else was happening for him. Lots of women crave sex with an elite soldier. If they could have seen Pete with his disappointing caveman body and the pungent unpleasantness of his body odour, or doing lengths in the swimming pool one afternoon, his thick covering of back hair floating on the surface like seaweed, they'd go off the idea. But what do I know? Maybe they'd like it. Maybe Pete is someone's dream man.

I told Craig about it the next day.

'Oh that's Pistol Pete,' he laughed.

'Why pistol?'

'Because five minutes with Pete and you want to shoot yourself!'

To tell you the truth, after a while the whole business of men using our store as a changing room and their general toilet habits began to get me down. Stripping naked was common practice for the guys, which I suppose was why Pistol Pete felt at home looking at me without a stitch on. For those who didn't know that a woman was employed here, the getting-changed practice went on until I found my feet and cracked down, demanding more modesty and less of all the dangly bits. Interestingly, not every man had such a relaxed attitude to body maintenance as Pete. Most of the starkers 2-2 men I ran into had the full Hollywood wax down there, laying the whole thing open to the public, so to speak. Just saying.

The store housed just one loo for everyone. There'd been no cleaners when I arrived and there were still no cleaners when I left, eighteen months later – short of staff, they said. So I cleaned as best I could with a bucket and mop and plenty of heavy-duty floor cleaner from the store. It was stocked in abundance, which was just as well. The loo was right by the front door, exactly one stride across the skinny corridor to the office and every man visiting used it while he was there. They rarely closed the door. If they'd started a conversation in the corridor or office and decided they wanted a pee, they'd step into the cubicle and carry on talking, one hand on the wall, leaving the door ajar. Then they'd come out while tucking everything in and zipping their flies, so I got an eyeful of their crown jewels. They literally seemed to have no idea they were doing it.

Craig rarely closed the door and Adie (whose toilet habits were too revolting to tell you about) never washed his hands – none of them did. The seat was always left up, and as for the ventilation, one filthy window would open if I stood on the toilet seat and stretched but otherwise nobody bothered, which was horrible if you went in there after Adie. I could have traipsed across in the wind and freezing rain to the QM building to use their warm and comfortable ladies' loo, of course. It was spacious and ventilated, with lockers for each individual to keep her make-up, hairspray and so on, and believe me, there were clouds of hairspray wafting around in there. I think there were four women in that department, with a cosy rest room complete with sofas and easy chairs where they ate their packed lunches from picnic cool boxes. As time went by they seemed to think it funny, or possibly suspicious, that I ate with all the men in the cookhouse instead. When I asked them why they didn't eat there with me, they told me, 'That lot don't speak to the likes of us – they think they're too good for us.'

Actually, I heard that a lot. The ladies on reception at the gatehouse said the badged guys didn't speak to them except if they had business up there, and the only other civilian females, young women at the telephone exchange, also said it was too daunting to eat in the cookhouse and the men would ignore them too. Happily, I had no such reservations. I had a few years on the lot of them, the confidence to engage and I knew how to talk to them – they were just young men, after all – and the idea that anyone would be interested in me was ridiculous. I soon found everyone there to be good companions on any lunch or dinner table. I was enjoying learning the job in the stores and that was far more important to me than scoring equality points. Not yet anyway.

XV

I walked to the camp gym on weighted legs. My skin felt tight and I was vaguely nauseous, like that churning feeling when you're waiting for someone special to phone. In my day, nobody could beat me for fitness – but that was fifteen, twenty years ago. I'd always been proud of my figure; I'm still slim and never willing to give up on it, but I knew I wasn't as fit as I was. My face was burning and I felt pathetic as I rehearsed in my mind what I'd say to the PTI chap to manage his expectations. Should I ask to be put into a side room so nobody could see me?

The instructor was shorter and cheerier than I imagined. I'd spoken to him on the phone and imagined a grim-faced type of guy with a brisk manner, but he put me at ease straight away.

'Hi, I'm Liam,' he said. 'My days, you look like you're off to play beach volleyball!'

They'd only told me last night I needed to come for a quick instruction on safe lifting procedures, which was nothing to do with being in the gym, but boxes had to be ticked on my civil service personnel file, apparently. I didn't have any gym kit so I'd dug out a pair of denim jeans, cut them off to make shorts and wore them with a white T-shirt and some old, rather grey tennis shoes. I felt ridiculous, as if I should be in proper leggings and a designer sports bra instead of bouncing around unfettered, and it revived memories of the time when I was a five-year-old little girl and my mother, an older parent who believed in modesty and personal dignity, proudly laid out a new school blazer with long grey socks and lace-up shoes to wear to my school Christmas party. When I got there, all the other girls were wearing pink hair ribbons, white socks and a flouncy skirt with net petticoats and I went straight to the toy cupboard and hid there, sobbing for the entire party. When Liam said that, I must have looked like I was heading for a cupboard to cry in because he added, with a beaming smile, 'That's a compliment, by the way.'

Off to a flying start, he showed me around. I needn't have worried about anyone noticing me because the place was like an Olympic gymnastics hall and I disappeared into it, an insignificant beetle scurrying across the floor. Vast and smelling of sweat, there was no motivational music playing and no TV screens in this cathedral to physical excellence. There was an astonishing weights room hidden around a corner and on the outskirts of the gym floor a couple of ginger-haired, pale men with beetroot-red faces, tall and bulky like Vikings, had what looked like scrap cars shackled to their waists with chains, pulling them behind them as they ran. With sweat and spittle flying, peppering the floor with droplets, they snarled with the effort. I was reminded that in ancient Rome, the sweat of gladiators mixed with dirt from their faces was scraped off and sold in vials to wealthy women who used it as an early form of face cream. Man sweat and skin grime. In a pot!

Here it was different. Unlike a standard gym where members would have an eye to both courtesy and vanity, everything here was a little bit *more*. Bigger, longer, the snarling louder and the sweat uncontrolled. Towards the back wall was a long bank of stationary cycles with people grimacing, heads down, earphones clamped to their heads, pedalling as if for their lives. This was no fancy civilian gym with all sorts of technology to plug themselves into. Nobody here was doing dry January or losing those vanity pounds, 'the ones only you know are there'.

Liam took me through a series of instructions on lifting very heavy items, placing them on surfaces of varying heights. Cycling and mountain climbing have always been my strengths, so my lower half was pretty strong, but my arms and back were pathetic. After thirty seconds my shoulders were burning. It wasn't the lifting, it was the overhead press to place the heavy box on a shelf higher than my head. It was torture. My job wouldn't be lifting the odd box onto a high shelf once a day: I'd be faced with several hours of this, day after day after day, up to my chest, then up over my head. Funnily enough, this was an aspect of my job the badged guys apparently envied, and I'm not joking. A whole afternoon pulling – no *hauling* – insanely huge pallets of boxes into the goods lift on the ground floor, trotting upstairs to haul them out again, stacking the boxes for the next hour and repeating the process, up and down the clanking stairs. Hauling, stacking, repeating was how we spent the afternoons, and to a lot of the geezers, it looked like heaven. I'd say to them, 'Yes, and you'd get just over

£1,000 a month for it.' Badged guys were on a lot more than that, of course. 'Yeah,' they'd reply, 'but great phys.'

Job done, Liam took me to a large area at the side of the gym with thick, padded mats. Some men were waiting for another instructor to arrive, a yoga expert, for a daily half-hour session which was gaining popularity. Liam asked if I would like to join in, not that it was anything to do with what I'd just been doing, but I'd mentioned that I did yoga and, frankly, anything was better than going back to the store, so I said yes. The yoga guy wasn't what you'd expect: he was 2-2 and the sort of huge guy who shakes the building as he lumbers across the floor, but I must say he was no stranger to the downward dog and his eagle pose broke box office records.

All around me were other areas where small knots of soldiers were silently stretching or using roller devices to ease sore or injured muscles. Across the floor on the other side and up a staircase was another small area with glass walls and a viewing platform, similar to a squash court. I was told it was for boxing. Having witnessed men doing real back-alley bare-knuckle fighting down at the training camp, I can tell you, it's frightening. We got used to seeing brutality down there because we were looking out through glass, like watching television, but I once witnessed something raw and unpleasant that shook me up. I was sent to round up stray coffee cups that might have been taken out of the mess to workshops and the gym and left there to grow mould, and I saw some hardcore, brutal training. I must have looked shocked and a little shaken, because later that evening I had a text from a lovely guy, Marksy, who'd been running the exercise.

Monica, hope you are OK. Not a nice place for anybody to be: we don't mean to be so cold about these things. We forgot how foreign and terrifying it could be. We are trained soldiers who have been indoctrinated to violence to a degree. I just hope you are OK. My sincerest apologies for not intervening, you should never have been there in the first place. Hope you are feeling better.

Once I got over being the only girl at the party and wearing embarrassing clothes, I knew my moment would come. The extreme stretching started – and it was *extreme* – and to my delight, I was way more flexible than any of them and found it easy. This was fitness for people who had to be the fittest, strongest military regiment in the entire bloody world. It was nothing to do with health and safety of course but Liam needed to go and suggested I stay and join any part of the gym if I wanted, as I was allowed full use of it. Put like that, I felt privileged to be training alongside them a couple of sessions a week. And there was nothing formal about it – there was no membership, the gym was a fantastic perk of my job and people could just join in any time of the day or evening or weekend they felt like it.

I got a tick in every box for having satisfied all health and safety requirements for a storekeeper, and I can't begin to tell you how I swelled with pride at that achievement. What was even nicer was that as the weeks went by, geezers would approach me in the lunch queue or join my table and ask if I would be at the stretch session that evening. I finally felt I had a place on camp.

XVI

'You're a customer now?' came a voice from behind me in the lunch queue. I swung around to see Pistol Pete, a wry smile hovering around his lips, the by-now familiar cloud of black curly beard and chest hair meeting somewhere under his chin like a balaclava, with only glittering brown eyes and a vague impression of nostrils peeking out from inside it.

I'd been musing on the comment from Craig about Pete and was trying to work it out. Five minutes and you'd want to shoot yourself – from whose point of view? Working with him? As a partner? On a night out?

'Hi Pete,' I said, half turning. We shuffled forwards, a place at a time, like teenagers in Starbucks for whom time is of little account. 'Yep. I need a decent lunch these days, with such a demanding job.'

The queue was strictly observed. Waiting for the doors to unlock was exactly the same tedious process we'd had down the road except this time I was a customer. This cookhouse was at least four times the size of the dining room down the road at the training camp and, in my opinion, not remotely as comfortable or friendly. The queue curled around in a graceful U-shape from the locked dining room door, past some vending machines and to the front door, where a gap was left to allow people through to the offices above and then the queue took up again on the other side. It could easily take fifteen minutes to crawl round from the end of the queue to the front and find all the best steaks gone; there was never any special treatment just because you were in the Regiment.

Eventually we took our places at the same table. The badged guys populated certain areas of the dining hall, which I had first assumed was a nod to their exalted status, but which turned out to be simply about being nearer to the exit, and far from the complex security precautions that sealed this place from the outside world. The geezers were ordinary, jeans-wearing, T-shirted individuals, shuffling through the archways that separated the serving area from the dining room. They each held a nine-inch plate of food, paused at the cutlery boxes and moved in a patient stream to fetch a drink from the line of machines. It was hard to comprehend that these were the men about whom scores of bestselling books and eagerly anticipated films and TV programmes had been devoured by millions; for whom the accolades 'fabled' and 'elite' were coined. These men inspire speculation, hero-worship and fanaticism from their followers, who, like the followers of God, love even though they will never see. Here, without the body armour and helmets, goggles and gloves, and equipment attached to their knees and arms and shoulders, they looked smaller, thinner. Some of these men are perhaps pasty and uncertain, others careworn and tired. A few were cheerful and energetic, baby-faced even. Down the road was the action movie, up here at HQ was different.

Pete sat next to me. We stared at the TV screen high on the wall. There was an item about one of those Castaway-type of programmes, where everyday people are dumped on an island and have to survive as one by one they're kicked off the show. Pete started a commentary. 'Well, for a start – I'd win,' he said, messily poking vegetables into his mouth, leaving unsavoury bits in his beard. He went on to explain how everything they were doing was wrong. It was twelve-thirty, he talked at length for an hour and a half, and when I looked at the clock again it was twelve-forty – well, that was the joke about Pete, anyway, but it was true.

After I had been on camp at HQ for a few weeks it filtered down that someone new was here as a fixture and the geezers were keen to take a closer look; I thought of their interest in me like an animal fascinated by a mirror. It was like any relationship founded on a shared situation; gradually, the men stopped giving me a wide berth and started joining me on my table. And here, I learned why the 'questions' thing had been such an issue. Nobody asked questions. Chat was always about what they were doing right here on camp, or their weekends, or their wife's effort at the London Marathon or some infuriating incident at Tesco. People talked about their families if they wanted to, but nobody *asked*. In my three years with them, nobody ever said, 'Monica, do you have any children?' or 'Are you married?' or anything personal except for one thing. At some stage, every guy would ask me, 'Where do you come from, Monica?' and when I said Manchester the response was always, 'You don't *sound* like you come from Manchester.' It was interesting. Now I could see why my cheerful and innocent enquiry into where a man spent Easter with his family and how many children he had must have rung alarm bells coming from a kitchen hand who drove a Mercedes and 'spoke posh'.

If life on camp could sometimes be a little monotonous, it could also veer from one extreme to the other. Sometimes it seemed like the most awesome place on earth, like when I had to take stuff to buildings I wouldn't normally go to and saw amazing things going on. Other times it was like a sanatorium in some European millionaires, playground, with men lounging around in flip-flops and expensive sunglasses. It was interesting, seeing men up here in 2017 who I'd seen down the road on selection in 2015. Now that they'd got over the 'I'm in!' frame of mind and were fully acquainted with the burden and responsibility of their status as elite, specialist soldiers, it was strange to see those formerly optimistic, animated people dealing with the reality of their ambition. They saw time stretching ahead of them in this rarefied new world they'd entered with their elite status, and it dawned on them that it would be a long slog for years. That's what some of them told me, anyway, but of course others felt the shift and loved it. It was an effort to imagine them as they had been, fresh and keen and determined, and added to that the marriages and relationships gone wrong or under strain and the odd, soulless dalliances with women obsessed with anything military, the dearth of fun and time off, the over-abundance of adrenaline, and a society here on camp populated with people exactly like themselves. Looking at them now, at all ages and stages of their lives in this legendary regiment, it was a life laboratory. As well as the cookhouse I met the men in the store or coffee shop, at the jet wash or the gym; the camp seemed to be full of unbearably cynical and ridiculously competitive men, feeding off one another. They felt invulnerable, and why wouldn't they? Getting into the Regiment was the crowning glory of their career. Living behind those gates gave them *carte blanche*. But in the never-ending cookhouse lunch queue they stood in line patiently with the storekeepers like me, pool guys, dog handlers, firefighters and men from the other regiments, and ate the same food that we all did. None of that bothered them. What set them apart were their skills; not what they were doing, but what they were capable of doing. And without much in their lives to cause them to question their viewpoint, and the supporting evidence of all those action films and books, it appeared that our lads' lives were already scripted for them, and they merely had to learn their part.

In the coffee shop, where you can easily spend a couple of hours with a single drink, the men sat in huddles. Some I hadn't seen before, very newly in, still had the gloss of perfection upon their faces as if, smiling down on the rest of us, they thought themselves unbeatable for now. Some no doubt imagined that the whole course of their lives would be as smooth as their travel arrangements, decided by others, paid for, and then issued by clerks. Many of them had no idea what they would do when they left the Regiment. But then, did it matter? For now, these young men were on the up.

I may not be an expert in the psychology of all this, but I think from what I've observed that the trouble with this sort of fame is that it upsets the balance of your life. If I got an amazing job, I'd be over the moon and able to tell everybody. I could write down my profession when asked, I'd have business cards printed with my job title. None of the geezers can do this. Maybe it didn't matter. Their families – the only people really in the know – must accept the change in their lives and, as I soon found out, very often the wives weren't happy about the closeted world of secrecy and suspicion and huge worry. For the guys, becoming badged wasn't something that stunned them with surprise and shock. Of course, they feel a thrill inside themselves, but they can't very well go on the town and have an 'I'm in!' party. And because the whole process of selection is so long and so uncertain, they never know from one day to the next if they will get kicked off the course; even when things seemed to be going well for them, they have no idea how they are really doing. The smallest thing can trip them up, so it makes sense to me that when the final day comes and they're told they've passed, they mostly couldn't believe it. I asked Zero once if he'd known, when the final stage was over, if he'd passed. 'No, you don't know even then,' he told me. 'It wasn't until we got back to Hereford we knew there were only three of us off the whole course who'd passed.'

So I think what I'm saying is that their status took a while to dawn on them. By the time the realisation came, part of them had been waiting, and waiting for a long time. Waiting for the moment when they realised that they really were different from everybody else. But for now, in the lunch queue at the cookhouse, these famed military legends weren't larger than life, but hovering to wait their turn for a plastic cup of orange squash like the rest of us.

I loved my mealtimes in the cookhouse, especially the atmosphere of calm. I was spellbound. Nobody was looking at his watch, eating quickly, rushing a drink down. If they were in a hurry, I couldn't tell. Everybody sat with friends and, refreshingly, there were no signs of mobile phones or devices, just a lot of people chatting. That's how I got to meet so many of the men, and, apart from the odd female soldier, I was usually the only woman there.

XVII

During 2017, the UK was subject to an unusually high number of high-profile terrorist attacks and distressing incidents, such as the attacks on Westminster and London bridges, and the Manchester Arena bombing. As a consequence, as part of my job in the quartermaster's department, I'd been asked to attend an enhanced security briefing.

The lecture theatre was housed in a 1960s-style building that reminded me of my old high school. It had a vast foyer with a flight of wide, clattering stone stairs on either side, the beautifully wrought-iron banisters, whose paint was now peeling and chipped, winding their way up rather grandly like something from an old Hollywood movie to meet a long connecting corridor above. The citadel-like structure echoed in an almost melancholic way, as if crying out for attention, yet for forty years this had been a place people merely passed through to reach somewhere else rather than enjoyed being inside. Corridors led past a seemingly limitless rabbit-warren of offices; each door had the inevitable security pad for access. As we headed around bends and sharp turns, it felt like we were passing through a vortex of concentric circles, starting big and finishing in a small, newly refurbished lecture theatre complete with pristine office carpeting and factory-fresh, tip-up cinema-style seating.

The Security Cell boss was an improbably young-looking guy called Gray. His bouncy nature and cool intelligence stood out above others who, you might be surprised to know, didn't always have much of an understanding of life beyond their regimental calling. Gray knew something about everything and his private passion bonded him to me from our first chat on the lunch table: he had a hedgehog feeding station in his garden, as did I.

I loved this about him. Whenever any of the men talked about their interests they were passionate. These men were fanatics. Fanatic temperaments and fanatic, straight-line thinking. I never knew any of them talk of a hobby without then going out and buying all the paraphernalia. Nothing was ever done by half with these guys, no job left unfinished. I even argued with Zed Johnstone about leaving a spoon in my own sink once, ready for washing up later. There was no such thing as 'later' for Zed or the rest of the geezers. Alex McQuoid, another friend, occasionally cooked for me but even if dinner were on the table and you were ravenous, everything had to be washed up and put away before you could start eating. God, that annoyed me.

I settled myself into the comfortable auditorium seating and looked around. Only about fifteen seats were occupied. These security briefings happened regularly as new people from other units arrived on camp and Gray was already there, setting up his laptop to project images onto a big screen. When the lecture started he spoke in a thin, strangely high voice, hissing instructions under his breath: clear, concise, but barely audible, his lips hardly moving. Gray rattled through the briefing, telling us what he must have said scores of times over the years, using tired-looking and outdated images to illustrate the points. It began with a film montage of security lapses caused by social media. Things like telling your grandmother your movements so that when she posts how proud she is of you, working in such-or-such-a-place with the Regiment, she is thus unwittingly revealing your exact location. Taking photographs on camp to delight your friends or maybe just capturing innocent-enough pictures of Regiment events, which might display some sensitive details in the background. Gray rattled through what those might be. It was riveting to me; there were things I'd never considered before.

He then turned to the question of unconscious bias, focusing on the fact that just as badged guys have no specific 'look', neither do terrorists. We were to actively challenge anybody on camp who wasn't wearing a pass. On the whole it was all important new stuff, some of it quite surprising, and I learned a thing or two, but I was surprised that around me most of the audience slumped in a desultory way. At one point Gray stopped and called to a young bloke from another regiment sitting higher up in the auditorium. He was dozing. I couldn't believe my eyes. These young soldiers joining had the privilege of being attached to this elite regiment for a time, yet they showed their disrespect by acting bored. I thought Gray might order him out, but instead he just said, 'I'm sorry you think you don't need any of this.'

Then Gray got to the bit about media and the press. I thought it was all very outdated and I was surprised to hear him make an unpleasant, off-colour comment about people who died on selection. He was alone on the vast stage, pacing slowly as he spoke, pointing at the screen or directing remarks occasionally to the largely empty auditorium. I'd picked up a pamphlet at the door in case it had information relevant to the briefing and was about to look through it when Gray stopped talking and looked straight at me. I put the pamphlet down and mouthed, 'Sorry.'

I stopped in the garrison coffee shop afterwards and ordered a poached egg on toast. It was the only place open until early afternoon, and 2-2 guys on the standby team would sit there most of the day if they weren't in the gym or sorting kit.

'Mind if I join you?' It was Gray. He dumped his bag on the other chair and sank down, exhaling theatrically.

'Hi, Gray. Great briefing today,' I lied.

'Did it do some good?' he asked, looking at me sideways, suspicious.

The cafe was full to bursting. The cheery smell of fresh coffee and toasted sandwiches filled the room, the windows ran with condensation and the queue stretched right back to the door.

'Well,' I started. 'Hmm... It was very useful. Probably more useful to visiting military, if I'm very honest, but you said a couple of things I didn't know.'

'Such as?'

I rattled off a few points I hadn't thought of and some which were new.

He nodded, looking at the floor, taking it in. I fiddled around with my coffee cup, moved my coat from the spare chair in case anybody else wanted to sit there. I turned my gaze to the TV on the far wall. Did Gray want to talk or had he just found somewhere to park himself?

One of the staff was shouting at the top of her voice *'NUMBER ELEVEN!'* I looked at the chalk board I'd been given: 11. I stuck up my hand and she weaved her way through the throng. I thanked her and reached for the brown sauce.

'Sorry, Gray, do you mind if I eat? I've had nothing since seven this morning.'

'So,' he started, not looking at me, 'you didn't have a job for quite a while?'

That was a strange thing to ask at this stage. I'd been a civil servant here for two years now, but I dutifully answered that no, I'd managed on my savings and money wasn't the reason I wanted the job.

'But how did your friends think you made a living?'

I laughed and flung my arms wide.

'They assumed I didn't need to work!' I said. 'But I don't honestly think my friends wondered anything. They didn't live in my town, for a start, they were mostly in London or Essex or Reading. And does anyone much wonder how a friend makes a living? They might wonder how they could *afford* certain things, like if you suddenly bought a yacht, but I don't think anyone thought about it, to be honest.'

Gray looked quizzical so I added, 'Look, I lived off my savings for nearly four years. It's old news now. I actually like working here very much.'

I forked some egg and toast into my mouth gratefully. Gray sipped his coffee.

'Why?' he asked. 'Why do you like doing these dirty jobs?' He still wasn't looking at me, his head turned slightly away from me, as if we were in a confessional.

I took a big breath and thought about it before answering.

'Well, I wouldn't say I *like* the jobs, but I'm enjoying learning something so different. Not the work, but the way people are here. The bad language, the way people just walk up and break in if you're talking to someone. It's all quite different.'

Gray nodded.

'They had a board about you.'

'A what?'

'A board. A special meeting, put it like that.'

The place was bustling now; coffee machines grinding away, the babble of conversation. It was a nice scene, a timeless one, mostly full of men who enjoyed each other's company bonding over tales of where they'd just been and what was next for them. Looking around, it reminded me of a Henry Fielding monologue of 1732 where he describes the King's coffee house as 'a rude shed and well known to gentlemen to whom beds are unknown.'

'Yeah, it's mad,' Gray went on. 'Just because someone's a bit different. Actually, you're an asset.'

'An asset? How?'

'Just – the life you've led. You could teach some of us a lot of things.'

He sat up and fiddled with his bag, then picked away at his fingernail. Outside, the sun was showing bleak promise and there was a distant, thin rainbow. 'Looks like it's brightening up,' someone nearby said, and the doors were thrown open onto the terrace outside as if releasing endangered species back into the wilds. It was the only really nice place on camp to relax, with its picnic tables and parasols. I stood up.

'You going?' Gray said.

'I need to get back. We're so busy.' I glanced up at the sky to see how long before the next shower and decided to put my jacket on.

Gray stood up too. I noticed slight changes in his face, it seemed softer and more relaxed. He asked me about a couple of items in our store and I said he'd need a special form, signed by the RQ. He wanted one of those stand-up desks that they all wanted these days. Most of our badged managers liked using stand-up desks.

I made my way out into the sunshine and looked for my car, which was by now pretty well blocked in by other cars. A note was wedged under the windscreen wiper.

THIS IS A NO PARKING AREA.
DON'T BE A NOB.
WE'VE NOTED YOUR REG.

Buoyed with my updated status after the briefing, I took positive action the very next day. Gray had impressed upon his audience that terrorists were unlikely to look as we imagine, and just because a man with an educated accent is wandering round the camp in a sharp suit and carrying a briefcase, it doesn't mean anything.

A fair-haired man came into the store, said hello without looking at me and pointed down the corridor. 'I'm just going to get some targets.' He had a certain self-assurance that he knew exactly where he was heading, he was wearing nondescript gym kit and had nothing but a bottle of water in his hand. There was no pass around his neck.

'I'll get what you need,' I said, trotting after him briskly. I didn't like his tone. 'Which size?'

He was fishing about in one of the large green boxes, grabbing a large quantity of cardboard targets. As he did so he was scanning the other shelves. I made a remark about this being a version of a wholesale place and this amount of targets would need a special docket signed by the RQ.

'I need to just write this down,' I said, smiling. I picked up the daily issue clipboard and asked his name and squadron or department.

The place was dark even with the lights on and echoed with every movement. He towered above me and I could almost feel him straining to get away.

I looked at the NATO stock number and wrote it down. 'And you'd like a box of twenty cardboard?'

He was making a move towards the door.

'May I see your pass?' I asked, fixing him with a firm challenge.

He realised he had no choice, laughed and held his hands out in submission. 'Must be in the office.'

'And where are these going to, please?' I said, looking at my clipboard again, then back up at him, pen poised. I wished Craig were here, but he was off at rugby.

He turned towards the door, impatient.

'And your name?'

'*ME.*' He said it with a confident smirk, as if I were a total idiot. As he headed out, Jules was in the doorway, and they obviously knew one another because they laughed and joked for a minute, then the guy went, and I was able to ask Jules who he was.

'Oh, Richard. He's the Regimental Sergeant Major. Why?'

'I just asked to see his pass.'

Well, that small story did the rounds. 'Monica asked to see the RSM's pass, and when she asked him who it was for, he said ME!' became a minor talking point for a little while and, as everything did on this camp, it resurfaced whenever his name came up. In case you don't know – and I didn't before I came to work here – RSM is only one down from the Commanding Officer.

So what? He should have worn his pass, it was the rule.

Actually, I didn't do too badly out of it, being the one person on camp who hadn't a clue who the RSM was and challenging him. I'm thrilled to report that Gray stopped me in the camp coffee shop a few days later and congratulated me for having paid attention to that part of his briefing.

'Well, you did say that terrorists can look like anybody,' I said.

XVIII

Ranger Judd was a man of intimidating charisma and perilous charm. He was also known as 'Judd the Thug', for some reason that hadn't yet filtered down to me. Quite what had propelled him into the limelight had been of doubtful authenticity, but with the advent of YouTube he had been unearthed on old newsreels from the 1980s as a flaxen-haired seven-year-old, padlocking himself to the perimeter fence of Greenham Common airbase in Berkshire to the cheers and hollers of 30,000 women forming an 'Embrace the Base' human chain. They were demonstrating against cruise missiles being stored on the site and the protest camp lasted an astonishing nineteen years, during eight of which it housed Ranger and his mum. He had been christened John in 1976, but his mother had changed his name to Ranger, meaning 'forest guardian' shortly after she committed herself to living in the peace commune. Five years later, young Ranger was still there, schooled in a tent, sleeping under the stars, and eating whatever food was donated, scavenged or stolen. This upbringing gave Ranger a mile-long advantage when it came to competing with a 120-odd other volunteers for selection and showcased formative years that every soldier secretly wished he'd had.

Nobody knew what form of Road-to-Damascus moment converted the young Ranger Judd from anti-nuclear activist and eco-warrior to one of the best soldiers in the world, but life in an elite unit like this was hardly bohemian. I could only assume that when push came to shove, he wasn't so much interested in The Cause, more the way of life. Sleeping rough and eating roadkill were skills that he was literally born to, and Ranger's brain tuned in, working out that earning a decent living that involved blowing things up and shooting people might not be so bad after all.

Ranger, known as Ray, had been in the Regiment for fifteen years when I met him; he was solid, as broad as he was tall and with the face and personality of a gravestone. There was no bedside manner with Ranger: he decided if you were worth talking to on any particular day, which didn't exactly bring out the best in people but lent them the glow of a chosen one when he turned his attentions to the fortunate individual of the week. This led to what I'd been warned was the intimidating presence of this man of few words and even fewer facial expressions. Ray Judd spent his time divided between his 'goldfish-bowl' office on the main concourse of the QM building (where it was rumoured he was merely looking at his computer to book his Tesco delivery slot), or in the camp coffee shop, where he was usually avoided by others. I spent time in the coffee shop too, but where people skirted round me because they weren't sure who I was, they avoided Ray Judd because they knew exactly who he was.

'You don't mess with The Ranger' was the accepted party line. Put like that, as if in a brochure for Outward Bound weekends for city teenagers, his title sounded like a tough old-timer giving team talks on campfire skills. He certainly had the body of an old-timer and I wondered if he ever felt a loss of masculinity or self-confidence, especially surrounded by fitter, more handsome, upbeat young men. Had he adopted his increasing scruffiness as an impermeable veneer of *ennui* in order to avoid any matey observations on the subject? I couldn't help thinking of the young Ranger, or John as he would have been then, swinging through trees and jumping over streams with the wild, carefree nature of the innocent during his years on the female-led protest camp at Greenham. But just because the boy John was free, it didn't necessarily mean that he was happy.

Whatever the answer to my musings on the subject, Ranger looked like he just brushed the crumbs off his shirt and rolled off the couch to go directly to jumping out of a plane before blowing up a few buildings, crushing a terrorist with his bare hands and returning to the couch to spread his newspaper and pop a can of beer. That is how he appeared, as an extreme example of a known type: the taciturn, restless, elite warrior with a hidden grudge.

His opposite in personality type was Kip Formby, who was vulpine, alert, worn out by his own vitality, hurtling towards the cliff edge strapped to a stick of dynamite. Kip Formby and Ranger Judd were the same age, forty-four, with different ways of showing their arrogance. Ranger was cool: Kip had swagger. Where Ranger was taciturn, Kip's life was based on posturing: he could never switch off the act or stop talking about his blue Regiment belt and the powers it gave him, shoving his superstar status in your face. When it came to expertise and knowledge of weaponry, everyone had to admit that Kip's internal database ran like the Summit computer. Kip was a livewire who made no secret of caring about his job and loving it, whereas Ranger Judd made no effort and yet all the men wanted to be him. Ranger was bored by banality, which stoked his inner extinct volcano to a dangerous point. He despised the fact that guys envied him his name, citing Zero Johnstone as a more worthy contender for sheer cool; but the other men didn't want cool – they wanted badass.

The final coup for Ranger's infamy on camp was his mother. Ranger adored her. She turned up to family days, a superannuated sixty-something hippy, smoking liquorice-paper roll-ups, skirt trailing in the mud, with long stringy grey hair, smudgy black eyes and a face that looked as if she had been left outside since she was born. Mother Judd didn't give a toss about anyone, a trait she'd passed on to her son. More importantly, her unabashed existence among the other preening, designer-clad wives and mothers verified his legend status.

Ray was counting the weeks until his departure out of the military. Far from the days of kicking doors in and enduring a beasting on Pen y Fan, his time now was spent in overseeing things in the quartermaster building and managing a rag-tag bunch of eight civilians and going to a gym session he and a few other older geezers arranged for themselves in a corner of a little-used hangar. I used to hear their music pounding and picture their circuits, far away from the serious stuff going on with the younger badged guys in the big, proper gym. When he was active in the Regiment the disagreements and antagonism challenged his ego, charging him like a dynamo. Here, with a soft-soap quartermaster boss, junior military or civilians like me, it must have been hell. He needed sparring partners, not sycophancy and obedience. If most of us get our energy from the beauty of life, healthy children and enjoyable occasions like Christmas, Ranger's energy was generated by pent-up fury. I saw him once, the velocity of his anger propelling him along the corridor to deliver a blast of invective against the younger soldiers for some accounting misdemeanour. He moved through the forest of life with the confidence of an elephant advancing in a straight line, rooting up trees and trampling thorns, but he ingratiated himself with me from day one.

Every morning, Ranger would hail me from afar down the long corridor of the QM department with a deep, 'Monicaaaaaa!', crouching slightly like a parent encouraging an infant to take its first steps towards them. He even asked if he could get me tea on two occasions. As my stand-in line manager, Ray knew my professional background but nobody else on camp did and I was keen to keep it that way. Details of civilian employees were known only to the civil service until someone was hired, and even after that, the people on camp did not know your date of birth, marital status or any other details which were not compulsory. He kept saying that I 'came from London' even though he knew I was a northerner.

'Yes, but you moved among those people,' he said. 'You've known some of the greats of society.'

'Who? Kylie Minogue and David Beckham?' I replied, joking.

'No. Rupert Murdoch,' he replied.

It was true. Rupert Murdoch, the billionaire media mogul and founder of Sky, Fox News, NewsCorp, 21st Century Fox and many more, had been my boss for twelve years. Unlike in this place, where it had taken many weeks before Ranger or the QM wandered fifty yards to meet me, I used to see Rupert Murdoch around the offices often, sleeves rolled up, having travelled halfway across the world to check on his staff and lend support. Sadly for Ranger and all the men here, where the Murdochs of this world had bank balances that did the talking, the status of the Regiment badge had to remain hidden, otherwise they could have given him a fair run for his money.

'What on earth brings the great man down here?' I said one afternoon, seeing Ray playfully scratching at the window for me to unlock.

'I'm shattered,' he said immediately. 'Played rugby last night – we lost, but I'm bloody sore today. Getting old.'

He certainly looked tired. His once-flaxen hair was mousey and thin on top, his balding head speckled with worrying dark spots and his entire skin appearing stretched beyond what was reasonable.

'You poor thing!' I exclaimed, mocking him a little. 'Need a brew?'

Few non-military people know the career system of a regiment like this one and, indeed, I needed it to be explained to me when I joined the staff. The elite soldiers who pass selection are still in the military for their allotted time unless they wish to leave; being in these elite units is entirely voluntary. So when they get past the door-kicking-in stage a range of other options are suggested, suitable for their rank and experience, which can mean a man in his forties looking at an administrative job or perhaps a special project where they might have to work alone or in a small group until their time is up. They are still in the army and they have a right to stay, all being equal, and that can mean people like Ranger settling into roles they probably didn't envisage for themselves back when they were enduring training.

Craig appeared from nowhere and held out a hand for Ray to shake. 'Ranger! How are you, Big Boss?' he exclaimed. 'Great to see you here! You'll have a tea – or a coffee? Here –' he grabbed the biscuit tin – 'have some biscuits. Or I have cake in the fridge, it was my birthday last week.' Craig was all over the place, steering Ray with gestures, bent forwards ingratiatingly as if royalty had just arrived and his task was to display a series of rooms containing exhibitions the distinguished visitors might wish to see.

'Craig, could you give Monica and me a minute?' said Ray, with a meaningful stare. He tapped Craig on the forearm, thanking him in advance.

'Hey! Of course, my buddy!' cried Craig, almost backing out with his head bowed. He glanced at me. 'My darling, I'll go up to the cookhouse and take the plates they ordered.'

'Give me half an hour?' said Ray, thumbs up. Craig gave a thumbs up in return. I carried on making the tea.

'Are you here for a reason, Ray,' I said, 'or just fancied a stroll?'

'Both really,' he replied, leaning on the fridge, adding, 'Wow, where did you get these biscuits? It's not even Christmas.'

I got out the teabags and a carton of milk, 'How d'you like your tea? Strong? Sugar?'

'Both, please, and plenty of milk if you have enough.'

I dipped the teabags into each mug.

'Here you go. Bit rough and ready. Do your own milk and sugar when you're ready, I can never work it out.'

I had put up my hair and tried to look a little more business-like. Drink in hand, we went into the little office two strides from the kitchen and I listened as Ray told me a slanderous story about one of the boxing nights they held every year – real black-tie occasions they were – and the big film star they invited who propositioned one of the hired waiters.

'Wow,' I said. 'It all goes on here.'

'He was what we call rough trade,' said Ray. 'It's a class thing.'

I glanced at the clock. My orders were piling up. Why had he come here?

'So,' I started, leaning forward on the desk and folding my arms. I said a couple of nice things about the store, adding that I was looking forward to learning.

'That's what I was about to say, Monica,' Ray replied, leaning back and looking at home. 'We liked the idea of having you here because you're keen to learn – and for your clear organisational skills.'

'Really?' I laughed. 'I thought you hired me for my muscle power, but basically you just wanted someone to tidy the place up?'

'Ha-ha. No, not at all,' said Ray, taking a sip of his tea. 'This place needs a fresh pair of eyes, Monica. I know you haven't done this sort of thing before, but we look at your character and capabilities. Though, I must admit –' he went on, casting an eye around the gloomy office with its yellow ochre walls from years of cigarette smoke, the wall clock high up and laden with dust, defying gravity, and notices stuck on top of other notices – 'this office could do with a bit of feminising.'

It was just us two sitting in the grotty but curiously cosy office and it did seem strange, I thought, that in this most lauded of regiments in the world, the standards should be allowed to slip so badly down here. Racing around to get records up to date and safety measures in place only occurred when an inspection was imminent. Yet it was a popular place. Some of the geezers' most intimate conversations had been in this store, and if they really wanted to be sure nobody was , they would suggest going to the back of the racking, where safety goggles and hundreds of toilet brushes were stored, and where they would spill the most intimate secrets. No wonder my good friend Steve Bond had said he preferred being down at the training camp. 'There's too many people gossiping up here,' he'd said in explanation.

'What's it like, going from the squadron itself to your job now?' I asked. 'Is it a massive transition, leaving active service and coming here?'

'Well, what do you think?' His hands dropped over the arms of the chair and he straightened his chest, uncrossing his legs. He appeared like a man about to assume an identity, checking that it all looked okay. 'Do I seem spoiled, out of touch?'

'You seem like a perfectly ordinary man, Ray.'

'Yet I'm putting on a face, like everyone does here,' he said, blankly.

The chill in his tone pushed me back, yet the sunshine lit up his flushed face, making it glow. It was a glow which could have been, in other circumstances, good health, but right now appeared like rising emotion.

'I am, as you must have guessed by now, a man without illusions.' He checked his pager and then his phone in case anybody was looking for him. His face clouded. Silence hung heavily. He wanted to say something, so I went very still.

'I was on a course last November, in the Brecon Beacons, and I was the only 2-2 there,' he said. 'It was a leadership thing, classroom stuff, and the rest were similar to me in rank but from other units of the army. I was the oldest, which didn't bother me, but at the weekend they organised an exercise on the hills. So obviously at first they were well ahead of me and I was near the last.'

'That must have been difficult for you?' I said. 'All the others off into the distance?'

'Well, I'm forty-four now, so there's no way I'm going to have the fitness I had when I was thirty.'

'I didn't realise you still had to do all that stuff?'

'Yes, but if you're badged, you don't think there's ever a challenge if you're being honest. In that situation you assume you'll be head and shoulders ahead. So I kept pushing on, and gradually I was picking them off.'

He gave a thin chuckle, as if he were making a bold claim. Thinking, possibly, about all the good years, the active years.

'Well, you had a drastic change of direction, Monica, didn't you?' he said. 'You've no interest in your old job now?'

This was a strange thing to say. Why bring it up?

'I've had several old jobs, Ray. Important jobs.'

'You know what I mean,' he said. 'Must have been used to the cut and thrust? Parties? Jet-setting?'

'So you're not referring to the six years I spent as the first woman training manager in a governmental public body?' I said, cupping my face in my hands. 'Or setting up my own business – that took me all over the world.' I smiled. 'I've had all sorts of different jobs, Ray.'

The clock ticked, the phone rang but immediately stopped before I could lift the receiver, and someone knocked on the door but I ignored it. His phone pinged, but he didn't look at it.

'You were in the media, Monica.'

'Hmmm... maybe.' I looked down at the desk. 'I don't want to talk about all that. '

'Fair enough,' he said. He stretched back in his chair, then crossed his hands behind his head and gazed at the ceiling. 'Think you may be a little late to cover up your past, Monica. That said, I don't think your presence worries anyone and you are judged on your performance, *not* what you did in any previous life. We know, but not people here in this store. Unless you tell them. My top tip would be to make good impressions with everybody.'

'I agree,' I said, 'and anyway which bit of our lives is really us, Ray? I've often thought about it. When you die, which photograph would represent you in an obituary? You as a baby? Your wedding day? Or as a very old man? They're all you. In obituaries they nearly always have a photo of a person when they were about forty, as if that was their best time. But it rarely was. You're a badged, specialist soldier right now. Is that going to define your entire life? You might spend many more decades doing something completely different.' I sat back. 'Like I'm doing.'

He went quiet for a moment, thinking. I didn't want to destroy his reverie and I wondered what he really wanted to say, so I didn't speak.

'So many scandals in the media,' he said eventually. 'Dishing the dirt on people. Kiss and tells.'

It was so quiet you could hear a pine needle drop.

'I mean, it's not right, is it? Like with us. Any hint of a story,' he went on, 'and they stick a winged dagger on it and it sells papers – they make a rumour into a scandal.'

'Is that what you think?'

'Well, it's true, isn't it? They hear a rumour or someone tells them something and they make something of it just because it's the Regiment,' he said darkly. 'Yes, I think they should lay off.'

He looked at me, quizzically, then looked down at his hands, picking at a nail.

I straightened up some pencils, deciding what to say.

'I don't think those people having affairs needed any help in destroying their lives,' I said. 'They're quite capable of doing that themselves. No one forces them to sleep around or fiddle their tax. People often say the media ruins people's lives, but they do it themselves.'

'But is it the public's business?' he said.

'When they're paid by the taxpayer, of course,' I said. I took a deep breath. 'That's how it is, Ray. If a politician can't be trusted to stick with his marriage vows or is a liar or hypocrite, how can we trust his political policies?'

Ray nodded. 'And the footballers?'

'Example to young people who see them as role models.'

He got up to straighten a calendar that was bothering him. 'Sorry, my OCD,' he said, and sat down again. He took a sip of tea then a touch of irritation clouded his face as his eyes fell upon a minuscule drop of tea that had left a stain on his uniform.

There was something about this scene which plays on my imagination to this day. It was if he were climbing over a fence just to see what was outside. When he got out, like they all do in the end, he'd be pining to be let back in. Eventually every geezer will go off somewhere else.

He reached for a tissue to blot the stain.

He turned and looked at me directly.

'So how did the media life happen?'

'Like a lot of things. I didn't have any burning ambition, but I was persistent. When they hired me I made sure they'd want to keep me.'

'You did well.'

I didn't know what to say. One of the tasks Ray had given himself when I came here was to get me up to scratch, and in my opinion he'd failed dismally. I'd said as much to the QM, in passing. Not those words of course: I wasn't a complete fool.

'It's not too different from you wanting to hide your regimental identity when you leave here, or maybe the way you've had to hide it now, all these years,' I said. 'First there was the peace camp and now here – hasn't it got a bit exhausting, Ray? Anyway, how did you decide to go for the army?'

He chuckled, remembering.

'Yeah. I was taking the piss actually, walking round Bristol with a girlfriend, I saw the Army Careers office and I went in for a joke – y'know, to horrify her. I said

I was going to join the army just to make her mad, but once inside they spent half an hour explaining things and I thought "Hey, sounds good." And you?' he went on. 'How did you unearth the job down the road?'

'On the internet, by accident. Searching for a plumber.'

We laughed. He smiled and shifted his position, thinking. He looked into his tea mug and saw it was empty. I remember that moment, his uniform, his blue belt buckle catching the sun's stray rays that breached the ancient vertical blinds at the window.

'Are you bothered about Greenham Common, Ray?' I asked. 'Because I think you are. I can tell you now that you being "unearthed" as an elite soldier isn't a story. Not for the media.'

'Isn't it?'

'Well, what's the story?'

He shrugged.

'Greenham Common protester's son... I'd have thought it's obvious.'

He shrugged wearily.

'Protester's son – then what? It's like Princess Diana's death; at the time people said we'd remember her forever and the country would never be the same, but that's not true. People aged twenty now weren't around when she died. Your background is a vague interest to a small number of people, but I'm afraid no editor would think it has any legs.'

'Really?'

There was a strange atmosphere in the room. What was he afraid of?

'I just like to make my own decisions,' he said eventually, letting out a deep sigh. 'Decisions on what people know.'

'I understand that,' I said, 'but remember, the protester was your mum. And nobody has photos of you now, in the Regiment.'

I couldn't ask him to leave. I couldn't even say I had work to be getting on with. He was the gaffer. I wanted to put his mind at rest; I was hoping there was no more to it.

'Look, I'm not an expert, Ray. It's not like I was a reporter or anything – I wouldn't know how to be – but I do know that what sells newspapers are free Legoland or theme park tickets, gardening vouchers or a chance to get a cheap holiday. Royal stories, soap stars, celebrities, you know. I'm sorry to burst your bubble, but stories about this place don't sell newspapers.'

'People love them.'

'No, they *read* them. If they're there. The public aren't thinking about you lot, I can promise you that. Only when those TV programmes come on about selection –'

'Which are boring and repetitive now,' he jumped in.

He got up, straightened his shirt, checked his cuffs, then reached for his jacket. He pulled his pass out of his top pocket and picked up his empty cup.

'The things I've done, Monica. The things I've done.'

At some point, if we repeat it often enough, we set our life stories in stone. Or other people set them in stone for us. The military often cite their army service as the best time of their lives. They will recall not only their best times and happiest moments, but their actions and battles and bitter rivalries too. Then somebody else throws in their own story, their own opinion on what went on and this means their life stories are revised in a way that they weren't ready for. Different versions can be called into question, challenged as if inaccurate or implausible. If this sounds complex, it's no more than the passage of all our life stories, but it can be confusing and lead people to anger and feeling hurt by being contradicted, and I've often felt that it's a form of abuse, to change perceptions of somebody by casting doubt on their entire lives. The media is often accused of dramatising events in this way in their reporting of all kinds of people's stories. Yet all stories hang like a drop of dew on a blade of grass, don't they? Strong yet bound to burst eventually.

I've often wondered since that day about Ray's words, but then I heard a lot of cruel gossip. *The things I've done, Monica.* Maybe some of it was true and he'd been worried sick about it, or maybe it wasn't, but as far as I was concerned, at that point he was a decent guy.

'Well, Ray,' I'd told him, 'I can only repeat that I don't think you have anything to worry about. It's not like you've murdered somebody.'

XIX

They say that in London you're never more than six feet from a rat. Well, I think we can beat that here at the store. There's so much tempting bedding material for all manner of rodents. We have a supply of several hundred rat boxes upstairs in bulk, and they're popular. Yep, according to the newspapers, this camp is state-of-the-art. I guess that must refer to the important equipment and capabilities of the Regiment, because these are the most ramshackle buildings and outdated facilities I've ever encountered at work.

As I said, the quartermaster department wasn't all James Bond with secret gadgets, but I was learning. Take binbags. How come all these special soldiers seemed to need so many binbags? More to the point, why did they take so long sizing each one up, discussing it with a mate, rejecting it and leaving a mess all over our shelves? All I could see were discarded binbags, then someone would order five hundred of one type of them. My 'binbag recognition area' was an attempt to solve the problem. I displayed each bag with its NSN and you should have seen the guys holding them up, deliberating on the relative thicknesses – it was like choosing an outfit for a hot date. They were to put things in, of course; transporting stuff, I suppose. Exceptionally long, thick transparent bags we called body bags, but it was just a grim joke.

My innovative 'padlock recognition area' was another improvement. We had thousands of padlocks, which weren't always used for padlocking things in the way you'd expect, and to make it easy for the men I made a display area. Everyone thought this was highly amusing and teased me until they saw that the place wasn't a mess and the guys could get what they needed in seconds.

Then there were envelopes. When I first saw box after box of different-sized padded envelopes it puzzled me, but they were used to send or carry all sorts of crazy things. Then there were boxes of alphabet letters or numbers, which men were always delighted to find. When a geezer sidled in hesitantly and said, 'I don't suppose you've got...?' I was ridiculously pleased to say, 'Follow me', lead them down to some dingy, dark corner of an aisle and up the platform ladder to retrieve a green box full of numerals or sticky signs.

Another favourite were the bales of rags. They went quickly. We used to laugh, Craig and I, at the idea that someone was probably a millionaire purely through collecting odd bits of rags off the floor of a garment factory somewhere, bagging them up and selling them off to one of the most elite regiments in the world, who couldn't get enough of them.

My life in the store was another world. I was learning fast and I loved getting fluent in the language and terms.

I've done loads of things back in the day, and often I would just walk in and ask if there were any jobs going, so I prided myself on being able to pick up a new job in a flash. Here, I was falling in love with stock codes. Code for a bale? Be. Para cord? Ro. Everybody wanted para or bungee cord, but some rolls cost hundreds of pounds and we only gave them to certain people. Same with batteries; some of them I couldn't even lift off the floor. Other batteries came in camouflage colours. The myriad ideas people had for using this kit was mind-boggling: wallpaper scrapers were never used for wallpaper.

Upstairs in bulk, we had targets. Some were just dots on paper and you'd laugh if you could see the way men would gather round the selection I brought out for them to inspect and take ages to decide on a type or colour of dot, talking between themselves, unsure. I don't know why I found it so funny but I did.

With Craig away doing outside jobs so much, raiding the numerous ISO containers to find kit we might have stowed away as surplus long ago, I ran the store more or less on my own. I suppose this was how I learned so much about the men and made so many friends, because they loved hanging around with their mates and eventually we'd get a brew on. I don't think it's how a store was usually run on camp, but the other stores were run either by young soldiers or the odd ex-military person in his sixties who'd been doing it for twenty years, and they didn't see anything interesting in listening to elite soldiers chatting about their problems like I did. We were often too busy to be chatting, what with the phone going all day long, but mostly I think the badged men just liked coming down here and that was the end of that.

This wonderful place trained me. I gained the ability to drive a forklift, and whilst the accounting course was a nightmare, I said to myself, 'I've learned Latin, I can learn this' and got on with it. That's what education is all about, isn't it? Transferable skills? Potential? Maybe they saw this middle-aged little woman and thought 'She can learn' or even perhaps 'She can bring something to us.' I don't know, but that's what was so great: this regiment, one of the most elite, specialist regiments in the world, takes a chance on people, and that was good enough for me.

XX

Monday morning I was to report at 08:30 to a bleak location along the perimeter road of the camp. My orders were to attend the forklift course for four days and pass the test on Friday. So I did what I always do: I decided I had no choice but to pass. I arrived for the course completely focused. By day two I went home in tears, on day three I told Ranger that I hadn't a hope in hell of passing, and at the end of the week I passed with top marks, only failing one point. Off I went to get my Forklift Truck Accreditation certificate, which I immediately waved in the QM's face, and at anyone else who was around. I was rather disappointed that they all seemed surprised.

The following week, another course. I'm going to call the accounting system TMGI. It was actually called something different, but even the instructor struggled to remember what the initials stood for. TMGI was the global British Army accounting system for all materials and stock, whatever it might be and wherever it was required in the world. It didn't just keep track of simple materials, such as the binbags and batteries we stocked in our store: the system accounted for anything from weapons to flags and everything in between.

There were six of us on the course, four of them 2-2. This is what I meant when I said that the geezers aren't just dodging bullets all the time. If they had responsibility for certain types of kit, or for stuff known as 'attractive to terrorists', then they had to learn the system like anybody else. We sat around a table set out with six big, serious-looking, identical computers. The room was windowless, airless and small. We each had a thick workbook full of ever more complex scenarios and questions. After an hour of learning the appropriate terms and log-in systems we were given a 'leg stretch' break and we all looked at one another in despair.

'I'd heard TMGI was the worst course in the British Army,' said one of the guys, 'but I didn't believe it. I'm not stupid but ...'

'Nothing is relevant to our department,' said another. 'It's like school.'

'Yep, there's a scenario here where I've received thousands of rounds of ammunition by mistake and how should I log it before returning it and what are the codes and what the fuck?'

'Well, lucky you,' I said, 'I'm just learning how to use it to issue a thousand mop handles.'

The problems got harder and harder, wrapping us all up in knots. Inevitably, a few of us formed a breakaway group of dissidents and we slightly took the mick out of it all, though we knew we had to pass or keep taking the course until we did. We remarked on the fact that the airless, windowless room must have been chosen specifically for this course to make sure you never, ever wanted to return.

On the final day, the assessment started at nine o'clock. The instructor told us the questions would be based on things we had gone over on the course, and we had all day to finish if we needed it.

I buckled down as usual and concentrated. The questions took a couple of minutes to read through and I soon realised that they were all the exact same questions and scenarios we had used in our lessons that week. You clicked to turn the pages on the computer, and after you had indicated your final answers there was no going back to adjust, so I read through everything carefully just in case.

After an hour and a half, one of the 2-2 guys got up, gestured to the instructor to check his computer, put on his jacket and left with a silent wave to the rest of us. Wow, I thought, clever bugger. At eleven-thirty, another 2-2 went, and by one o'clock, I was the only person still there.

I finished at three o'clock. It had taken me six hours, but I was fairly sure that I had worked through every detail. The instructor came to take control of my computer and started checking through my test.

'I suppose I'm the one with the least questions right?' I said, suddenly unsure. 'The others all left hours ago.'

The instructor shook his head. 'They cheated,' he said, smiling at me. 'So don't worry. You've done well.'

'Cheated?' I said, horrified. 'How?'

'You already had the answers in your workbook. What the others have done is not read all the way through and then work it out again; they've skipped straight to the end of each question past several pages, and simply copied in the correct answer from what they did this week.' He turned one of the other screens around so I could see what he meant. 'There are algorithms on the system which pick up when you're skipping pages,' he told me. 'You have passed TMGI with only one point deducted for not having a clear explanation of your question twelve answer,' he said, 'but otherwise you're top.'

I clapped my hand to my mouth. Had I really beaten the Regiment on this test?

'But they got them right?' I said. 'They were copying their own answers?'

Brian shrugged, tapping away at the keyboard, peering over his thick glasses.

'Oh, they got the answers right,' he mumbled, 'but that was yesterday. Today, they skipped the pages. If people don't pay attention to detail in the global stock control, think what could happen. I'm marking them all as fails.'

And he pressed the final button with a flourish.

Those two courses gave me confidence and taught me things I never knew I could master. I could now do my job better and be given more to do. That turned out to be a double-edged sword, because I soon understood the sort of accounting everyone else was doing, but an even *better* thrill was gaining a certificate with the British Army badge at the top declaring that I was now an official Joint Forces Materiel Accountant. Hurrah!

XXI

Badged men were elite, specialist soldiers but sometimes they weren't elite in every area of their lives, especially the younger ones. 'Baz' Atherton was a Liverpudlian of such immense stature and breadth that he wouldn't have looked out of place on a Victorian poster for fairground bare-knuckle wrestling.

'If I hadn't got in here, I was going to be a doctor,' Baz told me on the lunch table one day. 'I've no science exams but I'd do them first, and after being a doctor for a few years I'd like to go and be a scientist – Antarctic explorations, maybe.'

'But you came here?' I said.

'Oh yeah!' he said cheerily. 'I thought I'd go for the army, which was piss-easy and then I thought of here.' His eyes strayed over my shoulder to the distant walls of the cookhouse where old photographs of Regiment expeditions were displayed. Baz wanted to be on all of them and, while I admire anyone with ambition, from what he told me, there could never be enough mountains for him to conquer, enemies to slay and women to – er – squire.

The sort of day-to-day obstacles that the military faced, such as missing out on children growing up, being absent for funerals and anniversaries, were simply not on Baz's radar. 'You get through it, don't you?' he said breezily. At twenty-three, he'd already become one of the most fabled soldiers in the world.

By August 2017 the UK had suffered more terror attack deaths than any other EU country in March, May, June and September. There was no real sense of this on camp, but it was reflected in the huge increase in our workload. We were running out of kit, deliveries were coming in thick and fast, and I spent hours every day loading and pulling the pallet-truck just to clear the entrance. Supplies had to be taken away to make room for more to arrive. The entrance was constantly jammed with big white vans loading kit. Brilliant inventions like the pallet-truck made hauling hundredweights in and out of the goods lift childishly easy, and my forklift skills came into their own. I felt useful and vital. For my lunch hour I would sometimes eat for half an hour and then, if I didn't go for coffee and it was a nice day, I'd walk around for the other half hour, watching the men training or playing rugby on the beautifully kept pitches. Sometimes I called into the swimming pool and had a chat with Spike the pool man and Tom who managed things there. I'd met them when they'd come to the store for First Aid boxes or chlorine tablets. The firefighters would need bedding for their all-night shifts and the regimental quartermasters, who were working hard all hours of the day, often came to us just for some fresh air, they said. They adored poking around at the stock and I soon knew about their new babies, their holiday plans and their house moves. Sadly, then came the divorces and the bubble-wrap, packing tape and anger, moving to rooms on camp, but whatever the emotional temperature of the place, we were there for them. It felt precarious, though: one push either way and life here could be either in chaos, or sheer delight.

Baz had led a hardscrabble existence. He told me all about it once, his huge slab of a bashed-about face betraying no emotion. You could always spot him, chest puffed, entering the dining room and looking around as if to check that enough fun people were there to make it worth his while. He couldn't wait to tell me how he swept into the Regiment almost by chance, and now he was wondering what else they had to challenge him. He also talked for five minutes about the girlfriend he'd met on the internet. He found her boring, spoilt and vain, apparently, but she was good at sex so he didn't know what to do. He went on like this, describing his adoration for his three-year-old daughter, who lived a four-hour drive away, begat with someone he 'didn't want to be with', talking about juggling the job and satisfying his lusty nature. Listening to his complex but somehow endearing tale of the accidental outcomes of ill-considered decisions, these staggeringly convoluted situations made me thank God I had a dull life. Anyway, one day when we were incredibly busy with frantic latecomers twenty minutes before we closed, Baz came in for some special batteries. Craig said he'd get them from the battery store as he was going there anyway, and Baz leaned against the wall and settled in for a chat, disregarding the melee all about him.

'So you're intelligent, right?' he said, with his thick accent. He also had a huge mouth crammed with teeth like tombstones struggling for space, with the result that he sounded like he had a mouthful of food.

'Well…'

'What exams did you get then?'

'Er… English Literature, History, French, Music…'

'Music!'

'Yep. Music, Latin…'

'Fucking *Latin!*' He shook his head. 'Good effort, Mon. You must be so fucking intelligent. But what's Latin got to do with anything?'

I shrugged. 'A lot, actually.'

'Like what?'

I shifted my weight onto a hip and thought about it. Although I loved a chat, I wanted my lunch bang on time today and it was quarter past.

'Well, Baz, what a qualification in Latin tells people is that you can *get* a qualification in Latin, I suppose. If you can understand Latin and pass exams, it says something important about you, don't you think? And once you know Latin you can usually work out a lot of English words so –'

'Exams! Fuck!'

'And the same goes for degrees,' I persisted. 'Some people say a degree is just a piece of paper and a degree in, say, geography, is a waste of time, but –'

He shot his hand up like a child in class, begging to be the first to give the correct answer.

'It's saying, "I'm good enough to get a degree in geography – so now give me that fucking job in your bank!"'

He threw his head back laughing and clapped his hands together at the absurdity of it all.

I spent longer than I should have that day, talking – or rather listening – to Baz. The store was insanely busy with all the bad goings-on in the world and I was aware that I was needed, but Baz prattled on, arms folded, one foot against the wall behind him. He directed his thoughts over my head to some distant spot across the wasteland of the store. It was like listening to one of those old radios that needs fine tuning between stations and bouts of static. Bits of phrases were clear, others got lost in the noise around us and the speed of his narrative. He spoke in platitudes that came and went as his head turned, his words tuning-out as he followed the movement of people around us: 'What you see is what you get'; 'What doesn't kill you makes you stronger'. It seemed to me a process of filling space in the steady stream of vanilla phrases without any original, imaginative thought. But I got the gist.

'So, you're angry with your little girl's mum?' I ventured.

'It is what it is,' he said. His head swivelled around the shelves. 'Hey, can I have some cable ties?'

Thank God he didn't say 'Everything happens for a reason.' He was bored already. Girlfriends and Regiment matters needed mental navigation whereas *cable ties...* now you were talking his language. Baz bounded off and scanned the long shelves, which had every size of cable tie ever manufactured, and then froze, like a sniffer dog indicating to its handler a bag of cocaine. He'd spotted my display of ZX-54 Rust Penetrating Oil Compound.

Baz was a confused young man. He was rightly proud of his stunning achievements but, rather than being appreciated, to his mind they were treated like shit. He showered his daughter's mother with cash and anything she needed for their little girl, but she hated his guts in return.

'Did you ever say that you didn't want to be with her?'
I asked.

'Dunno. Maybe.'

'I mean, did you use those exact words?'

'Yeah. But I was within my rights,' he said, his face
clouding over. 'We were like brother and sister by that time.'

'Oh. I'm sorry,' I said.

'Yeah. Well, you know, I woke up one morning with this
incredible hard-on, and I was going to sort myself out then
I thought, hang on I've got a girlfriend in the next room so
I went into the bedroom and said can you help me out with
this, and she said I'm sorting the airing cupboard and I said
well, come on, two minutes! and she said okay then...'

Baz shifted his position and folded his arms, living
through the whole sequence of events as if he was giving a
statement to the police.

'... and she just climbed on the bed and turned over on
all fours, and honestly, Mon, that was it, no fucking effort.'
He pursed his lips and looked into the distance again, over
my head, mulling over the sheer incomprehensibility of it
all. 'She even shut the fucking curtains, Mon, I mean it was
nine o'clock in the fucking morning, who was going to see
us, but ... well. That was the last time we did it.'

We were silent for a few seconds. Should I tell Baz that
not every woman wants her early-morning bum under
scrutiny from close quarters in full daylight? That there
was the question of cellulite or possibly she was a few
weeks past her Hollywood wax? The more likely reason,
I thought, was that she simply didn't fancy him, especially
at nine a.m. with morning breath and such charming
foreplay. I stared at the floor with my lips clamped together

so he wouldn't see my trying not to burst out laughing. What an idiot! He wanted a performing dog willing to go through the routine, not a girlfriend. And he was surprised she hated his guts!

'Anyway – can I help you with anything else?' I said when I could trust myself to be composed. He shrugged and wandered off, coming back looking cheerful with an armful of expensive padlocks and safety goggles.

'Safety goggles?' I frowned. 'There's ten in that box.'

'Yeah, I know!' He beamed. 'I'm working on my car and … '

'Sorry, Baz. You can't just take stuff. Please go and buy them.'

He obligingly walked back to their place on the shelves. For Baz, who had already known a lifetime of being yelled at, beaten into next week and sent packing, being told no was nothing. He told me his grandfather had said that their family were 'Born low, stay low' types, but although Baz had proved them wrong on that, I wondered if it had stuck in his mind. He took another sweep of the store as I answered a couple of queries from other people and sauntered back, impressed.

'I've never been down here. Fucking terrible, our storeman, fucking useless cunt.'

'Whoa!' I said, holding up a hand. 'I've let it go so far today, but that's enough. No need for filthy language.'

'What filthy language? It's allowed.'

'Yes, well, allowing bad language is different from tolerating it,' I said. 'And it's not tolerated in here.'

Craig came back with the batteries and we did the usual paperwork. Off went Baz cheerily to his van, but seconds later he came blustering back in again, a force of nature so great that I could hear the front door hit the wall outside as he pulled it open. A blast of air tunnelled down the narrow corridor, noisily fluttering leaflets straining at the single drawing-pin holding them in place. Baz stormed towards me wearing a half-smile and held the face of his mobile phone towards me.

'Have you got a boyfriend?'

'What?'

'Have you?' He waggled the phone in my face. 'I wanted to cheer to the rooftops that you told me off for swearing. Good on you. I like strong women. I really like you.' He waggled his phone at me a bit more. 'Put your number in?'

'What d'you mean? You've got a girlfriend, you said?'

'Yeah.' He laughed out loud. 'You know how it is. She's nice and pretty and everything, but ... well, I'm a man, aren't I?'

That old chestnut.

'Sorry,' I said. 'I'm working.'

'Off camp then?' he persisted.

I looked away, worried that people would see this. It was a busy time of day, the big roller door was up and vans coming in and out. I could hear Craig talking loudly on the phone in the office and someone could drive in any minute and need me. I was aware that Craig laughed to his mates about me being very slow on the job, but it wasn't like that. Managing everything here mostly alone meant seven hours every day of physical slog. I kept the store phone in my pocket as the calls kept coming, chasing up items that were desperately needed, enquiring if something was even available to the troops and all the while stacking and palletising and going up and down the clanking store stairs dozens of times an hour to load and unload the goods lift. It had to be done at endurance rate, like a marathon, not a sprint. Craig showed up now and again and flung himself into it all headlong for an hour, but he had other responsibilities, like the camp rugby team training most afternoons, so it was rare to see him around after lunch. He had good qualities, you couldn't fault Craig for his sunny nature, but he just wasn't around much. Anyway, it was no good worrying about it. Right now there was the typical late-morning rush and Baz was practically pinning me to the wall with his eagerness to get my number.

'C'mon!' He was grinning, poised, spreading his legs and planting his feet firmly, blocking the corridor like a goalkeeper ready to dive either way.

'Don't be silly, Baz,' I said. 'Why on earth would you be asking that?'

'You're hot!'

'For heaven's sake.' I was irritated at his attempts to take advantage of me. 'Don't be ridiculous.'

I flicked through a couple of delivery notes. Somewhere I felt a stab. He was making fun of me. Baz flung his head back, laughing.

'Hey, you're hot. Just a bit of fun.' He moved closer and shot a glance left and right. 'I want to know what it's like.'

'What what's like?'

He waited until one of the firemen had gone past, holding a huge bundle of bedding, then he leaned in closer.

'What it's like to go with an older woman, M. No offence.'

I felt a familiar thud in my chest, the feeling of my entire mood deflating. Craig had come back into the store, looking puzzled at a delivery note, and a storeman was talking loudly to someone on the forklift who'd left the engine running. Corporal Eddy had slipped around the corner and was chewing his pencil, firing questions to someone at the end of his mobile. It was busy, and they needed me. I stayed still, barely breathing, looking down, hoping he'd get bored of trying to provoke me.

'I'm not a biological experiment, Baz,' I said in a low voice. 'I'm a woman, not an "older woman" and, as blunt as this sounds, it's not always about you. I'm not something to try out.'

He made a show of straightening his face to look serious.

'Hey, sorry, M. I really do fancy you.' He took a half-step even closer, so his huge chest was against me. 'Wouldn't you like to be blindfolded and tied up while I have my way with you?' he whispered.

'Not particularly.'

'You're not like the others, M, you have a confidence about your eyes and you talk like I've never seen before. You're really intriguing me.'

He came closer still: he must have been seventeen stone and I was actually backed against the big table that carried all our departmental demands in date order. He was breathing heavily. I was more bothered about him messing up my invoices.

'I'd kiss you all over,' he went on. 'I'm not a brash type – as long as nobody gets their feelings hurt and we're having fun, that's where I'm at.' He stood tall and raised his eyebrows. 'Can I do that?'

I didn't move. Brash type? What the hell was that?

'I'd hate that.'

'I'd make you enjoy it.'

That was it.

'Baz. OK, listen to me. I don't know what you've been told, but girls say and do a lot of things because they want to be cool. It's compliance. Women are afraid of not being fancied and that's all there is to it.' I wasn't sure I meant it, but I wanted to put him in his place.

Baz straightened, his expression frozen.

'There,' I said. 'Lesson over. You can go.'

He gaped at me, about to say something.

'Now, please,' I said very quietly.

He walked away a few steps, nonchalantly, then turned and came back.

'Look, vinegar face.'

He touched his finger to my cheek. I waited. He must have thought better of it, and he stepped back.

'The storeman with the big knockers, eh?' he said coolly, like some New York gangster. 'The crumpet isn't exactly coming out of the woodwork here, if you hadn't noticed. Sure you can't fit me in sometime?'

I didn't answer.

'That's a no then?'

I remembered what Charlie Rossall said to me that day in the memorial garden: 'Young guys, especially badged ones, they're like dogs. All they want to do is fight and fuck.'

I smiled to myself. Vinegar face, eh? I'll use that.

An hour later, Baz came back and apologised. He seemed confused and embarrassed by my response and upset that he might have offended me. He was obviously expecting horror and shouting and telling him to eff off. I made him a brew. He said he thought it was banter and I'd join in and not take him seriously. He was on standby, he said, and had all the time in the world. He was still the same Baz but being knocked back had bothered him, and he asked me if he was off-putting or not attractive. I felt sorry for him, so I said of course he was very handsome. Rejection wasn't something he was used to.

'I'm not rejecting you,' I said, 'it's…' I struggled to think of something suitable to nurse his bruised ego. 'I'm not rejecting *you*, just your offer.'

The next morning I had a note through the office door, and it made me think of the line in the camp poem, 'Always a Little Further.'

> **Morning Monica,**
> **Just wanted to see how you are feeling about me. I take it you think I'm OK looking. I know you are quite happy living alone and working etc, which is good. So are you happy with some company, coffee, drives, kisses, sex from time to time?**
> **BAZ x**

Being young is a strange time, learning how the world works, and being in the Regiment must make things worse for the youngest geezers. Over a third of relationships that lead to marriage start in the workplace, whereas meetings in bars, on holiday or online mostly result in flings. With on average one woman for every 120 men on camp at my rough estimate, and with most of the women unlikely to mix with the men like I did, these poor geezers didn't stand a chance of meeting anyone to have a long-term relationship with. I once asked my lunch-mates what they thought when they looked around the dining room and all they saw was men, and they simply shrugged and said, 'We're used to it.' Their only chance to meet anyone was down at the bars and clubs of Hereford every week. Young women in Hereford often said quite openly that they were looking for a 'Blade' and why not? Fit, handsome, shadowy, macho (oh, if only they knew), they would get tarted up and go for a night out with that one goal. The guys knew what they wanted but were then somehow perplexed when said young lady turned up some time later, pregnant, which is precisely what happened to Baz. While a child is always a blessing, maintenance payments and bitter arguments for the next eighteen years are, while not a certainty, certainly a warning.

These lovely elites needed to meet people randomly in a train carriage or lobbing bags of garden rubbish at the council tip or waiting for a prescription at Boots. If Baz told women that he was SAS, and I imagine he did, they'd be queuing up to 'try it out' just as he wanted to try me out. At only twenty-three, he didn't know what it felt to be a normal man, rejected for his mouthful of teeth. If he told a girl he'd be away and then back and then away again and not able to see her much, she'd simply say 'It's okay, I don't mind, I'll be here'. Plenty of these young girls try to sound like Cool Girls and hang on to their Blade boyfriends for sex, so these guys never caught on to the fact that they should make more effort with a woman they love if they want to have a lasting relationship. However much anybody rails against what I've just said, I'm afraid it's true. I saw the flipside of it with young women on camp who were seeing badged guys; they were always popping into the store in floods of tears, sobbing, 'He's only got a fucking *WIFE!*'

Once in the Regiment, and especially during the first three years, when they are under close scrutiny, developing a new relationship and making commitments is incredibly difficult. Many of the badged men would *like* to have a relationship, they told me so, and they envy their happily married mates with their sweet children. But they don't want the hassle of managing a girlfriend. Eventually she finds someone else, someone who's around a bit more reliably, so it's the guy who ends up heartbroken. Why put up with all the stress and tedium of keeping someone happy and worrying about who else she's seeing, when they can have no-strings-attached fun for the few days they're back in town? It doesn't mean they're bad boys, it means they can't cope with the problems of relationships when they're already coping with the constant training for complex systems of warfare that being one of the most elite soldiers in the world entails.

I can't criticise the excellent books written by ex-special forces personnel that talk about achieving mental endurance and resilience, and the ability to devise skillsets and strategies to be at the top of your game. It's important to be able to think clearly when everything around you is falling to bits but, as we have all found out during the course of 2020, amidst the COVID-19 coronavirus pandemic, sometimes things happen that turn our lives upside down and throw all good intentions out of the window. A sudden heart attack, the death of a parent or child, a cancer diagnosis or life-changing accident, redundancies, marriage breakups – there are so many ways events can overtake you. Mental health issues are better understood these days, and despite a resilient attitude and an endurance mindset, however elite you are, you are not immune. It always bothers me, listening to life advice from people who haven't lived very long, even though they undoubtedly mean well. I think that if your only experience of life has been in the armed forces, it's definitely not an effective blueprint for the rest of us. Even the strongest-minded soldier can be almost broken by a personal struggle.

One day, not too long after I'd helped him with bubble-wrap in the stores for his wife who was leaving him at Christmas, I saw Kip Formby again. With his huge black sunglasses and soft beige calfskin jacket, it was the first time I'd ever seen him out of uniform.

'Hi Kip.' I raised a hand, expecting him to drive on.

He pulled over.

'Out on parole, I see,' I said. 'Nice car.'

Whenever I'd seen Kip up here before he would ignore me or say a chilly hello. Today he seemed more relaxed. I straightened up and walked a bit nearer to his car.

'How are things, by the way?' I asked in a low voice. 'You were quite distressed last time I saw you.'

He looked away and gazed out of the windscreen.

'It's OK,' he said, sighing deeply.

Kip was a real hard man. He'd been in the Regiment for a long time and was exactly what you'd expect an elite soldier to be. Strong, self-assured, he took pride in his job – he loved every second of his life as a 2-2 and could talk into next week about it in his Northern Irish accent. But today he seemed different.

I waited. He switched off his engine.

'Why didn't you say you knew Mike Peller, Mon?'

'Would it have helped if I had?' I replied. 'And "knew" Mike is putting it a bit high.'

'High?'

'C'mon, Kip,' I said. 'I don't know Mike – I met him back down the road two years ago, and it took me about ten seconds to work out that he was a nasty piece of work. He's a type.'

'A type?' Kip seemed forlorn, listless.

'Yes. You mustn't think about him. He's irrelevant now.'

There was a long pause. I wasn't sure if I should go and leave him to get on and take his mind off things. He looked at me.

'Am I a type?'

'Course. Role model type.'

He laughed.

'And Mike Peller is self-centred.'

God, take away his annoying personality and Kip was achingly handsome. I could have looked at his face all day, but he was a dry sort of chap, never a bundle of laughs and almost … brittle. He always sounded like he was snapping at people and his gravelly accent had an edge. He was handsome, for sure, but that was about it; the grey was creeping in inexorably around his temples and it was only a matter of time before 'achingly handsome' would turn to 'bet he was good-looking when he was younger'.

'Have you sent her a message?' I asked. 'I mean a proper letter or a card, hand-written? That would be appreciated.'

He was already shaking his head emphatically.

'No chance. You don't know my wife.'

'I don't need to know your wife, Kip. I think you should send a personal message saying it'd be fantastic to take her out.' I paused. 'I think it'd be a good thing to do.'

'No.'

'Nothing melancholy. Upbeat. Short and simple.'

He sighed again deeply.

'What if she doesn't reply, M? Rejects me? Ignores me?'

'I know, but the thing about your fear of rejection is that she isn't thinking the same thing,' I told him. 'She's not thinking "I bet he thinks I'll reject him" she's thinking "He hasn't bloody well got in touch, not once".'

To my relief, Kip did at least raise his eyebrows as if to say, you have a point.

The pain of feeling excluded from someone's life is the same as physical pain. The idea of his wife with Mike Peller was the worst exclusion there could be – they'd be laughing together, walking together, eating and making love together, and yet the perception of what his wife was feeling was most likely wrong. She might be missing Kip. He wanted to be in touch but by failing to send her a message he was sending a different message, that he wasn't interested. And that was something she was also too afraid to explore so she did nothing either. I suggested all this to Kip.

'I can't do it,' he said. 'I can't take another rejection.'

You'd think, wouldn't you, that a man with his qualities and fortitude would be able to get past this, but his skillset had been forged for use with people like himself. For situations of conflict, not emotional pain.

'Look,' I went on, 'You're in the valley. You've come down one mountain and reached the bottom. You can keep going and reach the top of the next mountain. Don't you think it's worth it?'

'Hmmm… maybe.'

'It's doing the kind thing. To me, that's a virtue,' I said. 'And I think you're amazing, Kip.'

He looked at me. 'Amazing?'

'Well … you're interesting, funny, good-looking.'

'Standard,' he said.

We talked about it for a little while longer, but he wasn't having it. It seemed extraordinary to me that a man with such courage couldn't face the prospect of failure, but then the stakes were high. This wasn't just a battle, it was his whole life ahead of him, with or without his wife. And for the moment, he just didn't know what to do.

Then there was Jos, one of the guys I met in the memorial garden down the road who I'd see often in random places, like filling up our cars in the Asda petrol station. Well, two years had passed from our first meeting when who should come and join me in the cookhouse as I was alone at my late table for evening meal but Jos.

He looked rough – dog rough. He was wearing a baseball cap pulled down low over his brow, and his thick outdoor jacket was zipped over his chin, barely revealing enough room for him to eat. He sat down and started telling me that he'd recently had an affair and it had all gone wrong. His wife didn't know. To be honest, I was surprised at this news; I'd never had Jos down as a womaniser and his chat was always more about motorbikes than sex or drinking. He wanted to stay married, he said, but it had got complicated when the girlfriend, thinking him single and deeply in love with him, was introducing him to her parents and talking about the future together. He was trembling as he told me this, forking curry into his mouth, and he looked thinner than usual.

'I want to be with her,' he said. He was poking his fork around the plate, as if by stabbing indiscriminately, some food would fix onto it.

'So how do you feel about Colette?' I asked. 'You said you wanted to stay married.'

'I want her too, hundred per cent.'

It was almost the end of the evening meal service, mess hands were already wiping the tables and it suddenly felt miserable and soulless, like a seaside pier cafe out of season.

'It's carnage. I told her just before our holiday at Christmas...'

'Hang on, told who? Holiday with Colette or the other one?'

'Other one.'

'OK, right. So, you went away at Christmas with your girlfriend and left your family?'

'Don't.' He hung his head, then propped it up with both hands.

'Well, never mind that just now,' I said, keen to keep him on track. 'So what happened?'

'I told her I had a wife and she didn't speak to me for the rest of the holiday.'

I had to stop myself laughing. I put a hand over my face as if wisely considering his dilemma, but I was hiding my mirth. What an idiot!

'Yes, that's not good. And now?'

He looked up at me and sighed deeply, then stared at the ceiling.

'Well, she keeps saying she wants kids, but then I said if I already had one how would she know which kids I was going to be with on the weekend, hers or Colette's.'

'That's a good point,' I said. 'I agree, it's not hopeful.'

He was still poking around with his food and occasionally shoved a load into his mouth and had to lean over his plate to let some of it go.

'She's gone,' he said through a mouthful.

'Gone?'

'Blocked me, won't return calls. Hasn't read my texts.'

'Oh dear,' I said. 'We've all done stupid things in our lives.'

I knew Jos a bit; he was a nice guy who'd messed up. He liked a stable world around him and really didn't see why his wife and his girlfriend couldn't be completely happy with an arrangement whereby he carried on his life doing as he pleased and they just fitted in. Even the idea that having an affair meant he was unfaithful to his wife seemed to be a genuine mystery to him.

'Look, I'm not going anywhere,' I said. 'I'm living here in Hereford for the rest of my life, I like it. So any time you fancy a brew, the kettle's on. If you're busy and I don't hear from you, that's OK too. But I'm always here.'

'That's reassuring,' he replied.

Of course, he lost both women and, by default, his children, and it was so terribly sad, though I saw him quite a lot during the terrible floods early in 2020 when he often asked after me, and he seemed slightly happier.

Of course, I saw and heard a lot about their relationships when I worked on camp, but as I was in a place full of young men, I had to keep reminding myself that it was the *concentration* of men in their prime which contributed to the horror stories about broken marriages and cheating. Men and women all over the world cheat and have always cheated. It's true to say that it takes a certain type of man to go for the Regiment, but the emphasis on the hard training is only a small percentage of the complete story. The life is a difficult one, but then the life of a heart surgeon called out during the night or an oil rig worker away for weeks or a sewage worker on standby all lack certainty. There are plenty of happy marriages, especially, I found, when they buy their own house rather than living in military housing and put down proper roots in Hereford. It was the determination to stick together and embrace a career spent in Hereford that seemed to work for many of them.

And let's not forget the determinedly single man. Marriage and a family are not the automatic key to happiness when happiness can be found just as easily in solitude, as many of these men told me. Many of them hated Christmas, and really got angry about the 'all about family' emphasis and lived happy fulfilled lives in military service without any broken hearts, painful divorces or lawyers' bills!

XXII

Every now and again there was a moment in my job when I swelled with happiness and pride, and the inspection was one of those moments. I was utterly devoted to the Regiment and I may be blowing my own trumpet, but I can't do any job badly. I'd worked hard to straighten out the store; things were labelled properly, all the records were up to date and easy to find, rather like one of those TV programmes where an expert comes in to sort out a hoarding habit and persuade the homeowner to clear clutter. I felt like one of those experts.

The inspectors had come up from London and would be spending the next two days going through every aspect of the stores in the quartermaster department. They would be coming to our store first thing, which pleased me as it would be too early for anyone to mess things up. With them were the quartermaster and the chief health and safety officer. I was told to carry on with my work, but not to talk to the inspectors unless they wanted to talk to me. Basically, don't be too visible or distracting. They arrived at half past eight and I manoeuvred myself up into bulk stores, taking a broom to do a bit of sweeping so that I could get a look at the main men. Suddenly one of the inspectors walked towards me; the others were deep in conversation. It felt like the Queen taking a detour from her official route round a factory to ask a worker if they were getting their fair break entitlement.

'Hi, I'm Matthew,' he said, holding out a hand.

I quickly peeled off my thick safety glove.

'Morning, Matthew. I'm Monica,' I replied. 'You've come a long way today I hear?'

'Last night actually,' he said.

'Oh really, where did you stay?'

'Green Dragon.'

Pleasantries over, the inspector asked how long I had worked in the store, where I'd been before and what I thought of the camp.

'Oh, I just love it!' I replied. 'It's such a new world for me, and absolutely wonderful. I love learning new things and I even passed my forklift accreditation – I was so pleased that they would train me.'

I realised that I was overdoing it, but I wanted to sound enthusiastic. I wanted ours to be the best store, not for myself, but to please the QM and put our notoriously underperforming department in a better light.

'And you've done quite a lot here, I can see,' Matthew said. 'I came here two years ago and it needed improvements – it was pretty terrible, in fact. Your store is the busiest of all of them and it's always been a challenge.'

'Oh, they were so overworked,' I said.

I glanced downstairs and could see Craig below me on the ground floor, looking up anxiously. They had spent a week moving stuff that shouldn't have been there: certain goods that had been stashed away under the Regiment coffin (which was used for ceremonial purposes), personal lockers with contraband inside them had been cleared, they'd organised the TMGI system so things were 'managed' in order to be correct – you get my drift. Corporal Eddy had called himself 'the dodgiest of the lot' last week, beaming with naughty pride as he said it, and Adie's legacy of petty thieving had been hard to shake off.

Now the other inspector was making his way to us, followed by the QM.

'Excuse me, I'd better carry on with my orders.' I backed away, went downstairs and finished sweeping. If you didn't know what to do in this place or wanted to look busy, you grabbed a brush.

It was soon ten o'clock and I was dying to know what they thought. Before they left, Inspector Matthew wandered over to me and asked if I had a break coming.

'I'd like to talk to you some more,' he said. 'It's the first time they've had a female storekeeper and I'm interested in your experience. Do you have a little time to meet me in the coffee shop, away from all this?'

The walk over to the coffee shop would take a precious ten minutes off my twenty-minute break, so I drove up to meet him at bang on 10.15. Fortunately, the place wasn't full and we could find a booth and be private. I realised that I should have been paying attention to everything Matthew said, but I was side tracked – his hair was almost polished to perfection, his tie immaculate, his suit clearly bespoke, his face subtly cared-for. A woman can tell these things. I'd forgotten that seductive smell of aftershave, applied for a reason other than necessity. Nobody smelled like that on camp and I suddenly realised why my daily spritz of a Chopard *eau de toilette* made such an impact.

As I've said, you can always tell an elite soldier from his posture and his walk. Matthew was in the Regiment still but had 'gone over to the dark side' as they jokingly called it when their door-kicking days were over. I can look at any man in Hereford town and tell you who is and isn't in the Regiment and it's not about bulging muscles. Gym-honed bodybuilders look completely different from fit elite soldiers whose bodies go far beyond ten hours a week lifting weights. Our lads are long-distance, weight-bearing endurance soldiers. Even when they're roughing-it, growing their hair long and looking homeless, the geezers' colour is good, their skin clear from all that fitness. They look self-assured, steady and engaged because they expect people to listen to them. The soldiers, especially the surveillance specialists, might wish to blend in and be 'grey men' but it's not convincing as far as I'm concerned. They can never pass as nobodies. Shake hands with them – their hands are a revelation. They'll crush you to pieces with their grip. I suppose many years of doing tough jobs with their bare hands, gripping weapons or climbing rocks, leaves them so incredibly hard, it feels just like I imagine shaking hands with a gorilla would feel: a dry, calloused, bone-hard grip.

That was the giveaway about Matthew the Inspector. Coming from a smart London barracks he looked, smelled and dressed like he'd just got off a yacht and lived in a palace but when I shook his hand ... with my eyes shut I'd have said either elite soldier or trawlerman.

'So, Monica, tell me,' he started, 'I've been visiting and inspecting here before, and I can see that your store is a massive job with only – is it two or three people working in there?'

'That's right,' I said. 'Two labourers, me and Craig, the corporal who looks after several stores and the sergeant over us all.'

Matthew thought for a second.

'So what do you think accounts for the change from the last time I was here?'

I didn't hesitate.

'Oh, the culture,' I said. 'And I've thought about this a lot because obviously I could see the chaos, but everyone was working really flat out. I think the powers-that-be looked at the job as a category, nothing else. "Industrial, Skill Zone 1" is my job category and as long as you have the strength and ability to work under bad conditions, move stuff, supply stuff and so on, that was all that mattered. Thing is, though, Skill Zone 1 is the job, not the person. I thought a bit of customer service should come into it and we should also control the soldiers a bit more.'

'Control the soldiers?' Matthew looked amused for a moment, intrigued. I was enjoying this chance to have a proper conversation and it felt fantastic that someone was taking an interest in my job.

'Yes,' I said. I went on to explain how people like Craig, ex-military, were used to deferring to people of higher rank and wary of telling a badged guy to be more respectful of stock and not just help themselves. 'But being one of the most famous regiments in the world, this store should be held to a higher standard too,' I said. 'There's not even a trained clerk filing the vast amount of documentation we have, and all that's expected of us is picking and packing and hauling stuff around because we're on minimum wage. We were expected to pick the skill up and do it the best we can, but that's not the way to work in this famous Regimental store, surely?'

I looked around the coffee shop. I'd said more than I probably should have so I glanced at the clock and said I should be going. Matthew simply waved his hand and said it would be OK. We talked some more, and he ordered more coffee. I was way over my break time but a good report would be a tremendous coup – and even better if it was a *great* report, so I wasn't too bothered.

I arrived back in the store at eleven o'clock, turning the key in the lock. Why was it locked? Where was Craig?

I walked into the office and there was Jules, sitting in Craig's seat, doing her playing the bongos thing with her hands, rapping her palms on the desk in an impatient fashion while fixing her eyes on the wall clock high up on the far wall.

'Hi, Jules,' I said gaily, taking off my jacket. I knew I was in trouble. It was like having your mum waiting up for you to get home, then telling you you're grounded.

'This is – *un-acceptable*,' she said. She allowed a dramatic pause and looked at her watch for good measure.

I carried on as usual, taking my safety shoes out from under the desk and starting to change from my outdoor shoes.

'OK. Sorry,' I said, lacing them up. 'The inspector asked to talk to me about work,' I continued, opening my desk drawer for gloves. I changed my jacket to the heavy-duty one, zipping it up to my neck.

Jules looked at me, daggers.

'What did you think you were doing all this time?' she said, sitting back and folding her arms.

'I've told you, talking. He asked me to go, Jules – an incredibly important inspector from London. I was aware of the time, so I'm not going to say I didn't notice that I was late, but I didn't feel I could leave.'

'*Didn't feel you could leave?*' said Jules in her best shrill voice. 'You should have told him your break time was up.'

I couldn't help smiling. In fact, I had a job not to laugh out loud. Here was me thinking I'd done the department a huge favour by really selling it, fantastic public relations, telling the truth and outlining my ambitions for a better-run store and Jules thought I should get back to work to do ... what? Wait for somebody to come and ask for bubble-wrap?

'Where's Craig anyway?' I asked. I folded my arms and leaned against the wall, relaxed. 'Craig could have coped with anything, except he's not here.'

Jules wasn't used to subordinates questioning her. 'I don't know where he is, Monica, but he has a lot of duties with the rugby.'

'*Rugby!*' I wasn't having this. 'Craig is the senior storekeeper. Do you know that I, as junior storekeeper, shouldn't be left alone here for more than twenty minutes at a time? It's a dangerous place and if I fell...'

I realised my mistake the minute I said this. What if she suggested she stay with me every time Craig had rugby? That would be disaster.

'Anyway, Monica.' Jules stood up and held her watch up to look at it. 'That's forty-five minutes you need to make up as punishment. I'm taking it off your lunch break tomorrow. Fifteen minutes for lunch tomorrow, OK?'

I didn't care. Maybe I should have, but I didn't. I knew I'd been doing some good, not just sitting for nearly an hour gossiping, and so it eventually turned out. On the other hand, I decided that the situation between me and Jules couldn't go on any longer, as I couldn't face another year or more of these conflicts. Jules was a problem in my life and I decided I was going to take steps to sort it out.

A phone call came for the full stores personnel, including the military guys, to assemble in the big corridor of the quartermaster building at 14:30. There were about forty of us, and we stood in a big circle. Ranger came out first, then Kiwi, followed by two other RQs and Sergeant Jules, then the QM appeared. He was a big, imposing man, a quiet authority and very well liked.

'First of all, I'd like to thank you for the good effort you've all put in for this inspection,' he started. He then ran through a few details for each store, most of which didn't come up to scratch because of simple health and safety lapses, and then he got to ours.

'Monica, Craig,' the QM said, extending a hand, 'I have never known such a good report. There was one minor point about a fire extinguisher not securely fastened to the wall, but that was all. You really came out with flying colours. I want you to know, I'm well happy.'

Everyone looked at us. It was one of the most uplifting times of my life. '*Well* happy' he'd said. I've had bigger triumphs but I have never had a more significant triumph and a lot of it I put down to talking to the inspector in the coffee shop, praising the QM department for having the foresight to give me the job, train me in the forklift to help me take the extra work on, and letting me do things my way.

We all had a cup of tea and chatted for a while as a team, then I made my way back with Craig. I was nearly at the store when I noticed that Sergeant Jules was following us.

'Give me a moment Craig, OK?' I said and let him go ahead.

I stopped Jules in the middle of the car park.

'Jules', I said, touching her arm. 'Look – can we start again? We haven't been getting on and I'd like to change that.' I gave her a warm smile and she looked startled. 'I don't think we got off to a good start, but for some reason – my fault as much as yours, I'm sure – we've hit the wrong note. I'd like to rewind.'

Jules looked at me, unsure. 'Of course,' she said. 'It's a difficult job, this.'

Then she told me about her life – teenage children with their own problems, driving across the country every weekend to take them to see their dad, the stresses of her job in the army. I was incredibly sorry for her and I said so.

'It can't be easy working with me, I'm the first one to acknowledge it,' I went on, 'but I know we can make it work.' My jacket hood was up, my face screwed tight against the wind. It was a mad conversation to be having in a car park but where better? Nobody could overhear us. 'I don't know what you think,' I said, 'but going over old ground is futile. There's no point in trying to straighten things out or talk it through. Can we change the record, though? Start as if it's my first day again?'

And we did. Jules started to relax and even have a laugh from time to time and she became a huge support to me when things were tough. She left the camp in 2018 and moved on to her next posting, but I will always remember her with fondness.

Much later, when I told my story in the cookhouse to a bunch of badged men about being back forty-five minutes late for my shift, but all in a good cause, they looked puzzled that I was upset about being punished for it.

'But you were late, Monica,' they said, as if that was that.

'Well – yes,' I agreed, 'but I was asked to go by the inspector, and I could see this was doing our QM department the world of good – which it did.'

'Yeah… but you were late back. You deserved a punishment.'

'Even if I was doing it for the department, not me personally?'

'Er – yes!'

I laughed at that. They were right, technically, but they didn't see eye to eye with me about how those forty-five minutes were best spent. Back sweeping the store or getting the best report the department has ever had simply by playing the game? They were right, of course; in the military you follow your orders. I was just wired for a more commercial outcome.

XXIII

Cameron Moseley was fine on paper. Fifteen years in 22 Regiment, he was polite and articulate, soft-spoken and gentlemanly – and yet I felt there was something about him that didn't compute. Counting the days until his career was over, he seemed refined, self-centred and caddish, and expressed a fastidious distaste of a world he felt was inhabited by inferiors in an amusing way which didn't alienate people. Sometimes, however, he could go over the top. I once ran into him in a riverside coffee place in town that had life-drawing classes upstairs and hipsters drinking nettle soup downstairs; he made an entrance like the despotic ruler of a minor remote colony come to see if his subjects were getting enough food. However, I suspected that behind all his grand talk and lordly ways there probably skulked quite an ordinary, slightly shabby, grasping soul.

I don't know what made me say that. Maybe it's because of what happened next.

Cam was leaving the Regiment the following year. Only thirty-eight, he'd certainly put in the slog as an elite soldier. He'd been terribly badly injured a few times and I heard many independent sources relay tales of his heroism. Recently his back had been in a terrible state after an incident in London in 2017. To the badged men, retirement could be a relief or a dagger hanging over them. Some had a clear career path that could take them onwards to late middle-age but Cam wasn't the administrative type. He was staying for his twenty-two years in the army but that was enough. He didn't even explore any of the lucrative possibilities from commercial companies wanting his expertise; according to him, he had no expertise beyond kicking doors in and shooting guns. I sensed a certain inertia common among people accustomed to an institutional life; he seemed depressed. He was putting off any decisions until the day he walked out of the camp gates for good because, like a lot of people, he'd become a slave to his sexual needs. All it had done was land him in a mess and now the chickens were coming home to roost.

He called me out of the blue one Saturday. It was incredibly hot and I was cycling home from the shops. He said he'd rung 'Just for a chat.' Now, you may ask why any of the men had my mobile number, but it was common practice for us to give them out in case the store was locked and urgent supplies were needed. On weekends, one of the military would come in to see to it, but if I were only up at the cookhouse for lunch it was better to just call one of us to come back.

I stopped and sat on a wall to take the call, propping up my bike and taking off the heavy backpack.

'Cam?' I said, surprised. 'What's up? Something wrong?' I didn't know him too well, and it was strange that he was calling me at the weekend.

'I'm in Spain,' he said. 'It's raining.'

'Right. What's up, Cam?'

'I just wanted to hear your voice.'

Here we go, I thought.

'Ha-ha. OK,' I replied. 'So is everything alright?'

There was a long pause. I thought I could hear voices.

'Cam? You OK?'

Don't tell me he's having a heart attack, I thought. That had happened to me once – the person dying was 5,000 miles away and called me by mistake.

'Cam? Are you working? Or is it something else?'

There was another dramatic pause.

'Something else, babe.'

'Go on.'

'Sick of work, babe.'

'Ah.' I tried to sound soothing. 'I know. It's hard for you. Are you with anyone, friends?'

'No, on my own.'

God, this was going to take ages.

'And you're alright in yourself?' I said. 'Has anything happened?'

I heard him take a deep breath. 'Nah, nothing. My back's fucked a bit since the Westminster attack, and sometimes I can't move and have to lie flat for a couple of days, but I'm fine.'

'You don't sound fine.'

It wasn't very comfortable, sitting on somebody's low wall. Where was this going?

'You're the only person I like talking to,' he said. 'You understand.'

'Well, only a bit, Cam. I wish I could help.'

'I've got another year, M, then I'm out.'

'I know. Well, that's something,' I said, trying to be bright. 'Something to look forward to. Any plans?'

'I'm buying a coffee cart. Flog coffee in marketplaces and festivals. Good coffee.'

'Great.'

'I wondered if you could help, Mon?'

'Of course,' I said. 'If I can.'

'You'll help me?'

I laughed. 'If I can, of course I will. What's up?'

I needed to get home. I was wearing shorts, the sun was scorching my legs and I was worried about the tub of ice cream in my backpack.

'Well...' His slow voice had almost ground to a halt now. He really did sound as if his back were painful. How dreadful to go all the way to Spain for the weekend and be in pain. 'So, hey. It's a bit of a long shot. Are you free next week to have a chat? An investment you might be interested in.'

Oh dear, I thought.

'Just to give you the heads up,' he went on. 'It's investing into our coffee truck. And all in all, a good cause. But it'll require £7K. Basically, unforeseen circumstances meant I couldn't...'

He didn't finish the sentence. He sounded breathless.

'Have a think and let me know?' he said.

So that was it. I felt my heart sink. It wasn't the first time one of the men in the military had asked me for money. Seven thousand pounds!

'Why are you asking me, Cam?' I said. 'I'm a storekeeper.'

He laughed gruffly and it set him off coughing. Eventually he said, 'Yeah, but you're, like, a millionaire, M. You had your car done last week and you said it came to eighteen hundred.'

'It did, yes. I saved.'

It had kept failing the MOT on emissions so I'd needed a new catalytic converter and other bits and bobs. I wasn't exactly thrilled.

'Ha-ha. No, you said it like "Hey, well, it's eighteen hundred!"' He put on a feminine voice, mocking.

'Doesn't mean I was happy about it. I'm sorry.'

'You can't afford it?'

'Of course I couldn't!' I said. I'd saved every month from my pathetic wages. Anyway, I didn't want to say that I hardly knew him so there was no way I'd lend him anything even if I could.

'OK. Sorry, babe.'

It went quiet. I watched a few cars go by and heard the town hall clock strike. Was that it?

'I have to go, Cam. I have shopping here that's going to thaw. And chicken and stuff.'

'OK, babe. Take care. Bye.'

'Bye, Cam. Hope your back gets better.'

'Babe?'

'Yes?'

'It wasn't the money, babe. I wanted to hear your voice.'

'I'm worried about you, Cam,' I said, easing my bum off the rough concrete wall, wincing as the backs of my bare legs felt a graze. 'Please tell me you're OK?'

More silence.

'You're in Spain, you say?'

'Yeah, babe.'

'Well...' I was searching for something else to say. 'I hope it stops raining soon. It's awful to go away and find the weather's bad and –'

'Can I see you when I get back? Next week? I'm having a rough time here.'

I ended the call and cycled home, annoyed but also a bit concerned by the strange conversation. Still, I had things to do and asking me for seven thousand pounds had soured everything. I put my concern to one side. He was taking the mick.

A few days later I was at lunch and a man in Cam's troop joined my table. He started telling me about a fantastic big wedding he'd been to ten days ago.

'How was it?' I asked. 'Anyone I know?'

'Yeah, actually,' he said. 'You know Cam Moseley? Him. He's off in Spain right now, lucky bastard, on his honeymoon.' He threw his head back and cackled. 'Cost him a bloody fortune, stupid arse. His bird's got expensive tastes and chucked in a ten-thousand-pound hen weekend for him to pay. He even asked me to bail him out!'

'Wow,' I said, 'and did you?'

'Fucking joking? Cam's always skint. He's leaving service soon and hasn't made any plans. Stupid idiot's got a million kids too, three different women!' he cackled. His mates on the table joined him and soon there were lots of Cam Moseley stories keeping them all amused.

I didn't arrange to meet Cam. I kept it all at work and said he should pop into the stores for a brew, where hopefully Craig would be around too. He never came in and I forgot all about him, which is a little ironic because that's how a lot of them end up, forgotten. Perhaps it's because they don't learn to understand, as civilians do, about making connections with people and playing their part outside the Regiment. I couldn't begin to imagine how

Cam's marriage was working out because I suspected from what the other men said that his wife was one of those besotted with the 'Blade' idea of a husband, not a man earning his living running a coffee cart. Maybe I'm being uncharitable. Maybe the coffee business is a wild success and he's turned it into an empire. I truly hope he's not sitting on a street corner holding a cup full of pennies.

XXIV

Badged guys work all the time up here. If they weren't off training they'd be talking about training. If you're familiar with what they call the green army, and think it's similar, I can tell you this was nothing like that. I've known quite a few people in the armed forces, and their life is a peach compared with life in the Regiment. The geezers were away so much and home for such short bursts. I could recognise them in town on weekdays, any morning or afternoon you might see small knots of them around a table or maybe just two together, attached to a project. Despite their casual attire, hands cupping an Americano or munching an almond croissant, they looked hard at work. I could tell by their faces. If they're standing in the lunch queue, they're talking work. Off camp, phones are clamped to their ears the entire time.

Men in 2-2 are geared to notice everything around them, as was demonstrated to me one time when I was heading home from town on the bus. It was a very wet Saturday, the bus had stopped at the traffic lights and a throng of pedestrians with umbrellas had just crossed the road. There were so many people on the pavement outside it seemed like they could barely move. I was seated on the far side of the bus, the central aisle full of people standing. It was winter, and everyone was clothed in raincoats and Puffa jackets in drab colours.

I saw my friend Alex McQuoid in the throng outside. I suppose I noticed him because the traffic was jammed and the bus was stationary, so I was just watching the crowds. He was with his children and I watched them shuffling along for thirty seconds or so. Suddenly Alex stopped and his eyes darted about. He looked straight at the bus, and straight through the mass of people between us, directly at me. Our eyes locked. The bus moved on eventually, but days later, when I saw Alex at work, I asked if he'd seen me, and how he knew where to look.

'Course I saw you,' he said. 'I just sensed that someone was looking at me.'

'Yes, but the streets were heaving, and I was sitting down out of the way with a crowd of people between us,' I said, puzzled. 'You would never have expected to see me on that bus.'

He smiled. 'Yes, but I sensed I was being looked at.'

To me, that demonstrated the inbuilt instincts, or maybe the trained skill, of elite soldiers: be acutely aware that someone, somewhere has their eyes on you.

I've painted a slightly gloomy picture of life at the HQ, with rats in the buildings, nowhere to park and soulless conference rooms. Men home for a day or two then off again. That's not the whole story, however. The Regiment knows how to do things in style, and what with the black-tie boxing nights, summer barbecues and family days where they pull out all the stops on camp in terms of hospitality and entertainment, there were lavish attempts to reward the service and its families for their support.

During 2017 it had been busier than usual for everyone at work. There was never a feeling of panic or action, and in fact you would never have known outwardly that the Regiment were doing anything at all, but the pace for us in the main camp stores had accelerated from steady to relentless. Individual military storekeepers were in every day with long lists for me to fulfil, while Craig maintained the ordinary, day-to-day demands from the officers and sergeants' messes, such as setting up marquees for special events. There were often lots of special events and ceremonies going on here in the background.

Anyway, to reward us and lighten the load a bit, the QM arranged a half-day off plus an optional evening out for the entire department, like a patriarchal factory boss putting on a coach trip to the seaside for his workers. He even arranged a minibus from camp to top and tail the outing, so everyone could drink until dawn if they wanted. We all agreed on ten-pin bowling starting at two p.m., followed by a curry, then the plan was to hit the bars in town for the rest of the night. Ten-pin bowling is the sort of thing you can be terrible at and nobody cares, let's face it. I couldn't wait.

When Andy McNab gained prominence with his books about the Regiment in the early 1990s, the geezers used to be renowned for their nights out. Indeed, in his 1995 book *Immediate Action*, he recalls that the Regiment:

'was staffed by people who could tell the difference between work time and play time. When you're working, you're working and when you're not, then it's time to be the idiot – go out and get drunk out of your head or you can go home and mow the grass.'

I'm sure there are aspects of this that are the same now, but I'm also sure it's just not as often. It's nothing to do with the Regiment being different or there being different rules: young men have changed in the thirty years since that was written. Society has changed. Now with mobile phones, WhatsApp, Facetime and Skype, none of which were around back then, a lot of the men stay in their rooms in the evening and associate with their friends and family virtually. The old garrison bar within the coffee shop rarely operates, except on special occasions, and in the time I was working at the training camp I only saw the bar there used for one family day and a Christmas quiz night. Recently I asked some of the taxi drivers who line up outside the city bars if they were inundated every week with 'Blades', but they told me, rather crestfallen, that 'Nobody from camp goes out any more.' The 2-2s' habit of going out *en masse* has definitely withered and perhaps almost died.

That afternoon we set off towards ten-pin bowling around two o'clock, an eclectic mix of the RQs, the QM, and then down the roll-call of the department, including us civilians. It turned out that I was the only woman going: the event wasn't compulsory and the other ladies had decided it was a good opportunity to go home and spend an extra few hours with their families. The QM and Ranger took on the roles of parents taking their children on a day out and we had a lovely afternoon. I'm not naturally a team player and hate social gatherings, but I felt it important that I muck in with everything and not be standoffish.

We formed into teams for the bowling; Ranger Judd was with me and astonished me with his competitiveness. When he didn't get the scores he expected, he went back to the lanes quietly in the break while we were chatting and bowled a few balls to see how he could improve. Judd the Thug might have played the part of the impassive guy who'd seen it all, but watching his face when the cuddly, languid QM beat him hollow without seeming to try, I knew there was a fight going on inside Ranger: he had a score to settle.

It was all spectacular fun. The younger soldiers went mad with excitement and drank shots in the bowling alley bar at five in the afternoon; it was like tipping a bunch of starving toddlers into a vat of sweets. The curry afterwards was so-so, but I sat next to RQ3, Marc, who was one of those quiet types who goes home and mows the lawn. His main aim in life was to finish building the extension to his cottage somewhere in the Forest of Dean. When I asked him what he would do when it was complete, he told me he'd buy another plot of land and build another house. Quite a few of the 2-2s were countrymen. Luke, a neighbour of mine who was recently badged, had bought some woodland; he would take his old van and sleep outside under the stars. He was happy being in the Regiment, as fearless and determined and self-confident a man as you'll ever meet, but he hated being with people all the time. Sleeping outside as often as he could was the only way he could get through being this type of specialised soldier. Kiwi, another RQ, was perilously thin and the sweetest guy ever, and when I asked him if he missed the old days he simply said, 'One deployment too many.' He stayed in his office and never socialised.

Another of our RQs was Foster, outgoing, cocky, politically incorrect and with all the stereotypically arrogant traits that make up the image most people associate with the Regiment. The other guys didn't swear in front of me, but Foster had no such manners and the c-word tripped off his tongue constantly without his even being aware of it. He was very tall and gangly, with raven-black hair and a five o'clock shadow even when freshly shaved. It was an unpopular look, which US President Richard Nixon discovered to his cost when pitted on television against the fresh-faced John F. Kennedy. The American public were unnerved by his appearance; it was OK for a cop to have one-day stubble, but not the President of the United States. I felt that way about the quartermaster post. That was Foster's destination next year and although the Regiment was famously relaxed about the appearance of its working soldiers, once they 'went over to the dark side', as they called it, promoted to senior and important positions, they were expected to look the part. That meant, in Foster's case, he'd need to get a closer shave. There are geezers – and geezers who are down on their luck.

We moved from the curry house to a bar. By now it was seven o'clock and we were joined by a few of the others who had generously offered to be the skeleton staff for the afternoon, and the QM's wife. The young guys got more and more drunk; they were having a great time. Ranger continued to look bored and disinterested. We had a laugh, though. At one stage I was chatting to the QMs lovely wife who'd been married to him for over thirty years, explaining about the inspection and the QM testing me on a few health and safety questions.

Her jaw dropped. 'What? My hubby? Health and safety?' she cackled loudly and hung onto me to steady her mirth. 'He knows *fuck all* about health and safety! All he knows about is kicking doors in!'

By nine o'clock the drinks were flowing and Foster was holding court in a scruffy bar near the town hall. I suggested to him that as storekeepers were sometimes sent out with the squadrons when they deployed, he should consider me doing my bit and accompanying the next lot.

'No WAY can you go out there with all those men on a Sabre deployment, M,' he shouted across the bar, laughing. 'It'd be carnage.'

'But that's discrimination, Foster,' I shouted back over the loud music. 'All the others have gone. Why not me? I know what I'm doing now, and it'd be great to have me as their storekeeper.' I'm not sure I was being serious, but I didn't like the sexism.

I was beginning to dread the arrival of Foster as the QM next year. He was the type to want to make his mark and change all the rules, and one of my neighbours, a badged man who had been in Foster's squadron, gave him the sort of reference you never want to hear about your incoming boss.

'All you need to know about Foster is he's a cunt,' he told me during the evening.

Not another one, I thought.

'He's only got the jobs he has because nobody else wanted them. He's slimed his way up like a snail up your fuchsias, and you wake to find nothing left.' He took another swig from his bottled beer and leaned in closer to be heard against the thumping music. 'And he's vindictive.'

Great. Couldn't wait.

Half an hour later, Foster and I found ourselves paired up in the crocodile as our group swayed its way up the street to trawl the long line of bars on Commercial Road.

'So, M, no man?' he said at one point. 'Single? Or gay?'

'*GAY?*' I stopped dead in the street in mock outrage.

'OK, not gay. So what – you live alone?'

'Problem?' I asked.

'No sex?' Foster was slipping on and off the narrow kerb now. He'd had a skinful.

'I've never heard you talk about having a man.'

I didn't answer.

'I'm surprised it hasn't closed up, by the way. Your wotsit, I mean,' Foster wafted a hand in the direction of my legs. 'If you never have sex. I bet you used to be a nightmare.'

That's exactly what he said: I wrote it in my diary. How can you have respect for someone like that? But he was drunk and would probably be horrified if I played him a film of the night, as we all would. At work he acted like he once met a sincere person and he'd been impersonating him ever since, but when his guard was down he was a rat.

By ten-thirty I was exhausted and wished I had been in bed several hours ago. But to leave would have been to declare the outing a failure and offend the others. A couple of times I said I should be going and was met with howls of disagreement. The men's faces were red and flushed, their breath beery and their beards stained. At one point I looked across the bar and saw a table of newer badged guys each with a bottle of alcohol-free juice in their hands, looking forlorn. Poor guys, they were on the standby team; they'd probably thought it'd be nice to get out and instead found themselves observing a crowd of wasters getting off their heads.

At midnight a minibus from camp was waiting outside the bar. The evening was crumbling away and there was already a group saying goodbye.

'So amazing, *brilliant* time, just like the old days,' they crooned, stumbling down the steps of Wetherspoons. I left them all and walked through town, taking a moment to look at the stars – distant and eternal. Some of the other soldiers swayed past me, discussing whether to go to the infamous venue in town where a plethora of cheerful girls would be waiting, dead certs. I heard the next day that the Regiment bosses had stayed out until four-thirty. I had to be at work at eight a.m. as usual, but Foster, the QM, Ray and all the badged RQs never showed their faces the next day. It was just me and Craig, alone at the windswept perimeter of camp except for a few office workers, but even those military who turned up were gone by twelve.

I spent the day flattening cardboard boxes.

XXV

Where to begin with Alex McQuoid?

Every dog has its day, and that year, Alex was Best in Show. Tall, self-aware and assured, badged for eight years and the vision of an elite soldier, his opinion ratings oscillated so much that I often wondered if people were talking about the same person.

'He's a cunt!' spat Joe, one of the drivers on camp one day, upon hearing someone mention Alex's name. 'A fucking ocean-going, state registered *cunt!*' he added, in case we didn't get it the first time. Joe was a placid young man usually found larking around and smoking, but his eyes were blazing at the mere hint of Alex McQuoid. The drivers lived in a tight enclave down in a place I called Starveacre Lane, because it was too poor a patch of land to do anything useful with except shove us and our stores and the Motor Transport department here where nobody could see us. The drivers knew everybody and, given that a lot of their time was spent sitting in a large rest room waiting to be assigned a job, they had plenty of time to discuss everybody on camp in fine detail.

On the other hand: 'Ah, Alex... *lovely* man,' cooed the two smart ladies in reception, echoing one another. 'Such a *gentleman* and what a *fantastic* father.' They were every man's dream of the cool, elegant secretary: wise and influential, with immaculately piled hair and manicured nails, established in their jobs for years and gently formidable. They'd seen them all, from new recruits to old hands and out the other end, and they were accustomed to the vagaries of the geezers who signed and swiped and punched in PIN codes hour after hour as they went in and out of camp. These ladies loved Alex and that was good enough for me.

Alex McQuoid was Directing Staff. I never got the whole story because I still had the 'questions' incident at the back of my mind, but I'd first met him, like I met everyone, down the road in the lunch queue. He'd looked like everyone else: dirty combats, messy, bedraggled hair and smelling like the council tip. He didn't act like everyone else, though. Alex could start a fight in an empty room. No, he'd *build* a room first and then start a fight in it, alone, so determined was he for action, so addicted to adrenaline. He was a restless customer. The orange juice would be too diluted, the bread not fresh enough and he soon made his displeasure felt when the chicken had gone and we were down to sausages. It was no surprise to learn that he was close buddies with that other moaning minnie, Kip Formby.

If the two men had been in one of those TV programmes about Selection, Alex and Kip would be fighting for Chief Instructor status but the fact was, they appeared to share the role. Imposing, with an easy smile and self-assured bearing, Alex's pale freckled face and chestnut-red hair were neither here nor there but he was well-read and interested in life, and considering that we met when I was washing dishes, he was unconcerned about the difference in our status. I think it was his reluctance to impress me with his astonishing military record that impressed me. Alex only needed to be himself.

Strange then that Alex as a man was lacking in a certain personal self-confidence. I clearly remember him telling me about one of his students on Selection who was now a newly badged trooper. They'd passed one another in the cookhouse and he called Alex 'mate'. Alex was seething about this but knew that he shouldn't be. He talked about it for at least five minutes out in the road after lunch, working out what to feel. The trooper was the same age as Alex and he used to be an officer in his previous regiment, therefore senior to Alex, but once in the Regiment all previous ranks are left behind and they started back at square one. There must have been a huge conflict of emotions there: rank versus experience. I suppose it's the same for all of us when somebody more junior is promoted up to our level or above. I suspected his mates would have taken the mick if he'd told them how he felt, so I said I didn't blame him and I'd be bothered about it too, and that seemed to calm him down.

Always on the alert for a female of the species, like a tiger sniffing the trees for a scent, Alex could be sitting in an airport lounge and if an attractive woman had crossed his path heading for, say, a flight to the North Pole and he was catching the next flight to the South Pole, thereby offering zero hope of a sexual encounter, he would still do his best to catch her eye. If it resulted in a brief second glance from her, that was enough to keep him going. Working amongst hundreds of combative, self-assured and increasingly younger, fitter men must have been demoralising, so if there was a remote possibility of a confidence boost, however small, nothing was too much trouble for Alex. Like many of these elite soldiers, he felt a remote possibility was a gamble worth taking.

Alex and I had bonded over a chat about raw, unpasteurised milk, of all things. He was instructing on Selection and I was refilling the milk-dispensing machines in the course of a hectic lunchtime, dwarfed by a crush of men reaching over one another. I forget how the conversation began but I mentioned that I got raw milk straight from the cow for myself, and when I said it was totally fresh and untreated, he was hooked. I brought back four pints from the farm for him to try. Alex loved anything close to nature; he would have lived off leaves and roadkill if he could. He and I could talk into the night about nutrition and feel we'd only just scraped the surface of a subject that we both loved.

We began cooking for each other from time to time and Alex was heroic in his efforts to play his part. For two years he was instructing on Selection and I felt awkward when he suggested it was his turn to make a meal as I knew he'd been run ragged all day and must be exhausted. But he saw it as a refreshing break, to talk about something else.

'The course is running and time is in short measure,' he texted one late afternoon. 'I'll get something for us on the way home. We had salmon last time – steak? Chicken? Fish?'

I replied that anything would do as I was conscious of his time.

'Prawn curry?' he replied.

We ended up with steak, pan-roasted vine tomatoes and sauté potatoes and the whole thing was delicious. He was still flecked with mud, stinking of guns and looking worse for wear when I arrived at his house, but as the steak sizzled, he showered in the downstairs bathroom in three minutes flat, like all the badged soldiers can do, and reappeared in his towel in enough time to flip the steaks, pop the vine tomatoes under the grill and go to put some clothes on. I had sat with a glass of wine as he carried on talking to me with the door open.

He told me stories of passing selection himself some years before. He'd been a smoker, he told me, though he gave it up a while ago. 'I got into the Regiment and thought, "Yeah, I'm in the SAS!"' and he mimed a sort of comedy, cigarette-smoking young geezer. We always talked into the early hours even though he would be back instructing the next morning, and it was just the most welcome break from my dull job. Alex was an elite soldier, but I never saw him as any different from other people; he just had an entirely different life experience from mine, that was the great thing, and I think we were both fascinated by one another in equal measure.

Alex was the sort of man who fills a room. A restless guest, always shifting, studying my framed photos, picking them up and asking questions, lifting a pan lid to see what you're cooking, opening your fridge: you know the kind of person.

By May 2017, I was up the top in the store job and loving the fact that I could get home at six p.m. and still have a couple of hours outdoors for a cycle or walk. We kept the huge roller door at the store open all day to let the sunshine and fresh air in. People passing stopped to put their heads in and often stayed for a brew. It was so different from my job in the kitchens at the training camp.

Around nine o'clock one evening, Alex texted saying he was at a loose end. The tragic and shocking Manchester Arena terrorist bombing had happened just days previously, and he was on the standby team. I texted back that it would be great, as I had the next day off, and he replied, 'Be round in 15', correcting himself immediately with 'Oh, was just gonna say, 20 minutes. I need to walk to my car. Poor time analysis from me.' And he added a laughing emoji.

He came to my house, straight in as if he owned the place, dumping a folder and his brown canvas messenger bag onto my kitchen table. He headed to my cupboard for a couple of wine glasses.

'I've brought a great bottle of red which I think will be outstanding,' he said, pulling it out of his bag and fishing about for my corkscrew in the drawers below. You know someone is a good friend when they know where to find your bottle-opener.

'I didn't expect you to be around tonight, of all nights,' I said.

'I almost didn't phone as I was going up north, but at the moment I'm glad I waited. I'm no longer required, I don't think,' he said. That was what these things were, to people like Alex. '*We are the Pilgrims, master; we shall go ...*' The unwritten next line was surely '*wherever you tell us to.*'

We settled on my sofa and he immediately shuffled about, shaking his shoulders, bedding down and grinning, saying with the satisfaction of a child with an ice cream, 'Well, this is nice.' He was wearing a checked shirt, khaki shorts and a huge black wristwatch. His hair looked unwashed, and he smelled the way that a lot of them do: musty. There's a particular smell that comes off the weapons and settles in their hair, like somebody who's been sleeping rough and can't clean themselves up.

He talked about his girlfriend problems. Despite everything I have just told you about him, Alex was besotted with a stunning young woman who lived in France. He visited her every couple of months and I thought their situation was heart-wrenching. He was in Hereford until 2024, so if they were to be together, she would have to move here and leave France and her huge house and fantastic career. He spoke of her with love, but I could picture her side of the story: Alex was a soldier, away a lot, a guy with four children who would always come first, and an ex-wife (never good news) – a man who would travel for hours every few nonths for outstanding sex, basically, which was all well and good, but I didn't hold out much hope for their chances if they decided to be together in Hereford, stuck in traffic, queuing in Sainsbury's, realising that a fifth child might be tricky.

I asked him how his marriage went wrong. It was dim in my sitting room, and quiet. We were facing now, mirroring one another, both with legs tucked underneath, both with an elbow on the back of the sofa, resting our heads in our hand.

'I made the classic mistake of thinking I could do better,' he said, taking a swig of his wine.

'Because you were badged?'

'Hmm, probably. It wasn't a decision of mine, not a conscious thought. It's not as if I wanted better but I thought I *deserved* better.'

So that was it.

'Someone who didn't treat you like the squaddie she married fifteen years ago?'

I listened to his whole, extraordinary story: the births of four children in succession while also going through Selection and the first few difficult and uncertain years in the Regiment. Getting in is only the start. After that, he described it as 'squeezing every last drop of work out of them'. In the end, though, Alex's wife didn't just reject him; she lit the fuse and annihilated him. He discovered that she had found someone else, a local gas engineer who came to sort the boiler while Alex was away and stayed for a brew or two. It is one thing for a badged man to lose out to someone richer and fitter but quite another to see your missus slumming it with trade and, by comparison, finding him more appealing.

He poured more wine and fussed about in my cupboards looking for snacks. I made toast and we settled again.

'What's it like, M, getting the boot from your job at two days' notice?'

He turned to look at me, a movement that surprised me for some reason. It felt like a giant spotlight had just been swung around and focused onto me. His eyes were bright, but not alert. For a moment I could picture him in battle, his face on fire, his eyes taking in everything about the dreadful scenes in front of him. This was the same face, the same eyes, with barely discernible signs of fatigue. This is what getting old looks like, I thought: it's in the eyes. They lose muscle tone; they don't register surprise. Look at the eyes of a teenager and, however miserable they might be feeling, their eyes are taking in the world – learning, analysing, poised for something new to happen, alert for the voice of authority to come and spoil their fun. By the time you get to Alex's stage in life as a specialised, elite soldier, highly trained, it seemed that not much was new. These men appeared to others as if they had seen the world, yet to me, they had merely nibbled around the experience like dieters nibble around a chocolate bar, just tasting the edges, pretending not to eat it because of the calories. That's how soldiers saw the world, or at least that's how I thought of them, nibbling away at it. Never really getting to the crux of life, a life where one supports oneself entirely. They would never be cast adrift, to find their own way home. Never receive a phone call saying sorry, the army's closing at the weekend, you'll have to find something else. It seemed at that moment as if the vital faculty of existing was ebbing out of Alex like sand in an hourglass; slowly but inexorably until there was nothing left, and part of that, to my mind, was the sheer inevitability of their role and lack of real decision-making. Too much security isn't always a good thing.

'It wasn't nice,' I said. 'I got another job that time, but a year later I was living in Bristol and one afternoon out shopping, I had a call.'

I told Alex all about it.

Alex looked down at the sofa then he said, almost in a whisper, 'That was it?'

'Yes. I walked home and it sunk in that I had three more pay cheques, three weeks of pay, then nothing.'

He reached out to touch my arm in sympathy, but my legs were in the way and he brushed against my trousers and it turned into one of those awkward moments. I pretended I hadn't noticed.

'So what did you do?'

'Everybody has disappointments in life, Alex,' I said. 'You can't have a life without disappointments.' I took a deep breath. 'Anyway, if it hadn't been for all that, I wouldn't have moved to Hereford and I wouldn't have got the job on camp and you wouldn't be here. Have you ever thought of those things, the fork in the road? Strange twists and turns of fate?'

I got up to go to the bathroom and winced at how stiff I was as I straightened my legs. 'Anyway, right now you're on standby for terrorist situations, which is pretty bad. My situation years ago of losing a couple of jobs was nothing.' I deliberately decided to sound light and bright.

I noticed that while I was out of the room, Alex didn't flick the TV back on, or check his phone. He was nursing his empty wine glass when I got back, looking at the ceiling, head nestled comfortably in several cushions.

'How is it, having four children?' I said, when I'd settled myself down again. I hadn't been sure whether I could break his reverie, but wherever his mind had been in the past five minutes, it didn't look a nice place. His brow was gently furrowed and his eyes slightly narrowed and it put me in mind of a sleeping dog twitching with dreams. I wanted to bring him back into the room with me.

He blew out his cheeks and looked away as if searching for the right words.

'Not easy, M. Not easy.' He got up and fetched the bottle of wine from the kitchen. He came back and went to pour me a glass, but I put up my hand. 'Work in the morning Alex, early.' He sat down again. 'How does it work then when you're away so much? How does your ex feel?'

'Angry,' he replied without needing to think. He raised his eyebrows and looked sideways at me. 'And I don't blame her. It was bad for a long time, but now we get on OK. It's just that I can't always be there to do alternate weekends, half the school holidays, that sort of thing. When get back, sometimes, it can be difficult. I can be home a few hours and she's throwing the kids at me – not that I mind, I love them obviously, but my accommodation isn't very child-friendly, and the guys I share with suddenly have four kids on them for the weekend.' He raised his eyebrows and shook his head. 'Carnage,' he said and then laughed. 'Fucking carnage!'

Alex always found peace and calm in my house. He enjoyed the chat and my company and the fact that I wanted nothing from him. He drank most of the wine and I opened one of my own bottles. We put the TV on at one point and caught the tail end of the news, but he was more fascinated with Donald Trump than the national news. He thought the way the man blasted through any opposition, pushing everyone out of his way, was great.

By eleven o'clock Alex had a completely different aspect, refreshed and serene. With the curtains closed and the light from the table lamp with its soft peach glow, he looked almost languid. It had been an idyllic evening. I gave him the guest bedroom and he fell asleep almost instantly, pager on the bedside table.

My alarm went off at five the next morning. I took him some coffee and perched on the side of his bed. And we watched the news, which was all about the terrorist event, he didn't say anything or appear particularly engaged. Mind you, no one expects trauma doctors to be riveted by the news about a twenty-car pile-up on the M4. He was more interested that day in the weather forecast for a trip to see his children. I believe that these men, these special and formidable soldiers, whose lives are ordered by others, are not plugged into a situation for its own sake. They have other duties which take them into completely different responsibilities. They are trained to do what they must do, but I don't think they're desperate for action all the time. Their turn comes, they know it will come, so they save themselves for that moment when it is their turn to put themselves in the firing line.

It was nice, having a guest. We still had half an hour before either of us needed to leave for work, and Alex was already up and running with his moans.

'You get no thanks for anything, in this job,' he muttered. 'Nobody ever pats us on the back and says well done.'

He took a sip of his coffee, swilled the mug around and downed the lot, holding it out to me for more.

'What do you think about it, being classed as "elite"?' I asked.

'Well...' He stared at the ceiling for inspiration. 'You get used to it. It's only the papers that say that, and books.' He poured more coffee from the cafetière.

'I suppose...' I started, 'I suppose out in society you're one in a million, but there on camp, there are hundreds of you.'

I had known Alex only two years at this point, but he was eternally troubled; troubled mostly by his own pugnacious character. Alex wasn't well thought of by many of his peers, and he knew it. He seemed to have it in for everyone, once complaining that 2-2 guys were competitive even to the point that they competed without realising it, to be the fastest walking back from The Area to the cookhouse for lunch. Alex hated men calling themselves 'geezers'. He scorned the guys who shook hands every time they met. He loathed the new trend for long hair and beards and wanted to bellow 'Get your fucking hair cut!' Alex McQuoid was a perpetually angry man. It's a reasonable rule that when someone expresses a burning hatred for someone, it's reminding them of themselves. I wondered if Alex McQuoid had been a lonely, needy child and his language towards the newer geezers suggested he felt betrayal. A little lost boy casting around for validation and eventually finding it in a secretive, anonymous organisation, only to discover people coming in behind him, turning his security upside down with their own, newer rules. I wondered if the trend of handshaking was something he felt left out of: maybe it was also underlining his advancing age?

'What makes you happy, Alex?'

I thought he might say 'my kids' or 'the woman I love'. He looked away for so long, I thought he might have drifted off to sleep again.

'Alex?'

He turned under the duvet and brought his face so close to mine, I could almost make out every hair of his morning stubble.

'What makes me happy,' he started, 'is watching the face of some bastard I've just shot, seeing his eyes glaze over as the last breath leaves his body.'

He looked back at the TV. Then he stretched, flinging his arms in the air and exhaling, sinking back under the duvet. He blew out his cheeks with an air of resignation.

'Nah. What makes me happy, genuinely happy … is a bowl of Coco Pops.' He turned his face to me. 'Have you got some?'

Alex and I had a relationship made in heaven: I liked looking after people and Alex liked being looked after. Simple as that.

'Are you happy right now, Alex?' I said.

'Course I am,' he said, yawning, 'this is great.' And he pulled the duvet even higher, stuck a hand behind his head and reached for the TV remote.

I got up and paused in the doorway.

'Well, tell your face.'

Late the next day Alex sent me a text.

Monica, today has been hectic and I never got a chance to say thank you for your lovely company. As always, an amazing evening.

I thought a lot of Alex. Plenty of people hated the mention of him and the c-word was coupled with his name more times than I had ever heard in my life. I daresay people had their reasons, reasons which might make me think twice if I had known what they were, but I didn't so I speak as I find. He was a tough, uncompromising guy, I know that. Maybe he had been intolerable to work with? My dear wish is that Alex is well, and one day he will wash up at my front door for a catch-up with a bottle of outstanding red wine, because of all of them, he was the deepest thinker; a man who was willing to stretch his thoughts around corners, to take the energy required to do more than follow orders. He had his faults, but so do we all. He was just such a three-dimensional figure: incredibly funny and a great cook, a great warrior too, by all accounts, and a terrific father. I hope he worked it out with his girlfriend so far away: he deserved to be happy.

I only saw Alex a few times after that evening. He was deployed, and a terrible tragedy happened when one of his best friends was killed in action. The last time I saw him was as a pall-bearer at the funeral on camp. In the store the following day, it so happened that a guy in Alex's unit was there too. He started going on about Alex with the c-word and, even though I was only listening in, I felt annoyed for him.

'Isn't there *anything* you admire about Alex McQuoid?' I said.

'Yeah, there is actually,' he replied. 'He's managed to stay out of jail all these years, so I admire him for that.'

XXVI

I think it was the drabness that made everyone so negative. The men wouldn't have seen it, of course, most of them so long in the military, but there was nothing here to stimulate the mind: no beauty or culture unless you count the fabulous statues here and there about camp. It was a step up from training camp, but the architecture was nothing to write home about. The cookhouse was drab and functional, the stores and offices were gloomy and stark and even the workforce lacked any variety. The people you saw were mostly men, usually the same age, give or take, and all schooled in the military way of life. I understand it, of course; and I had joined their world and made sure not to criticise it. I'm only telling you because it really hit me in the face when I came to work there.

It's like this: I worked in London for many years, five of those years in Southwark at a fabulous building called the Blue Fin. It was so modern and extraordinary that film companies hired it for futuristic movies and TV adverts. Right next door was the Tate Modern art gallery on the banks of the Thames, and if you walked south towards the famous Borough Market you could take your lunch and watch people in boats going by. When you mention working in London people automatically assume it's glamorous, but you don't have to be rich or privileged to enjoy these delights – you can be unemployed and skint and still spend a day in the capital at no cost, enjoying a variety of scenery. The young people I worked with were interns or assistants, deputy this and that, and some simply washed the cups and ran errands. Salaries were pitiful. Many people commuted for up to three hours every day, spending thousands a year on season tickets from Essex or Berkshire or Brighton. I travelled a 140-mile round trip every day before email made it possible to work from home more. When we were told, inevitably, that a contract couldn't be renewed because of budget cuts, or there were staff redundancies, everyone took it without self-pity or complaint. It didn't mean that people weren't upset, or in some cases devastated, but we all knew that life held no promises or certainty. We went home and hit the phones looking for another job, all the while paying council tax and sorting childcare with no income. There was little real glamour in that world, just a lot of hard work, long hours, average pay and insecurity, yet we took it on the chin.

Here on camp there's the security of a guaranteed job and pay at the end of every month. The men know what year they'll be leaving, they can plan. There's no uncertainty in their situation. Housing is provided along with medical and dental services. Meals are ridiculously cheap – I'm talking two pounds for three courses – and almost everybody leaves camp at noon every Friday. So why did everyone appear hopeless and drag around moaning?

I don't think the men felt appreciated. There was the odd slap on the back and 'good effort' but that was it. The 2-2s put their lives on the line and give everything for their country, which to my mind is all the more reason to occasionally give them a little more praise. I once told George, the Warrant Officer back at the training camp, that Ben, one of the chefs, had single-handedly fed the entire group of Regiment Reservists who'd landed on us for the weekend at no notice. His effort was completely astonishing and yet George just looked at me stonily, saying, 'Which is exactly what he should have done.'

The Regiment is full of the most extraordinary, highly trained people, but I can see why so many of them struggle when they get out into civilian life, especially if the army is all they've ever known. It's hard for them to get the language right, to understand the tone they need if they are to get on in the world; they have to learn all that, just like I'd had to learn their ways of speaking. It's all very well these so-called hardcore military experts talking about going through hell and 'getting on with it', cultivating a mindset that doesn't need praise and validation, but real life isn't about going to war. Hardly any of us ever need to do it, just as hardly any of us spend our lives as veterinary surgeons or priests. Those are specific skillsets. The skill absolutely everyone needs in abundance is the ability to get on well with our own species. Life is about playing the game and understanding how to motivate people of all types, and that's something I think the military just can't do. There are no old people here, and no children. Hardly any women. Of course, these men have private lives and families, but the bulk of their time is spent with like-minded individuals living in the same town. They're like the inhabitants of a medieval village, unaware of what's going on in the next village along.

And yet …

I never felt nostalgia over any of my London jobs, or missed them when I was away on holiday, but I missed this place dreadfully when I had a week's leave. It's like parents having a much-needed break from their children but who are unable to stop thinking about them – eventually they go home early to be with them again. And I know this is ridiculous, because I really didn't have much of a role there, and anybody could do what I did, but that's how I felt. Concerned for them. Geezers weren't demanding nor entitled but they were needy, with everything about their daily lives worked out for them. I doubt they'd agree, but somebody in the Regiment was always there to pick up the pieces and help them. Doctors and physios are on hand, and welfare officers. It's still hard for me to identify the emotions I had towards these men, but I think that while the public image of them is of extraordinary, almost superhuman beings, they really did seem a bit helpless sometimes and, in that regard, I felt desperately sorry for them.

Yes, I think that was it.

XXVII

For the most part, being a storekeeper suited me fine. I might even say that it brought out the best in me. I keep hearing that it's low-skill, as if the person doing it has no education or training, but it's the job that's low-skill, not the person doing it. Anyone can do this, which is why I liked it. After years in meetings and travelling and deadlines, this job was right up my street.

But there's the solitude. Craig was too frantic to talk to most of the time, Corporal Eddy too young and giddy and Sergeant Jules was hardly ever there. Three nice civilians occupied a health and safety department housed in a ramshackle Portakabin round the corner, but they were never there. I can't claim I was immune to all this isolation, but I could live with it. The store is a gaunt place, well away from the flashier buildings nearer the entrance a good walk away. It's embellished with a pile of litter outside, mostly packaging that escapes from the massive bins; no matter what the weather's like by the entrance gates at the top of camp, it's always worse down here, or so the joke goes. That's why I liked talking to the guys in 2-2 when I got the chance, when they came in to look for a bit of kit or see what we'd got. Sometimes I got so immersed in my own company alone in the store, if someone came in it was a shock.

That's how it was that afternoon. As I stood contemplating where I'd left my thick safety gloves, Jim Campbell snaked around the corner. He wore his leather jacket, as always, and looked benevolent, as if nothing in this world could trouble him. He had a beautiful wife, so beautiful in fact that nobody could understand what she'd seen in this shambles of a man, but I imagined she'd fallen head over heels for him back in the day when he was parachuting out of planes all dressed in black with guns strapped everywhere. I couldn't even imagine him doing anything like that, but I'd heard many stories about his outstanding bravery and heroism.

It was Thursday, and soon Jim would be down in town, drinking. He wasn't a sociable person, but he liked his drink and, better still, he loved pubs, proper boozers, the rougher the better. Jim was from New Zealand and had been in the Regiment since the year dot. He was very senior, with lots of projects on the go and was one of those men who never stopped working, though you'd never have known it. His lack of discernible energy gave the impression that, far from enjoying life as a soldier, he would prefer to do nothing at all, but that couldn't be further from the truth. He was an exercise in frugality, gifted in fortitude, but every talent has its downsides and, although this encounter I'll describe was before he told me about it, his marriage was about to end due to his passion for work. He had an extremely regular existence, with holiday bookings three years ahead, and he had coffee in town at the same time every Saturday morning. There was a story, no doubt apocryphal, that at a Regiment dinner he was obliged to attend, someone asked him where he was going on his holiday and, half an hour later, he replied: 'Why do you want to know?' His mind had been somewhere else.

Jim's mind was constantly on fire. A cauldron of swirling thoughts and ideas inhabited him to such a degree that apparently facial expressions and physical labour would have stolen precious energy. He put me in mind of the great Isaac Newton, who, when asked how he had discovered gravity, replied: 'By thinking about it.' Forced into a kind of lockdown during the plague of 1665, Newton isolated himself completely, sure in his belief that making observations and thinking about things was a better path to knowledge than reading books, and thus he laid the groundwork for the theories and laws of science that make him famous to this day.

'People don't think enough,' Jim said to me one day. 'If a person shuts themselves away and does nothing but work on a problem and doesn't do anything else, they'll find a solution.'

Jim didn't mean to be rude. He just didn't have the capacity to take a natural interest in other people's lives. I once heard him explain the square root of a vector to a hapless young Lance Corporal and he started to glow, but on everything else it was about focus: when you are at his level in the most elite specialised regiment in the world you need a high level of focus and there just wasn't enough space in his head for small talk.

One season was giving way to the next, and that autumn was busier than ever. There wasn't a single lull in the store and Craig was on extended leave to accompany the Regiment rugby team to play abroad somewhere, so I was doing most of the work myself. Sergeant Jules had me by the throat with one demand, one instruction after another, though never following through or staying long enough to even sign something. She only needed to add a signature once a week on eight racking registers, but these were now in a two-month backlog. Having said that, Jules was a straightforward person with absolutely no side to her. I never heard her gossip about anyone, which must have been a first on camp, and as I got to know her better, I realised that her job in this regiment was probably overwhelming, given the problems she had told me about in her home life and this being a special type of military establishment.

When Jim came in that morning holding three massive empty water containers, I was glad to see him. He always brought a sprinkling of calming dust with him, and a sense of things that were done properly. I can't tell you much more than that, but Jim was an important man.

'Morning, Monica,' he said softly, with his usual disarming smile. 'Any chance of some water? We've taken over a village next door but there's no taps.'

'Of course, Jim,' I said. 'You'd better do it yourself. I'll never lift those whoppers when they're full.'

A 'village' was the ironic term the geezers had coined for four or more Portakabins or redundant shipping containers moved into a group, with a useful green space in the centre. To get in you'd squeeze through the small alleyway created by the structures. It variously afforded comfort, privacy and peace, though facilities were lacking.

'What are you up to, anyway?' I asked, leaning against the corridor wall while the kettle boiled. 'You're not secretly growing cannabis in there, are you? Pretending you have a super-secret project to save the world?' I pushed myself off the wall and went back into the kitchen to check on the fresh milk situation.

I often say I just worked in the store and knew nothing of what was going on, but of course I did. If you were in you were in, as far as the geezers were concerned, and anyway, I was fully involved with their supplies. They probably thought it was all a bit boring, but sharing details of their lives with me wasn't uncommon, probably more to unburden themselves than anything else.

Jim put his heavy water containers onto the floor.

'It's just something we're doing, and we need space and a bit of peace and quiet. Come and have a brew with us when we're properly settled in.'

'I'll hold you to it,' I said, putting teabags into mugs and getting the milk ready.

'Er... can I use your toilet? We don't have one.'

I put my hands on my hips and did a playful glower. 'Does this mean all three of you will be coming in to use the loo several times a day, Jim?' I said. 'Because if so, I'm going to make a list of unacceptable practice – beginning with leaving the seat up!'

What started as a patch of scrub and empty ISO containers next door to us became, over the next several months, clipped and orderly – lush, even. In the first couple of days the three men on Jim's team came to ask if we had desks, coffee tables, chairs, lockers and even waste bins and a microwave, all of which we did have stacked away in the musty containers which hadn't seen daylight for years. As autumn ground on and my work became frantic, I almost forgot about Jim. He spent a lot more time now up in the big important building on camp, plotting and planning major things, and I went a little more to the gym, enjoying the stretching sessions. I'd joined quite a group of the geezers by now, most of whom had injuries or had simply done too much training, and as we sat on the huge mats, we chatted while we eased our hamstrings and calves and backs on special roller things that hurt like hell. I felt completely at one with them by now, and even took the gentle jokes about my poshness in good grace. ('You have class, darling,' said James, a guy from Poole who was doing something on camp for two years. 'Your energy is very watchable.' That was funny.)

One day, Jim brought me a little plastic bag of tomatoes, the sweet end of a crop he and his two mates had been tending all summer. I'd been too busy to take a look at their village, but I could just spy sun loungers and I joked that hanging baskets would be next.

'Bloody hell, Jim, is that Portakabin-on-the-Wold? Why don't you get this lot thatched and do the job properly?'

'Funny you should say that,' he replied, donning his sunglasses and stretching his arms back, 'but I've asked the carpenter if he can make a bench.' He grinned like a man who was genuinely happy and fulfilled.

I brought tea out in mugs and passed the biscuit tin around. 'You'll be inviting *Gardener's Question Time* here next, Jim. I see great things.'

'Well, let me show you around.'

When Jim opened the door of his 'tin can', as he'd called it, I clapped my hand to my mouth in amazement.

'Wow Jim! You've got a ski lodge here,' I said. There were easy chairs, a new sink with taps, plus kettle and toaster. Toaster!

He beamed.

Men like Jim Campbell were as much a demonstration of the supremacy of the Regiment in the world as any of the active Forces. Three months later, at Christmas, Jim came into the store to look for a brew and tell me about his wife leaving. He wasn't a workaholic in the accepted sense; it wasn't that he needed it, but he was dedicated to his country and the cause, and his scraggy-looking exterior disguised a prodigious mind. Jim Campbell always felt that there was more work to be done, and although I had no idea what he was really like to live with, I think any human being would be worse off without his company.

XXVIII

'**D**O IT!'
    I looked up, alarmed as I jammed on my brake. A good-looking man with a blue lanyard was standing on the corner of the road. He was wrapped up warmly against the bitter wind, hunched up with his hands in the pockets of his fleece jacket, and I had just seen the red 'No Entry' sign on the road I was about to turn into.

He waved his arms again.

'Do it!' He laughed out loud, throwing his head back, amused by my caution. I held up a hand helplessly and pointed at the sign.

It was my first time on the big camp, in 2016, and I was up at HQ for a security briefing. I already felt overawed: the grid system meant that I could go round and round and still not find the building. I was running late.

'Choose your moment, look around, see if the coast is clear then make a dash for it,' the handsome guy said, crouching to get level with me.

I shook my head. 'Sorry,' I mouthed through the window, gesticulating in big exaggerated circles, 'I'll think I'll go around. Thanks!'

I next saw him a year later. He was in the cookhouse and raised a hand in acknowledgement, which I thought was very nice. We met at the sauces area and he told me his name was Matt.

Months must have gone by before I saw him again. This time we were on the same table and he overheard me saying that it was soon to be my birthday.

'What date?'

'Fourteenth of August.'

'Kidding!' Matt exclaimed. 'So's mine. Where are you from?'

'Cheshire. Well, it's Greater Manchester these days.'

He slapped a hand down on the table. 'Me too!'

'What, you're from Manchester?'

'Tell you what,' he said, 'I'll give you a present, birthday twin, in August. Promise.'

'I think there's a good few years between us,' I laughed, 'but thanks. Amazing. I've never met anybody with my birthday.'

He held up a hand. 'August fourteenth club.' We high-fived across the table. He turned to a friend. 'My birthday twin,' he said, and cocked a thumb in my direction.

I had an opportunity to talk to him the next day at lunch. For once he was alone as he came in to eat very late. There was some old newsreel playing on the TV about the assassination of President Kennedy in 1962 and, in passing, I said something about liking the style of Jackie Kennedy's pillbox hat, which the papers took to calling a 'Jackie O' hat some years later when she married Aristotle Onassis. Matt piped up that he liked that style of hat on a woman; he thought it sexy.

It was nice, talking to him and to the other men who sat with me. I was still in the early stages then of my time in the store and the tensions were beginning to drag me down. I don't know how I'd have coped during those months without Matt occasionally showing his face and talking to me as if I was at least a member of the human race. He always had a cheery smile and asked if I'd been back up to Manchester recently. I'd tell him I'd been up to Cheadle to keep my parents' grave tidy.

Then, in March 2018, I had the biggest shock – Matt's face was looking out at me from the front of my morning newspaper. I hadn't seen him since before Christmas as they'd all gone away, but there he was: killed in action.

The funeral was at the end of April, and in the previous week his comrades returned. Around the corner from us were the tailoresses' cabins, and a steady stream of cars arrived outside the store, bringing Matt's squadron who were bearing their best uniforms, needing a button replacing or a seam mending.

Matt's funeral was the biggest I've ever been to. All work was suspended that day, except for a skeleton staff. I did Matt proud by making a special effort, buying a small black pillbox hat like the one he had admired on Jackie Kennedy. It had a discreet veil over the brow and I wore a simple black skirt and silk blouse. The day itself was unusually warm and the sun shone without a break, its rays lighting up the camp as if illuminating their brother on his journey. The little church, St Christopher's, was full; a marquee had been erected outside with a video link to accommodate what must have been a couple of hundred other people from the Regiments and there was still an overspill, with at least another fifty personnel having to stand outdoors. I was seated somewhere in the middle of the marquee.

The entrance of the coffin to 'Ride of the Valkyries' was suitably apt for Matt. I nearly cried when we all stood to sing 'I Vow to Thee My Country'; it was a thrilling sound, the massive swell of male voices almost carrying along the pomp of the occasion. I nearly thought twice about hitting the high notes, to save the attention I might draw to myself with a distinctive female voice, but then I thought I must do justice to the occasion and belt out the hymn. Eventually it was just me, soprano high above the basses, doing my bit at the line '…till we have *built* / Jerusalem!' in the final hymn when the blokes couldn't quite make it.

It must have taken half an hour or more for us to process from the church up the camp driveway. Men parachuted down in honour of Matt and when I looked over to where the pall-bearers were waiting to bring the coffin out of the hearse, I witnessed the men I knew as these rather devil-may-care buccaneers behaving like everyday soldiers. I wish I could describe what an extraordinary sight this was. Seeing my friend Alex McQuoid standing to attention on command, closely shaven, proper haircut, marching with the other five men towards the funeral cortege, arms stiff and clenched hands, firm in his soldierly stance of attention, stamping his feet, head high. It was incongruous but moving, as if Alex and the others had just demonstrated a hidden skill. I couldn't take my eyes off them. Military photographers in almost glamorous black suits and ties followed the entire proceedings like paparazzi, hiding in trees and bushes, snapping away discreetly near the grave for an hour, capturing the whole ceremony for regimental posterity only. I wondered what Matt would have said if he'd seen them.

Matt was only thirty-three when he died. It was such a tragedy and I felt heavy inside that I wouldn't say happy birthday to him in August. He'd promised me a fairy cake. Matt was a hero, a friend; he lifted the spirits of ordinary people like me without weighing up if I had enough status to be worth knowing. He was a dedicated soldier, a credit to the Regiment, a devoted son and brother. I will always remember him outside the cookhouse, encouraging me to drive the wrong way up the one-way road. 'Choose your moment, look around, see if the coast is clear and make a dash for it,' he'd said.

I'd like to think he led his life like that.

XXIX

I breezed into the quartermaster building, signed for my key and took a detour to place a special order for something. As I rounded the corner of the corridor I walked straight into Ray and the QM standing, mugs of tea in hand, chatting as they did every morning. The QM was a lovely chap, very tall and broad, in his early fifties, blue Regiment belt gleaming to enhance his rather imposing presence.

'How are you, Monica?' he asked. 'You're looking bright as usual.'

'Well, I would be,' I beamed. 'Happy autumn equinox!'

'Autumn what? Isn't that when the clocks go back? It's not yet surely?'

'Ah, no. It's September 22nd today and strictly speaking the equinox is later. Maybe you should find out the exact time? By the time I sign out at home-time?' I paused, a cheeky look on my face.

The QM looked at Ray and back to me.

'OK, absolutely.' He made a gesture of flicking the pages of a book feverishly onto the palm of his left hand, grimacing with effort. 'Put me under pressure. I like it.'

We had this thing going, the QM and me. He'd spent many years in the Regiment and done all his door-kicking-in, happily relinquishing all that to newer lads. He was a fantastic man, very approachable with a wonderful endearing nature, which is why I had a laugh with him. I swept on to order the stock, and as I was walking back down the long wide corridor of the building, I ran into a former neighbour of mine, James Devon.

'James, hi!' I greeted him. 'Haven't seen you in ages.'

'How are you, Monica?' James had a slow, wide smile and a quiet, slightly sibilant voice. He spoke with a straight face, barely moving his lips as if someone were operating him from a hand in his back. Six foot five, and one of the younger men to get into the Regiment at the time, he was now just thirty-four with ten years under his belt.

'How's it going?' I said, grappling with the load of paperwork under my arm.

'It's all good.' He leaned against the wall. 'I've been away. Another deployment.'

'Thought I hadn't seen you. How's Kate? And your little boy?'

'All good, yes, all good. Thanks. And a baby now.' He suddenly looked serious. 'I was going to say, what are you doing this afternoon?'

'Ha-ha. Is this a date?' I teased.

He smiled his impeccable college-boy megawatt smile and courteously replied that he'd be happy if it were a date but no, he just wondered if he could pop into the store.

'Course you can, James. Need something? You can talk or have a look around while I stack shelves – or something else suitably glamorous.'

More civilian staff were arriving for the day, with greetings and banter and dogs everywhere. Dogs had to be either in a cage or tied up securely in offices, but at this point of the day there was a sort of ceremonial doggy meeting where they rushed up and down the long wide entrance area, slipping and sliding on the stone floor, barking with excitement. James seemed delighted at the sight. His clean-cut appearance was incongruous on a camp populated by the studied unruliness of the baseball-cap-wearing newer geezers with their tattooed bodies and long hair.

'Must go, I've left my car outside blocking everyone in as usual, I imagine,' I said. I didn't want to be seen talking to the guys, not here anyway. Not in work time. They were funny about that; the work time, not the chatting to guys.

'See you later,' he said.

Homecoming for these extraordinary men could be fraught. The very word 'homecoming' suggests a happy event, taking place at an appointed time on a specific day, but for many of them it could be a long and difficult process and 'getting back to normal' wasn't clear-cut. These weren't men who could always keep in touch while they were away, not even exchange emails or regular letters with their loved ones, so for months, lives on both sides would be devoid of any news. Returning to a home that had been carrying on without them could be confusing, even when they'd done it many times before. Simply going into the house could feel momentous, with its everyday memories and events that he hadn't been a part of. I suppose that moment was when everyone had to make a commitment to reality. And who knew if his family had been sticking by him?

I couldn't help going back in my mind to Kip Formby and Jim Campbell, two of many whose marriages had fallen apart partly because of the frequent absences. Were these men afraid of being displaced?

'Come in, James,' I said later on that day, locking the door behind him and pulling the curtain across, switching off the corridor light. 'I'm just moving some boxes upstairs, but if you don't mind talking while I carry on?'

He followed me down the narrow, dark corridor. He looked up, as people did, taking in the sheer strangeness of a place that seemed to be sealed in time, forgotten. Up there, under the roof, cobwebs hung in long catenaries, turned black by the weight of dust that had gathered on the threads spun over the years. The ceilings, as high as a house, were impossible to reach with a vacuum cleaner. We crossed the vast, echoing ground floor, which now appeared empty since I'd worked some order into the place. James burst into a long laugh, his brilliant smile lighting up the place. It always made people smile in return.

'What are you up to today?' he asked.

'Well.' I put my hands on my hips and took a deep breath, surveying the scene as if weighing up my options. I was wearing thick, padded gloves and indicated several pallets of boxes which I'd just hauled out of the goods lift. 'That's three hundred boxes and I have to stack them – there.' I pointed at the expanse of brick wall.

'Wow,' said James. 'Right up to the ceiling?'

'Yep.' I laughed. 'But I have my radio and earphones,' I said, pulling them out of my pocket, 'so I'm soon to be tuning into Radio 4 to keep me company.'

'And this is your job today?'

'Well, it's my job this afternoon,' I said, pulling off the band on my ponytail, fluffing my hair out and putting it back up again. 'The morning is fraught with squadron storemen coming for their orders. That's why we close in the afternoon, so I can get on.'

James shook his head slowly and looked around at the long rows of neat boxes and stacks of things on poles like brushes or mops, then the fridges over at the far end of the gloomy store.

'Wow. I didn't know about this place,' he said, blowing out his cheeks. 'Hey, that's not a coffin over there, is it?'

It was. Right over in a corner by our personal lockers, was a coffin. It was usually covered in a sheet but that hadn't come back from the laundry yet.

'It's not a proper coffin to be *used* by anyone, silly,' I said. 'Come and see.'

We walked down to the far end and James lifted the lid, grimacing at the massive supply of black armbands.

'It's for funeral practice,' I told him.

I enjoyed showing him around. 'It's a supply chain,' I said. 'There's no reason why you should know, all you guys need to be confident of is that you have everything you need, right down to the smallest detail, whether it's foot powder, insect repellent or para cord.'

I took off my gloves and safely stowed away the pallet truck. James ambled around, looking at the labels on boxes, rows and rows of them; different sizes of the same thing, crates and boxes and canisters of everything they used on exercise or operations.

'I wish this were my job today,' he said, but then gave a dry laugh. 'I'd listen to my music, lift the boxes all afternoon, nobody to bother me. Nice bit of phys. Sounds like heaven.'

'Yeah, heaven for one afternoon,' I said. 'Come on, sit down, if you're staying.'

James was another notable personality on camp. When I read about badged men who are fitness fanatics and spend every spare minute training, I think of James. Boxing, rugby and football were big on this camp and James was a superstar of the boxing ring. A true Brixton lad, he'd gained a scholarship to a public school for his final two years, been knocked into cultural shape and these days competed with me for who'd been the first to see the latest National Portrait Gallery exhibition.

'You wanted to ask me something?' I said. 'Here, help me pull these boxes into a bit of a stack.'

He hauled a few into an amusing sofa shape in seconds.

'What's in the boxes anyway?' he asked, tapping them. He stretched out his endless legs and propped himself up on one shoulder, clasping his hands.

'Solar showers, I think. Yep –' I checked the label – 'solar showers. I'd never even heard of them before I came here. Nobody ever asks for them, and suddenly we get an order for six hundred.' I smiled and shrugged. 'Here, would you like one?' He took it like a new toy and put it in his pocket.

'So this is where everything comes from?' he said, shaking his head. 'I've never thought.'

'That it's all here back at the ranch in Hereford?' I said. 'And it's me sending them to you all those thousands of miles?' I beamed. 'I hope that will make you think next time, about us grafting here for you!'

He went silent, pondering what I'd said.

'It's a nice thought, M. Piece of home. You should sneak a message into your cargoes sometime. For the lads.'

It was dim and quiet up here. Our fire escape was open for fresh air and there was a lovely view of the woods rising up into the distance.

'I can't believe you work alone down here,' he said suddenly. 'Sure I'm not disturbing you?'

I shrugged and smiled. 'Most of my time is wasted here anyway,' I said.

'But this job? And down the road in the kitchen? Why d'you do it?'

'Work's work, I suppose,' I said. 'Are you just killing time this afternoon, by the way?'

He pushed his chin down into his jacket collar and zipped it up, higher.

'I've got some personal admin, that's all. Some stuff to take to the clerk. Thought I might eat here tonight, so I'm just doing bits and pieces... ' He seemed to run out of energy for the conversation and I decided to leave any chat for another time.

When people are convicted to a long prison term, it is usually reported that they show no emotion. That suggests that they had no emotion to show when the opposite is more likely. Facing a barrage of thoughts racing and tumbling over one another, nothing clear, nothing to get hold of, the mind is incapable of engaging with anything outside itself. They become compliant, obedient. When I was a prison visitor they told me these things. Here, on camp, the badged guys who were the most ebullient, the outgoing ones never short of something to say, never allowed time to question their thoughts, sort them out, categorise them. James was doing this now. Being deployed had been a way of escaping his responsibilities. Now he was back, he obviously didn't know where to start. His silence, his apparent lack of emotion, hid a cascade of thoughts, all jostling with one another, vying to be first on the list.

'I'm knackered,' he said, looking up from under his eyebrows, almost apologetically. 'Like my bones hurt.' He looked around the huge store. 'It's great up here. You're lucky, M.'

I crossed the floor and wedged open the fire door which was clattering backwards and forwards with the breeze blowing through. We were in full sun and the whole area was suddenly bathed with dancing multicoloured hues. James's skin looked dull and cratered from weight-loss but nothing could detract from his handsomeness. Everything suddenly felt perfect: an afternoon set aside, stretching ahead of us and there wasn't a better way to spend it. Every cloud had been blown away and we had nothing but unhurried chat. Yes, I should have been working, and I did, continuing to stack the small, light boxes while James talked. Right now I was probably the only person on camp who had time for him.

James didn't want a deep philosophical discussion about the meaning of life. He just wanted to get this stuff out of his head, as if in a confessional. Our minds can be cesspits of terrible thoughts; sometimes degrading, sometimes cruel, other times lustful and obsessional, or charitable and loving. We often describe people as laid-back, charming, elegant, easy-going. It doesn't mean they don't also have cruel, bitter, horrible thoughts and grievances as well. Maybe James was at that place where two roads were diverging in the wood and he was plagued by indecision? It is often said that sticking with something, as these men have to do in the military, is 'getting on with it'. Facing up to things is seen as the better way, but I wonder. In normal life, people often stick with something for other reasons than duty: fear maybe, inertia, depression. I wonder sometimes if walking away isn't 'giving up' but instead challenging the status quo? Taking the decision that you won't put up with things? It can take enormous courage to quit.

James wandered over to the open door. Upstairs could get ridiculously hot even on autumn days and we opened the doors every afternoon for a bit of fresh air. Beyond the tin roofs and office-views of the other elite Regiment, there are breathtaking views of hills and fields and cattle and trees: it's a bucolic, timeless scene. I watched his long, tall body silhouetted against the bright sky from the gloom of the musty store. I wondered how he would look in twenty, thirty years' time. He leaned on the iron staircase railing, crossing one leg over the other, settling onto one hip. Usually taut and upright, he subsided gratefully.

'This place sucks the life out of you,' he said.

I understood why they liked to come down here. I'm not saying I was fantastic or anything, but Craig would never have sat here like this. Craig has his own worries; a wife and growing teenage family to feed and clothe on twelve hundred a month. An elderly, impoverished mother hundreds of miles away. He had no time for the inner turmoil of the primped and preened, well-paid geezers who had everything provided for them. Craig was respectful of their status, but unimpressed. They didn't look pampered to me, but to Craig, if you had money, you had everything.

He would only go so far in satisfying their requirements, and emotional support was definitely a step too far. 'What the fuck have they to moan about?' he used to say, walking away and angrily flicking on the office computer. Looking at a blank screen stopped him exploring the subject. Took his mind off things.

'How is it being back?' I asked.

James was still looking away, as if the answer to his dilemmas lay somewhere in the distance. He'd been away for most of the year and I'd seen his lovely, pregnant wife walking their son to school past my house. She'd looked increasingly drained and pale and lacklustre. It's one thing to have support from the Regiment and welfare departments and know that your husband is doing a wonderful duty to his country, but the wives and their entire families also must serve their country by keeping home happy and welcoming, freeing their men of extra worries. That was the message. But wives missed their man next to them at night. Missed intimacy and affection, the sort you don't get from children and parents and welfare officers. I couldn't have done it.

'Honestly?' He shook his head solemnly. Then he opened his arms helplessly. 'There's jobs saved up for me. Fix the fence, fix Rory's bike, paint the utility room. Help Kate. Visit people. Go to work and get into my new job.'

'And Kate?'

He turned around.

'Fantastic. It's good being back. I missed her actually. I missed the seasons. But I don't mind being away. When you're away, there's only work to think about. Here at home, there's work and family and chores, people want to catch up ...'

He came back into the gloom and, walking towards me, he looked an incongruous figure in a place where we all wore cover-ups, overalls, thick boots and gloves. He looked immaculate. My jacket was zipped up to my throat every morning, sleeves pulled down, hair tied up. James's neat and clean leather jacket, the pristine jeans and crisp white T-shirt were the first personal clothes he had worn since last year. His hair was freshly cut and he looked exfoliated and scrubbed.

I sensed that James was undergoing a process of re-evaluation of his life, a re-evaluation that might cause him to make some poor decisions. He'd said 'I'd missed her *actually*' when he mentioned his wife, as if there could have been some doubt.

'I didn't tell you, but I've got another kid, a daughter, in London. She's twelve. Her mum and I weren't together...' He shrugged as if nature had played games with him, and he hadn't been told that there was a bit more to sex than having a good night out. He ran a hand across his face, fatigued. 'I wish I hadn't had children, M.'

I didn't answer. I think he just wanted to say it out loud, to try the phrase on, see how it sounded, or maybe see how it felt to say it. The store creaked, and I heard a box flap snap along one of the aisles.

'It's OK, it's rats,' I said. 'Come on, James, sit and talk to me. Or sit and be quiet with me, I don't mind. I'll carry on if you like. Nobody will ever know you're here.'

I sat, not looking at him and not doing anything more than resting my eyes on the outside, like people who sit on a beach, staring out to sea. I wanted him to know that I was easy with him being there and expected nothing from him.

Eventually he said, 'I knew Glynn, my best mate, for twenty-three years. We spoke of many things, knew each other really well – all our secrets, y'know? Well, he was killed, four years ago.'

'I'm so sorry,' I said. 'In action?'

'No.' He took a deep breath and shifted his position. He folded his arms tightly across his chest as if consoling himself, still focusing out of the fire exit. 'Car accident. What bothers me … We had years of knowing each other and we did so much but I can only remember one thing. One stupid thing, M. He said he liked ironing, and it was a mad conversation because I said I did too and always did the family's ironing. Then Glynn said he ironed everything, even the towels and tea towels, because they stacked better.'

James laughed, a wide laugh, displaying his even, gleaming white teeth.

'That's all I can remember him saying, M,' he said, face clouding over. He dropped his head. 'It came back to me again and again. Of all the things we talked about, all I can remember is that he liked to iron his tea towels. I can see his face when he said it. I can see the lines on his face and the exact colour of his sweater when he said it. Ironing his fucking tea towels.' He looked at me, his brow furrowed. 'Why is that the only thing I can remember, M?'

I looked at the floor. 'I don't know, James,' I said quietly. 'We're all the same, I think.'

'Yeah?'

'God yes.' I looked at him. 'When you're more relaxed, maybe one day when you're not in this lot, you'll find yourself sitting out in a deckchair thinking about Glynn and all sorts of memories will come flooding back. And other memories no doubt, that you didn't even really know happened.'

He looked around him and at the gloomy sight on the floor below us. He closed his eyes, briefly. 'This is nice.'

'The lost corner of England,' I said.

From far away, downstairs, I heard a rattle of the door. Then a bleep. Then a key.

'Must be Craig.' I said. Sure enough...

'Darling! Darling!'

'Up here, Craig!' I yelled back.

'You OK, darling?'

'Yes!'

'I NEED TO GO UNLOCK THE PAVILION DOORS FOR THE ELECTRCIAN!' he yelled.

'OK!'

'You're alive then, darling?'

'YES!'

'Just checking!'

We heard Craig leave and lock behind him. James got up, shaking out his legs and grimacing at being stiff. He bent a foot backwards to stretch out his thigh muscles. 'I should go,' he said.

'Brew first?' I offered.

We went down to the kitchen, not daring to put on the light in case someone thought I was in. I filled the kettle. James leaned on the fridge, relaxed, watching.

'Was there anything else you wanted from the store, James, I forgot to ask.'

'Nah,' he said. 'Just wanted to hide away for a while.'

I made the hot drinks. We stayed in the dark, comfortable exactly where we were.

'What's the worst thing you've ever done, M?' he said, out of the blue. It was that kind of afternoon, our conversation like a bunch of balloons set free, landing where the wind took them.

'Blimey,' I said, 'let me think.' I made a face, but my eyes were smiling that embarrassed sort of smile when you're not sure whether to say it. 'Probably so many things I can't remember, James, to be honest, but I've a clear memory of some Dior shoes in a sale – *in a sale,* mark you – half price at £700 a pair, and I was so thrilled I bought all three colours.' I laughed at the stupidity of it all.

James laughed too. 'Fair play, M.'

'I wouldn't do it now. That was fifteen years ago. I look at those shoes, only worn a few times, and can't understand what I was thinking.'

We went into the office to sit down. 'Your turn,' I said, pointing my mug at him. 'Entertain me with your worst bits. No war stuff, mind.'

'Knocking one out on the M4,' he said immediately.

I burst into laughter then clapped my hand to my mouth.

'No, you *don't!*' I said, giggling. 'Do you?'

'It's been known.'

I couldn't stop laughing, bending double with my head on my knees. I wasn't sure which bit of me was embarrassed, then I realised it had changed our relationship very slightly. Too much information, maybe.

'That bit between Heston and Reading services, thirty miles. So boring, M.'

I gave a playful shrug. 'I'm not going to ask if it affects your driving ability.'

'I'm blue-light trained, M.'

'And it's an emergency?'

'The worst.'

I threw my head back and guffawed again. Not really at what he said, but because he wasn't embarrassed saying it.

'Oh well, we get through life the best way we can,' I said. And I giggled again and it started him off and we got into one of those waves of laughter that just when you think you've stopped, the imagination takes over and off you go again. James the Geezer, driving and doing 'the Barclays' at the same time. I'm laughing again now, and it happened three years ago.

His pager buzzed and he gave an exasperated sigh, pulling it out of his pocket. I re-did my ponytail, fishing in the desk drawer for a mirror. God, I looked tired. I tried not to look at myself too often these days – once in the morning and a tidy-up before mealtimes. If you don't like what you see, don't look, my mother used to say.

He put his pager back and got up. 'People move on,' he said. What was he referring to? Was he afraid that the Regiment would move on without him? Or that he had moved on from the Regiment? His wife? Something else?

'I'm quite strong, really,' he said, 'which helps when you're swimming against the tide. But I sometimes think "Did I really do that? Why?"'

He could have meant anything. Having a child with someone he didn't care about, maybe he had an affair, maybe it was something to do with being a soldier? I couldn't imagine James Devon having someone on the side. But then I couldn't imagine him being aggressive or dragging people across the floor and yelling at them to put their fucking hands on the wall. What you see is rarely what you get in life, I knew that much. Whatever was troubling him, it was eating away at him. These men, I thought, they can't have a quiet rant about work in the pub, unless it's with other geezers, and even then they have to be mindful of who's listening. They can't ring an old schoolfriend and talk it through. Not warfare. Not stress. It's secret. They can tell their wives, their mum even, but would they understand situations of conflict, if indeed it was anything to do with conflict? We were warned in security briefings about casual talk with family who might post their pride in you on Facebook. Everyone is told to talk more about things that bother them these days, but how can *they*? Talking to other geezers, or anyone in the military, come to that, was usually through banter, taking the piss, whatever you might call it. That's their way.

'Are you a religious man, James?' I asked.

'Nah. God? No.' He flashed a look at me. 'Why?'

'Just asking.'

He shrugged. 'Well, if there was a God, how can he allow all this terrorism and atrocities in the world?' he said, shaking his head and looking at the floor. 'Where was God during the 9/11 attacks, for fuck's sake? Or any of the terrorist stuff. God stands back and lets people get beheaded?' He raised his hands and slapped them back down in frustration.

'Do you believe that God exists?'

He shook his head vigorously, looking at the floor. 'No.'

'So – then how could God have stopped them? It's hard to lay blame on God if there's no such thing.'

He laughed. 'Human nature, huh?' he said, squashing the teabags I'd left in his mug, and swigging the dregs. 'What's God to you?'

'My conscience,' I said gently. 'That moment when you're balancing between something you should and shouldn't do or say. I suppose a conscience is there for a reason.'

'Suppose,' he replied, thinking. 'So what else do you believe in?'

I considered for a second then decided to brighten up. I smiled and slapped his arm playfully.

'I believe in you, James! Great things are coming for you, I know it. And you know Devon means Warrior of God?'

'Kidding?'

I shook my head. 'Nope. I remember it from somewhere.'

He laughed. 'Except God doesn't exist!'

We laughed and, as if the universe heard us, sun suddenly shone through the windows in long beams, exposing everything to scrutiny. The cobwebs up high, the dust on the desks. I looked at James's face while he checked his phone. He looked tired. Outside, a sudden blast of squally rain overwhelmed the spill of sun. Giddy with light, the car park and roofs blazed briefly and in seconds the whirl of rain shut it down again. I wondered if James was briefly in a world without perspective. Lost. Disorientated at coming back to a place that had been carrying on without him. How can you recalibrate your mind after spending most of the year in some hellhole with people exactly like yourself? Had their wives or parents ever seen their husbands or sons like that, in body armour? Of course not. Nobody knows what they look like at work; even their nearest and dearest will never have seen them with all those guns and radios strapped to their bodies, or fighting on Selection or being kicked around. This secret world stifles everything that makes them who they are.

'I like this place,' James said, returning his coffee cup to the sink and holding it under the running tap, ensuring that every corner was washed and rinsed and then wiped dry. He hung it up on the crude nail above the sink and ran his damp hands down his trousers. His phone pinged. They needed him back.

'Well, come again,' I said at the door, like a hostess seeing off her last guest after a party.

'Sure?' he asked. 'That'd be nice.' Then suddenly he remembered something and pulled out the solar shower pack from his jacket pocket and grinned at me like a naughty little boy. 'Do I need to sign anything?'

'Dear Leader!' I said, as I tapped my knuckle on the wall of the QM's office just before I left for the day. I always called him 'Dear Leader' in the style of North Korea.

'Ah! Monica!' The QM looked up from his desk. '21:02, am I right?'

'Well done you!' I smiled as if talking to a seven-year-old.

'And as you know, it's traditional to raise a glass of dandelion and burdock, Monica.'

'And the only day when egg-balancing is possible,' I added.

He shook his head.

'That's the spring equinox, Monica. C'mon, everyone knows that.'

'10:28, March 20th, of course, what was I thinking?'

Oh, the endless fun of competitive fact-finding those senior geezers provided!

XXX

Sometimes I get so immersed in my own company on camp that if I unexpectedly run into someone a bit like me, it's a shock. There's a lovely woman in welfare, Sonia, who comes here to bring bedding from special emergency family accommodation. I've met her maybe four times and she talks about her grandchildren. A couple of women from the sergeants' and officers' messes pick up monthly cleaning supplies and we pass the time of day, and there are two fantastic and beautifully dressed women, Charlotte and Jane, who have worked in reception for years. We've started having lunch in the garrison cafe together once a month. It always involves a lot of laughter, mostly about the camp and the crazy people here, and once or twice I've been invited into their little secure goldfish bowl on the gate, where they talk about their lives, but never for more than ten minutes because there's cameras everywhere and I'd get another roasting for being out of the store, and there's only so many times you can get indignant about breaking the rules.

Apart from the surveillance regiment, Special Forces was only open to men to apply until the last few years. I've no idea how many women are now applying, but when I've been asked if I think they'd get in, well, of course they can. To my mind, having been very close to the way things work, it isn't the tough stuff that's the hardest to bear. Lots of women have everything it takes to pass Selection but that's not all there is to it.

Getting in is one thing: they have to *stay* in and, I suppose, that's where I have my doubts. In my experience, women don't compromise as much as men do. Women can pass Selection and be fit and strong and bloody-minded; naturally, women *can* do all of this. But are they *likely* to? I doubt it. This isn't about equality, it's about gender. Mothers are certainly less comfortable about leaving their children for months on end, not necessarily because they miss them more than fathers do, but because they know their children will pine for their mother. Life in the Regiment is a slog and, personally, I think they're worked into the ground. Plenty of *men* would not tolerate a job where they didn't see their families for months on end, so I don't think it's really about men versus women, but different personality types. Some want the life of an elite soldier and others wouldn't consider it.

People will say that not staying in the Regiment is 'not being able to hack it'. There's always the criticism, isn't there, that if someone won't stay it's because they couldn't do it. But couldn't isn't *wouldn't*. People can grind on doing the same thing, and as I've pointed out, being in the Regiment isn't all hardcore skillsets and training mindsets – it's staying the course when they take you off all that stuff and it's time to move on. I think that if the elite regiments can use the skills that women can bring to the role, it will be a huge success. I daresay that's already happening. The main problem as I saw it, at the time of my leaving, was the old status quo of the entire establishment. They rely a lot on doing things by the book, evident in the way they deal with just about everything. My opinion, for what it's worth, is that sometimes they should put the procedures and rules aside and actually talk to staff like normal people.

XXXI

The place was always busy, but it was usually a case of crowd control more than anything else. Craig had a jaunty way of dealing with people, starting with, 'Hey, buddy, whatever you want, fuck off!' and then he'd smile and slap them on the shoulders and send them to help themselves to whatever they needed. And I know why he did it: we just couldn't manage with only two pairs of hands and the phone going every few minutes.

On one of those very busy days, important kit was coming in which we didn't usually see very often and I'd been called endless times to escort delivery lorries, often being persuaded at the gatehouse to 'take an extra one while you're here', so I was driving all over camp trying to find a space for them to park. In the spirit of 'all pulling together as a team' I'd spent that wet, stormy day going places on camp I hardly knew existed.

In the store, 2-2 guys who'd been told by Craig to go and have a look for themselves were tearing open boxes, one after another when they found that it wasn't what they wanted. It was carnage. We couldn't operate on a self-

296

service basis. Alex McQuoid was in the corner, balanced on a pile of sandbags trying to reach a blocked-in shelf of stuff, and reaching his arm backwards while facing the other way, as if he were pulling tickets for a raffle.

Two generators, £6,000 each, a special order for abroad, had somehow gone missing after they were supposed to have been accepted into our store. I had escorted the driver on that particular day – reception always had a record – and I was said to have signed for the delivery. Maybe I did and maybe I didn't; I was signing for a huge amount of kit that day. The fact was, nobody knew where the generators were now. Soon enough the whole QM department was looking for them. Long-forgotten ISO containers with specialist equipment were being prised open, just in case they had been put there by mistake. One by one, the RQs Marc B, Kiwi and Foster appeared, tasked with 'having another look', and the whole thing was still dragging on two weeks later.

'What would they have looked like?' I quizzed Marc. 'I mean, are they generators that I'd recognise? There's generators and generators, surely?'

'They're the sort you'd take camping or they have at festivals, that type of thing,' he explained. 'According to the driver, who didn't know what was on the pallet, they were both together and covered all over tightly with black plastic sheeting.'

'So I wouldn't have known what was on the pallet?'

'Definitely not,' he said.

Next day I had a bright idea. I went to the little office in the QM building where three clerks sat all day ordering stationery or something. I asked to see the signature again.

The department had requested paperwork from the delivery company, and it had all been enhanced in a forensic kind of way by one of our departments, and it definitely didn't look like anything I would have scribbled.

'That's not my signature,' I said, perplexed. 'Look.' I signed a blank piece of paper. 'I always write my full name. I never put M instead of Monica, never. I never write initials; however sketchy it needs to be.' I wrote it again and stood up with a flourish.

Well, for some God-only-knows reason the senior clerk, a plodding type of man, ex-army, took offence, and then someone else called my signature into question and the clerk got shirty.

'Why are you speaking to me like that, Derek?' I said. 'I've just come here in a friendly way to see if I can help a bit more. There's no need to speak to me like that.'

His face turned red.

'Come with me to the RQ,' he said, coming around the side of his desk, straightening his tie and pulling his shoulders back.

'For heaven's sake,' I said. 'I'm not going anywhere. I've got to get back.'

That was all we said.

Next day, Jules came to say that Ranger wanted to see me.

'Sit down please, Monica.' Ray had my file in front of him. It noted reprimands for a long tea break with the inspector when he had asked to see me, the 'asking questions' incident, and now whatever Ray was going to say to me would be given a note in the file. In my working life before the camp, I hadn't had a single question mark over my conduct in thirty years. Here, I'd been carpeted three times, if you'll excuse the expression, by the SAS. You have to admit, it was all getting a bit rock 'n' roll.

'These generators, Monica. Sit down, please,' Ray began in a tone of voice I hadn't heard before. 'I've had a note from Foster about the dispute you and Derek had yesterday. I've had a chat with Derek about this and I'd like to hear your version.'

'It wasn't a dispute, Ray,' I said. 'We had words, I've no idea what got into him, and I was merely trying to be helpful about this generator matter. Frankly, I wish I hadn't bothered. What I *am* bothered about,' I went on, 'is the actual disappearance of the generators, especially as they're worth £12,000, and I've been racking my brains to help. They came into our store but I haven't a clue what happened to them; it was a massive delivery that day. I just had another idea about it yesterday and popped in to tell them. OK? That was it.'

Ray held up a hand.

'It's not that, Monica.' He closed my file and leaned forward, clasping his hands on the desk. What he said next I simply couldn't believe, especially not from a badged soldier at his level, and indeed it was so extraordinary to me that I can clearly recall every word and detail of the scene three years later.

'Foster is concerned about raised voices in the building. It can be very upsetting to a lot of people. We have to be careful about the mental welfare of staff, and Foster is clear about this. Two people having an argument in the corridor can be bad for mental health and I am speaking to you about this. I'm afraid there will be a note of reprimand on your file. And Derek's, of course.'

I had to stop him. As well as the RQs like Ray and the QM, who were all badged, working in the quartermaster building there were two clerks: Sue, who was also a club bouncer at the weekend, and Rachel, whose daily routine was sticking two fingers up at the bosses behind their backs and not talking until noon because she was, as she put it 'arseholed the night before'. And then there was Ross, the sergeant. Ross was a six-foot-four Glaswegian rugby player who peppered his conversation with *fucking this* and *fucking that* to fill in the gaps of a dull tale of drinking and losing money on the horses.

And Ray was suggesting that overhearing a mild disagreement on a perfectly legitimate work topic was bad for their mental health?

'*Really*, Ray?' I said. 'Ross? Sue? Have they said they're upset? Complained about their mental health, have they?' I found the whole idea laughable and extremely unlikely but it occurred to me that it was the sort of thing he could write on my file as a reprimand. Frankly I didn't know what had happened to him when we usually got on so well, but I was about to discover that it was coming from someone else.

Ray lowered his head and looked at me like a bull about to charge.

'Monica – the *quartermaster* feels this way. We cannot have this sort of behaviour.'

'Well, it's ridiculous,' I said. 'I can't take it seriously.'

He raised his hands.

'I understand, Monica, I do. You've worked in London in a cut-throat world, you're more robust.'

'Correct. It's also a world where people fall out all the time, say their piece and forget it five minutes later. Nobody calls them in to explain, wasting everyone's precious time like this.'

'Well, we have a different way of doing things.' He went on, 'We have to find ways to solve disputes and keep everyone here happy.'

'OK, Ray, so can we talk about the generators because that's why I came over here yesterday in the first place.'

'We're probably going to write it off.'

I was dumbfounded.

'Are you serious?'

I felt personally insulted at my efforts to help everyone out. I didn't believe the pathetic ruse about upsetting staff, and his peremptory way of closing down the whole matter. Something was up.

'Look, Ray, OK –' I took a deep breath – 'they're stolen. I can't prove it, but I believe it to be so. We've torn this camp apart. Someone with access to a key took them. It's the only explanation.'

He shook his head but looked at me intensely.

'Stuff is disappearing out of those gates regularly,' I went on, 'you have my word on that. Nothing expensive or of great account until now, but that's not the point. Put together, it's a lot of stock and a lot of money. When Adie was here he offered me duvets, batteries... even a new washing machine when I mentioned that mine was on the blink. Obviously I didn't take it, but he would have let me have it. He was running a protection racket about the whole thing.'

'Monica...'

I could tell he was irritated, but there wasn't much that could be done. I was sensing somebody who didn't want to go down the road of taking steps over theft because there was a lack of imaginative understanding, lack of emotional depth. He could only do the job he'd been trained to do, like a dog. Those terrifying German Shepherds who can kill a man with one command wouldn't have a clue how to sniff out explosives.

'I've told people, Ray –' I mentioned five people I'd raised concerns with – 'and all they'd say was it's always gone on in the army.'

I'd mentioned it to the girls on the gate at coffee, and they said, 'Oh God, yes, everybody steals in the army.' I told the *security cell* people and they just smiled at me and agreed it goes on. I knew it was hopeless. This was nothing to do with 2-2, they had more than enough on their hands, but it seemed to me a case of 'while the cat's away'. In this extremely relaxed camp, where people did a lot more of their own thing, something had been allowed to slip on the logistics side, and for a long time too.

I'd found it shocking. Something inside me was fading away. It was hope. It was trust. I felt as if I couldn't trust anybody. If this had been a firm, a business, it would be a different story. It was easy, here, to give up on a search: nothing terrible would happen, no jobs lost, no wages docked, no reprimands. It was nobody's money. I could see something in Ray's manner, and the other RQs – the loss of the generators was an inconvenience but writing it off was the easy route. The QM had a big budget and a couple of clicks on the computer stock control would deal with any audit, or so I assumed. I'd done the TMGI course, after all. I knew how these things worked.

Ray just gave me one of his searching stares.

'OK, Monica, you need to understand something.' His voice had gained an edge.

'Yes, the military has its rogues. It's always been the way. They're terrors, but they do good work. We'd be lost without people like that, working for decades for the good of the service. So, if they take home a few toilet rolls or bin liners, well, it's best to turn a blind eye. I'd advise you to stay over there, in your little bubble, do your job and let other people do theirs. We have important things going on in this camp.'

'Absolutely,' I said, 'and it's because of the important things that I'm here today instead of turning your "blind eye", Ray. I could have stayed in my office and I wouldn't have suffered any consequences, not like now. *This* is how you reward conscientiousness.'

'You need to let this one go,' he told me. 'Four of the RQs have been to your store, right?'

'Yes.'

'And found nothing.' Ray sat back and dangled an arm over the back of his chair.

'Exactly! The generators have gone, that's why – they've been stolen!'

I got the steely look again.

'Forget it, Monica. These things happen.'

I couldn't have it.

'It's disgraceful,' I said. 'Calling people terrors – that's what I'd call little boys who pour your perfume down the sink as a prank. We have all just spent nearly three weeks looking for expensive kit when we could have been supporting the "important things" on camp. I've got two shipping containers to fill for deployments and, you may not have noticed, Craig is never there so I'm working alone.'

'Monica –'

'It isn't just the £12,000 loss, it's the time and expense of all of you lot coming over to search high and low for it.'

'Monica.' Ray adopted a familiar, patient posture; I'd seen it before when George had a go at me for asking questions. 'Monica, you are robust, but listen to me.'

I looked at his face, then at the headdress behind him with its Regimental winged dagger badge, a photograph on the wall of his entire squadron, and back to his face. He was like a terrorist interrogator deciding to take the soft route for a moment, to mollify me.

'Monica. This is a great department. We have all these different people doing things I don't understand; people who have been here for years. Great civil servants. They know their jobs better than I can ever know, and I let them get on with it.'

He lifted a hand and described little circles in the air with his finger. His voice had a soft tone, hushed and slow, lilting, as if telling a child a bedtime story.

'There are little bubbles of industry on the camp, Monica. A bubble over there,' he paused drawing his circles, 'a bubble opposite here,' another pause, another circle in the air, 'and over the road there's your little store bubble and all the other stores – all bubbles of industry who go about their business on their own initiative, working hard, achieving what they need to achieve. And then they go home. They don't spend time going between offices, nattering away. They probably don't even know what each other does. But here's the great thing, Monica.' He leaned forward even further and clasped his hands again. 'They get on with the job and don't *need* to know what everyone else is doing.'

He sat back and regarded me.

I didn't move. Nice speech. Ray hadn't a clue what our jobs were.

'And that's the reason they get away with taking stuff,' I said.

A couple of 2-2s who had been waiting outside in the corridor put their faces round the open door, then tapped on the glass in that way people have when they're impatient, like when you rattle a toilet door even when you know someone's in there. Ray rose to his feet, the movement releasing a waft of stale air. He gave a slight flash of his eyes, as if confirming his lordship over me, and moved to the door, kicking the wedge away from the bottom of the door with an unbelievable force, so it clattered shut. Whatever he was about to say, he required privacy. Quite suddenly, I loathed him.

'So what you're suggesting is that I see these things, these criminal things, and you want me to do nothing about them?'

Ray hissed out a deep breath, as if gathering himself.

'It's not that,' he said, wearily.

'Why did you hire me, Ray? Yes, it's a store job, but I don't just come here to do a job, I come here to work. Do you even know the civil service list of core values? Leadership, working together, managing a quality service – *quality* service, Ray –' I put my hands on my hips, emphasising that point – 'and delivering at pace. Putting the obligations of public service above personal interest. These values apply just as much to storekeepers and kitchen staff as government advisers,' I said finally and waited for him to respond.

Ray said nothing. He looked almost belligerent, so I added, 'What you're expecting of me is to break these rules, these core values? That I turn a blind eye to criminality, consciously breaking the code of integrity and honesty? There are supposed to be bonds of trust between staff and their line manager, but right now I don't trust you.'

There. I'd said it. Ray was concentrating on every word, but I could tell he didn't give a damn. He always went to the gym at three o'clock and it was five-to.

'Why are you in such a foul mood?' I went on. 'We were talking in a perfectly normal way the other week. Am I part of some kind of diversity experiment, because right now it looks that way!'

'What diversity experiment?'

'Hire the female to keep your numbers up. Better still, hire the older female. You were there, on the interview panel. You knew perfectly well that I'd been in leadership roles. You took me on knowing I'd be full of ideas, that I'd challenge you... God, Ray, I've never once minded this job or thought it beyond me or beneath me, same with washing dishes. I wouldn't be here if I thought I was too overqualified to do them. I'm just annoyed that you expect me to become some compliant little person, turning a blind eye when I know it's wrong. You must be furious that the civil service picked me when you could have had a nice young man.'

He looked at the desk, then out of the window to the long queue down the corridor. His eyes were bleak. He must have had other worries.

'No Monica. I'm not.'

I should have realised that my accomplishments wouldn't travel. There was no place for moral growth here. I went to the glass door.

'Monica –' He held up a hand to stop me.

'An important part of security clearance for all of us,' I said, 'is honesty. I'm going, Ray. I did my best on the generator search. I hope you find them.'

I didn't care what he thought. How far will an existence take you when it's founded on the way other people think of you? I didn't mind being branded a troublemaker when I was sure I was doing the right thing. These people represented a different way of thinking. The people who didn't get into any trouble were the ones who didn't give a toss about the job, staying silent as if that were a virtue. Now, even talking about the way the store was run was a subject apparently beyond discussion.

I went back to the store, which was locked. Craig was off helping the officers' mess assemble staging for a ceremony. Outside, the trees shivered soundlessly as the wind blew. Trucks and cars slid past, occasionally turning but never stopping, like those little trucks you see at airports, transporting luggage up and down, same speed, same tempo. Seamless and effortless, that's how this camp appeared to me. Even when things were happening in the world, they were so well prepared that there was never any sense of panic or rush. During terrorist events the geezers were out of the traps and on their way in under thirty minutes yet it wasn't like calling out the fire service or an ambulance: there were no blue lights. Things just happened here and were dealt with. I wanted to stay. I'd only come for a few months back in 2015 but I was still here three years later. However many drawbacks there were, I'd stuck it out and I'd learned. I hadn't a clue about the military before I came here. This camp, secret and hidden from the world, had been my saviour. I'd learned that I could learn new skills and ways of thinking, which is surely what personal progress is all about?

I went back into the store and stood alone in its vastness and felt lonely. I was stuck. Stuck with a hierarchy above me who didn't want to change and grow and improve because they were coming to the end of their time and I suppose there was nothing in it for them.

Worst of all, worst of everything, Ray really didn't seem to care. I saw him ambling along to the gym ten minutes later, laughing with Foster and Mark. They were all amnesiacs living in the moment, like cats.

I thought back to a day in the store, talking with him. 'Well, what do you think?' he'd said. 'Do I seem spoiled, out of touch? I'm putting on a face, like everyone does here.'

What had made him say that?

Was it his reputation as the cool guy with the name everyone wanted, living up to his badass reputation?

Ranger's refusal to see beyond his usual boundaries demonstrated to me yet again that perspective blindness or 'rules are rules' mentality on camp. The danger of groups of people with the exact same perspective is that they become ever more certain of their rules. These men weren't challenged on any blind spots so they could never hope to see them, and even if they did, there sometimes was no point in doing anything about them, hence 'turning a blind eye'. Here in the camp stores they got through chaos rather than avoiding chaos in the first place because it was how they'd always done it. The disappearance of the generators and the success of the petty pilferers was because the pilferers could predict how they'd get away with things – and let's face it, cross one line and you can cross them all. Found out, it would have reflected back on their bosses for not knowing, up and down chains of command. It was easier to do nothing.

When I finally locked up for the day, switching off the lights and making sure everything was off in the laundry room, it was raining. I thought of Pistol Pete, innocently getting changed in the laundry room one afternoon and getting caught out by me. That was funny. The rain drummed on the long line of metal bins running alongside the buildings. All over camp I sensed plants opening up, drinking for their lives. I felt like that.

As far as I know, the generators were never found, and twelve thousand pounds of taxpayers' money had to be written off. If I'd been working at Marks and Spencer's or Sainsbury's, someone would have been arrested by now.

Maybe the generators were found. Maybe they were there all the time.

Maybe lots of things.

XXXII

It's still early days, but there's a type of grief that time cannot alter, nor soften, nor render us philosophical. Sometimes we just can't find peace, struggling with great jags of sorrow and frustration which come from nowhere. My grief was for Andy Flynn.

A highly valued member of the specialist surveillance regiment, he had served his country in Afghanistan and tours around the world; he was a hero, an elite soldier and linguist. He was also heartbroken. And I cry bitter tears because there's not a damned thing anyone can do about it now.

I first met Andy not long after I bought my house in Hereford. At the time I had no job and precious little to do except ride my bike about and go swimming; I was deeply depressed, thinking that I might never work again. I clung to a sort of routine that included walking down the hill every morning for the newspaper, and that's where I first saw Andy, sitting outside the village shop. Over the next year or so I would see him there a few times, and if the weather were bad I'd scuttle past, clutching my rain hood and throwing him a quick 'Hi.' When it was fair, I'd stop and chat and Andy would stretch, hooking his armpits over the back of the bench, waving away any suggestion that he had things to do. We'd talk about nothing, passing the time of day and, to be honest, I thought he might be unemployed, like me. Eventually I went for the kitchen cleaner job that everyone was so suspicious about and when I got there, there was Andy Flynn. It was one of those terrible moments when you recognise a face, but you can't remember which part of your life they fit into. It was quite a surprise to me that he was a soldier, but even more incongruous and somehow unsettling was seeing him so confident on his own territory. It threw me. Outside, going about our business in the village, we were equals. Suddenly, the context put us firmly in our places: Andy the senior soldier, the hero, and me, the kitchen cleaner. It was like coming home to tell of the old woman you chatted to for ages on your hill ramble, only to be told that she was the Queen.

'Andy?' I gasped. My heart was pounding. I quickly pulled off my long black rubber gloves and tucked them into my apron pocket. I was red-faced and perspiring, my hair frizzy from the steam coming out of the bucket. 'Sorry, I'm not exactly open to the public right now,' I said, trying to back away into the kitchen. 'Fancy meeting you here.'

'So, Monica – what do you get up to at weekends?' he said, leaning back in his chair, stirring his tea.

'What, when I'm not here?' I said. 'Erm, well... I love hillwalking, and cycling, of course. I keep a spare bike right here on camp, actually. I love the great outdoors, birds, trees...' My voice trailed away. I felt dull. I should be saying that I loved nights out, gin, girls' weekends, spa days, skiing and travelling. Everybody loved travelling, didn't they? But I didn't say that in case he asked me where I'd been.

'Sounds good,' he said, looking out of the window. 'Great afternoon for it.'

I shrugged. 'Well, it'll be nice if chef lets me knock off early,' I said. 'Three o'clock, hopefully.'

'And you live in town? Been down the Wye by Fownhope?' Andy asked. 'It's not far from you. I often go there, it's beautiful.'

'Er, no. Don't know that area. Where is it?'

He told me that Fownhope was a small, picturesque village close to the River Wye and gave me directions.

'Sounds brilliant,' I said. 'I'll definitely go there, maybe today even, or tomorrow.'

'I might see you down there sometime,' Andy said. He got up and pushed his chair back then said something strange.

'You shouldn't stay too long in this job.' He turned to leave but paused at the door. 'You don't belong down here.'

'I don't intend to,' I replied.

Three years later, in May 2018, I had left my job. Going down to the river at Fownhope had become a favourite place during my years on camp when I wanted a blissful, non-demanding walk by the mighty River Wye. There was always something to see and it was hard to know when to call it a day when the scene demanded one more corner to be looked around, or ten extra minutes to see where a track led.

On that day in May, before I had handed in my resignation, there was Andy by the river's edge. I almost didn't see him, standing in last season's long withered grass watching a couple of swans. They were nibbling at the bank, dredging and sifting the water and occasionally nuzzling their beaks together, dipping and weaving in a show of bonding. I decided to have a few polite words, ask how he was and then leave him to it. I picked my way through the long grass and joined him.

'Hi Andy.'

'Hello, Monica!' He smiled, emerging from his reverie. 'You want monogamy, marry a swan,' he said, tipping his head at the courtship display. He leaned and embraced me like a friend and, in spite of his wearing sunglasses and being pretty much dressed like any other man, his bearing and stance felt instantly recognisable.

'It's been very warm this year, the spring,' I said. 'I'm up the top now, Andy, I work in one of the stores.'

He seemed amused. 'Wow, how's it going?'

'Not bad,' I said. 'We have bad days, but never bad weeks. It's the store right next to your place actually. Surprised I haven't seen you there.'

'It's not "my place" any more,' he said, looking into the distance.

'What isn't?'

'You said that your store was next to my place up the top, but it's not my workplace any more.

'Oh?'

'I'm not working there. On camp. I'm not actually in the army now.'

'Oh. Oh, I see,' I said, matter-of-fact. 'Well, what are you up to now?'

He asked if I had time to sit for a while and he looked for a spot, kicking aside a few brambles, small stones and dry animal droppings. He sat down cross-legged and I did too. We hugged our knees into our chests.

It was one of those early May days where the seasons were all awry, still straddling spring and summer, days of boisterous weather, the sun warm and the shade cold. I looked up to judge the fast scudding clouds to see how long we would be given our warm sunshine before the big billowing cloak of shade flung us back into the chill.

Andy Flynn. There's a heaviness inside me when I think back to that day. A sort of melancholy, as if war had been declared but the sun was still shining and nothing had happened yet, although we knew it was only a matter of time. I pulled my small backpack off my shoulders.

'Look, I've got a flask of tea here if you want some. Or you can share my sandwich?' I pointed to my backpack, which I'd put on the ground, and started fishing about in it. I held the flask up to him.

'Fancy some? Or I have a small pack of three biscuits if you fancy? Custard creams? There's not many problems that a custard cream can't sort out,' I went on, prattling like an old woman, diving deep into the backpack again for a teaspoon.

'OK, thanks,' he said. 'You first.'

'No, don't be silly. You've been here longer. Sorry I've only got the one cup. God, this is so nice, I've been on my feet since five. Fabulous seeing you here, Andy.'

Looking back now I can see why the exchange that was to follow was so important. It was my only means of building up a picture of how Andy was really feeling and it had a big effect on me. Not many people would have known Andy's true role in life, nor mine actually, so we depended on one another, even in small measure, to hold one another's secrets.

'Look Andy, I've rather landed myself on you. Would you rather I went and let you be? I'll leave you the sandwich and biscuits if you like.'

Two women came walking along the path with dogs on leads, and though it was completely stupid we both stopped talking until they passed, even though we weren't actually saying anything. We waited until they walked round a bend of trees and disappeared out of earshot. It must have been part of Andy's natural instinct to say nothing when strangers were about, and it had become mine too.

We were sitting close, our legs almost touching. I hadn't noticed until that moment, but the ground around us was all thistles and stones, so we were crammed together on the only tiny patch of comfortable grass. I could feel the warmth emanating from him, smell his breath; it had that sour, metallic odour of nerves, the inside eating itself away, depleting all the body's energy and starting on the reserves. The closeness was that of friends, we were touching but rather than being embarrassing it was like being jammed next to someone else on the bus where there is no added meaning to it. The sun had gone in and as he turned his head to watch some other people pass by with a dog, I noticed that his hair had been fashioned into a crude parting with his hands and it needed a brush. With his knees up, I could see the sharp outline of his kneecaps.

'I wasn't too good after Afghan, M,' he started and looked at my face. He turned on his side, stretching out his legs and crossing one over the other so he was angled towards me. He was propped on his elbow, cradling his head with his hand. There was one lone yellow buttercup in front of him, which he picked and twirled.

'Nothing bad – well, it was bad, but ... y'know...'

I nodded.

'And it got worse. I could've hacked it if I hadn't been on a particular job but I was away with work so I couldn't kind of *absorb* it like you can at home. Sit and think about it. I couldn't sleep.'

I was a Samaritan volunteer for five years and we used to get a lot of Falklands veterans in. I could never claim to be a professional or an expert, but Samaritans all had more than two years of ongoing training for bereavement and PTSD clients, most of whom were daily callers. We listened and befriended, sometimes going to see them regularly in their own homes. I knew to stay quiet as Andy talked.

'So I got some sleeping tablets, that's all. There was no opportunity to go to the Med Centre. It didn't seem that bad a thing to do.'

I turned on my side to face him.

'It wasn't a bad thing to do.'

A slight breeze caught us, one of those gusts that come from nowhere. I pulled up my collar.

'Look, I mustn't bore you,' he said. 'You must have places to be.'

'I don't have anywhere to be, Andy. No hubby. No dogs to walk or aged parents to visit.' I smiled. 'My washing's on the line and the fridge is full. It's a bank holiday weekend. I can lie here for the rest of the day.'

He told me what happened. It was an incredibly sad and personal story so I'll spare the details, but eventually I said, angered by his story, 'How can you trust people who can't be trusted?' I was looking at the sky through my fingers. What I really wanted to say was 'They're a bunch of tossers,' but that would have been to trivialise his story, as if a standard phrase would do when it deserved greater analysis.

I reached and put a hand on Andy's shoulders and he raised his head a little.

Two swans had glided up to the bank to get at the few crumbs of sandwich I'd thrown away. I watched them nuzzling each other's bills. Andy did a quick look round at me, as if he'd been startled from sleep.

'Sorry, but I'm still here,' I said softly, and chuckled. I kept my hand where it was and soothed him with circular movements between his shoulder blades. It helped me as much as it helped him.

'Hope you don't mind me asking,' he said, 'but you were suffering from depression when I first met you in the village?'

I nodded.

'Did you ever feel it was all too much? Life, I mean?' he added.

The sun came out again. I looked at the sky again to judge how long we might have the pleasure of its grace upon us. Not for long.

'Yes,' I said. 'For a brief moment. New Year's Eve 2013-14.'

'I must have known you then?' he said.

'Yes.'

A few more minutes passed, the sun disappearing and then reappearing from the fast-moving clouds as if offering a treat and then taking it away again.

'Wish I'd known,' he said. 'Did you think of ending it?' He wiped his eyes and nose on his jacket sleeve, unselfconsciously.

'Ending it! God, no,' I said, surprised. 'I'm a Roman Catholic. So I couldn't take my own life. It's the worst thing you can do in my religion.'

'Oh, yeah,' said Andy.

'It shows you have no faith in God to help. So I had no choice but to carry on living.'

He was silent for a moment, imagining it.

'God,' he said eventually. 'It's a jail sentence.'

'Hmm. Well, if you keep thinking about it, it might be, but to me it's as obvious as being told you can't kill. You don't go through life pissed off because you can't kill anybody.'

'You didn't ever question it, though?' he said. 'You had faith in something that might just be an old tale, to frighten people?'

I chuckled. 'Yep!'

Andy sat up.

'See, that's what faith is, though, isn't it?' I said. 'Belief without evidence.'

'Blind belief?'

I nodded. Knowing what I know now, I wish we hadn't talked so easily about my beliefs, but the fact is, I had no idea what was in his mind. Depression is a dreadful thing anyway, and very personal. I remember feeling utterly desolate when I knew I had to carry on living whether I liked it or not, and the idea of the rest of my life feeling as bad as I did was devastating. But it had to be borne, there was no choice.

He turned over to lie on his front, supported on his elbows.

'You must have had some disappointments in your life, though, M, that made you question everything?'

I turned to my backpack, squashing it slightly to make a pillow for my back. I wanted to lighten our mood. 'Well, put it like this,' I said, 'I've got a card in my desk drawer at home, one of those massive, fancy ones, and it says, "To the man I love at Christmas". I bought it in 2011.'

'Wow,' he said, straightening up. 'Really? You never sent it?'

'Not yet.'

'Bloody hell, M. What happened? Old flame? Couldn't bear to part with it? Oh, sorry – he didn't die, did he?'

I shrugged and chuckled. 'The card cost a fiver, Andy,' I said. 'I'm damned well going to get my money's worth one day.'

We fell silent and watched a small group of teenagers pass by, giggling about something on one of their phones. Andy looked lost again.

'The things one person can do to another,' I murmured, 'it's unbelievable really. One decision and things are in shreds.' I put my hand on his arm and gently tugged it. I thought he was feeling past it, depressed. Unsure of his future maybe. 'Your life's not over, Andy. You'll know it's in shreds the day you die, but – look at you.' I tugged again, that sort of gentle, playful tug a child gives their mother's hem to get her attention. 'Come on. You've got so much.'

Shame is one of the most powerful emotions there is. Shame is not like guilt. Guilt is private, it's about the failure of your own values. When we feel shame, it's really about how we think others see us. A sense of being scrutinised or rejected can spark it. I know, I've felt it. It can drive you towards weaker, smaller things that you can crush. Or violence against yourself.

Eventually, we got up. It wasn't really the day for sitting outdoors for too long. We walked together up the track to where I'd parked my car and Andy said he was going to pop into the village pub if it was still open.

'What are you off to do later?' I asked, as I threw my backpack into the boot.

He smiled. 'I've got some DIY to do. Make dinner. Then, who knows? Watch TV or something.' He kicked a pebble.

I put my hand on his arm.

'Some people, y'know, if you asked them to describe their ideal day, would say what you've just said.'

He shook his head and looked at the ground. He was so good-looking. Such a brilliant smile, he could give the sunniest day a run for its money.

'I'm not making light of this,' I said. 'You're amazing, Andy, remember that. When we used to cross paths in the village and I was feeling desolate, your smile kept me going. Try and hold on,' I said. 'This isn't all there is.'

He kissed me on the cheek.

'No, *you* hold on, M,' he said, holding my car door, 'and find someone to send that card to!'

Why didn't I give him my number and say call any time? Why? I know why. I thought we'd simply had a philosophical discussion sitting by the river. I have conversations about death and beliefs with friends all the time. He'd talked about his anger at being left to rot by the Regiment, but I thought that he would go on to a new life and he'd live to eighty and it'd be a distant memory. What a stupid, stupid thing to think.

Actually, that's not the reason. I didn't give him my number because I know it suggests something else. You can give out your number and say things to men if you're thirty, and you can do it if you're sixty – but somewhere in the middle you risk being seen as something else. Desperate. An 'older woman' trying it on with a man in his thirties. I'm not saying it would have made any difference, but it might have. What I had, which very few other people in his life did, was an inside understanding of the Regiments and the camp and the whole structure there. But anyway, I didn't give him my number and tell him to call me for fear of being thought a 'cougar' – ghastly word – and for that, and thinking only of myself, I'm sorrier than I can possibly tell you.

That was 8th May 2018. Ten days later, I saw social media posts that Andy Flynn was missing and the next day I heard that he had taken his own life.

There was so much more to Andy's story that I didn't know, things that maybe only he knew. I can only tell you my own account of Andy Flynn, another gospel if you like, according to how he was feeling on that May afternoon. He didn't need to lie to or impress or explain anything to me. Andy could talk to very few people, and the few who would have understood were inside those fences and walls, a place he was not now allowed inside. That was the worst bit. Excluding him. What a horrible, brutal process. The bosses and line managers have procedures, they 'play it by the book', looking up online what they should say, what form a reprimand should take. There's nothing personal about it, and I know that myself. I'd had another reprimand since the 'questions' incident, which ultimately came to nothing, but at the time my line manager Simon talked to me like a stranger, as if we'd never laughed with each other or shared tales of his children and their holidays. He just told me to go home and wait for a letter. The letter said I mustn't talk to anybody about it except a partner, but I didn't have a partner so I just stayed home and stayed silent. For me it was a storm in a teacup, but for Andy, being ostracised like that was to deny all the service he'd put in, the heroism. It was to deny who he was, Andy the linguist and surveillance specialist. Left to do nothing but worry, not knowing, being warned *not to talk about it*, waiting for the outcome of investigations. It's mental cruelty.

Some say that not enough is done for those who have served, but I believe that it's the wrong help that's offered. Apart from practical help, what many of them need is someone close who understands, who is actually there for them, in person, any time, no notes taken or appointments to discuss their anguish. Everything with the military is a process to be followed, and that's understandable as the military is such a vast organisation, but human beings aren't processes. At the end of the day, I couldn't help thinking that Andy was being treated like a highly valued and loved family pet dog who takes an uncharacteristic bite at a child one day and, without anyone seeking to understand the cause or work out what to do in the animal's best interest, the dog is put down – immediately.

XXXIII

All the new quartermaster ever wanted was to be the boss. Many like him slid successfully into senior Regimental administrative roles as they got older, or out into the world for pastures new, but Foster needed something more. Managing budgets and staff was never going to satisfy a man who needed to be visible, so he adopted the demeanour of a Mafia boss running his empire from a prison cell.

Many of us go through life wearing a figurative lifejacket, and Foster's was that of a puppeteer with a suitcase of characters he brought out to suit his mood. With Ranger Judd gone as my line manager, shuffled off unexpectedly to another post, Foster had ultimate power as the QM over the new incumbent and the rest of us. Ex-military types like Craig and some of the older account managers automatically understood the line of succession and Foster's authority. As long as he was issuing orders, Foster maintained a sense of power. But that was tricky with outsiders like me, and others like the tailoress and the new female storekeeper; we had the privilege of being able to walk out when something didn't suit us. His need to be seen to be having an effect meant Foster pulling my strings now and again, for all the good it did him.

The new boy was Simon. Where Ray had been around every morning as a dynamic presence, Simon was the polar opposite of his predecessor: neat, reserved and with a habit of staying in his goldfish bowl of an office, emerging only now and again to go to the gym. We soon discovered that Simon wasn't a pushover, however; he acted like a man temporarily on remand who couldn't face the reality of his fate, who popped out to the shops every now and again expecting to see everything in order when he got home. I recognised in Simon something of myself when I first worked down the road. Biding my time while I took it all in, working out a suitable strategy. It had been effective, to a point, and I saw Simon's quiet demeanour masked a man quietly deciding on his next move.

Foster, meanwhile, had since worked out that being QM carried very few significant day-to-day decision-making opportunities that would satisfy his lust for power. He called us all together one afternoon to make his killer pronouncement: things would be different with him in charge, he said. He was reconsidering the Friday early knock-off time for civilians and he would limit the number of dogs brought into the department.

Dogs didn't interest me very much, nor anybody in my store, but I was pleased to see that the knock-off time issue was confidently seized by Jo, who was the clerk and also the trade union rep. I thoroughly enjoyed seeing Foster struggle with the intricacies of the Working Time Directive, explained patiently by Jo in her quiet, firm tones.

Contractually, we all had to leave camp by four o'clock on a Friday and, in practical terms, it was hardly sensible to keep us all working when every military person on camp, bar the men on standby, had left camp at midday, she told him. Then she added, with devastating finality, that keeping us until four p.m. would mean one of the corporals from Royal Logistics Corps would also be obliged to stay, as only a military person could control the signing in and out of keys and attendant security paperwork. Was Foster prepared, she asked, for telling a young lad he couldn't get home to his missus and baby in Devon or Manchester until nine p.m. if he was lucky?

The new line manager had only been there a few days when I knocked on the glass of his open door and popped my head in.

'Hello, Simon,' I said. 'I just wanted to say hi. It's great that you're able to be with us now after all these months with your stand-in.'

He was only about forty-two and hadn't expected to be in this new job. Suddenly he would never fight again, just sit in his goldfish-bowl office and maybe go to the gym in the afternoon. I looked at him, his huge, hulking frame and big round face, the quiet voice and soft features almost blinking into the light of his new world and wanting to go back down the burrow.

He stopped what he was doing and smiled. 'Hey, yes, thanks a lot. There's a lot to learn,' he said. 'It's all very new.'

'Well, I'm Monica,' I said. 'I work in that big store just over the way. Come over if you need anything. We can show you what there is. And you're the gaffer, so you don't have to put any paperwork in – I'll do it for you.'

Where Ranger had an open-door policy, Simon quietly clicked it shut every morning and didn't emerge until lunch. I did admire his keenness to learn about his new domain, though. After a few weeks, I think he settled in to his new-found status as manager of a small band of civilians. I'm not saying we became best buddies, but certainly Craig and me were able to have a laugh together with him when we had a quiet half hour in the store, and Simon would sometimes follow me around, chatting as I pushed the ladder platform about from racking to racking, counting stock. He would ask about certain items and whether they were popular with the squadrons or not. There was never anything personal, unlike chats with Ray, but he was interested in the store and how it worked, which I appreciated.

XXXIV

In December 2017 a wave of extreme weather hit the UK, a foreshadowing of the 'Beast from the East' that would blow in the following February, and Hereford got its fair share of heavy snowfall. My car was snowed-in and I was delighted when lovely James Devon came round in his huge 4x4 work vehicle, having offered to pick up as many civilian staff as possible. It was all very jolly, especially seeing the geezers shovelling snow to make footpaths to their offices. Pre-Christmas celebrations on camp always started with something called 'bunfight.' I can guarantee that if you think you've been to extravagant Christmas work parties, you've seen nothing. Each department would have a party and there'd be a sort of trawl around visiting different barbecues and gatherings all day long. In theory, we could all join in but in practice there was still work to get through. The store had to be ready if needed and the lads on standby couldn't drink. By all accounts, bunfight was almost a chore, especially for the more senior geezers with time to spare and no good excuse not to partake; they almost dreaded the obligation. I wasn't too disappointed not to take part.

It was freezing in that gloomy corridor, waiting for the meeting to begin. That was where I started writing down my story. The meeting was about my resignation, among other things. I knew I'd miss this place dreadfully, but it was time to move on and wash up on another beach.

I'd liked working there; in fact, I loved it. It had entertainment value and learning opportunities in spades. I learned about terrorism, conflict, the military way of life and discovered capabilities I didn't know I could stretch to, like the TGMI course and the forklift accreditation. Outside the cookhouse there were always notices for free language courses, things like French and Arabic – anybody could go, if they wanted to. I think I'd have stayed if there were a chance of moving up to better posts, but there was nothing suitable really and I couldn't imagine still stacking boxes in ten years' time. I wanted to see what else was out there in the world for me.

I worked on camp for over a thousand days and I've only covered a handful of them in these stories. I talked to hundreds of the SAS yet I've only told you the stories of a few; the ones who represented ideas and problems and events that scored themselves on my memory. I know I've told you about some of the cheeky ones, and perhaps that's cheeky of me, because in three years I probably came across only half a dozen men who behaved inappropriately. The others were complete gentlemen. There was so much more to all of it than I could possibly tell you here.

I loved the Regiment because they put up with being worked into the ground and simply got on with it. We were all just people who worked around one another, all pieces of the same orchestra, working together to make a crazy sort of magic. I've made friends against all the odds and I'm the richer for it.

On my last day I cleared my desk and locker but felt no sadness. It was inevitable. I chatted with Sergeant Jules and Corporal Eddy for a while in the store next door, then Craig came in to see me off. As I was leaving, I met Zero coming round the corner.

'Hey, going to town?' he asked.

'I am,' I said, 'but my car's full of stuff.' I got in and put my seatbelt on. 'I'll see you around.'

POSTSCRIPT

Of course, I could never go back after I left, in May 2018, and I miss it even now, almost three years later. Somewhere on camp, there's a long, framed photograph of the entire quartermaster department taken in 2017. We all trooped out to the cherished war memorial in the centre of camp and stood or sat in two rows, the QM centre front. Next to him were Ranger Judd and there was Kiwi and Marc and Foster either side, wearing their uniforms with the fabulous blue belts and sand-coloured berets with the winged dagger badge. The last person on the end, sitting down, is a dark-haired woman wearing a bright pink silk blouse and black trousers. That's me. Nobody told me there'd be a photo that day, or I would have dressed a little more in keeping. Unfortunately, you'll never see it and neither will I. We weren't allowed to have a copy. But somewhere on camp it's there, the 2017 staff of the quartermaster department, and I'm extremely proud to be among them.

Although I left my job, I haven't left my Regiment friends behind and I'd like to bring you up to date.

Camp was on lockdown during the 2020 coronavirus pandemic. Yes, just as the rest of us had to stay at home and observe the two-metre rule on social distancing, so did they. The men on the standby team stayed at home unless needed; as you can imagine, they were frustrated to be doing nothing. My neighbour Joe told me he didn't know how the unemployed did it because he was near the end of his tether. In line with the rest of the country, the camp gym was closed too. Suddenly the pretty little country lane near to my house, which also happens to be challengingly hilly, was swarming with men with unfeasibly honed and carved physiques ploughing up and down it; dawn, noon and nightfall. To stave off boredom, they'd do it all again on bicycles, and I noted them as they warmed up, walking past my house on the shortcut to the lane, swinging their arms and pausing for quad stretches.

When they didn't fancy another run, they followed my neighbour Nathan's lead, turning his garage into an upmarket training area for his boxing passion. I could hear him from inside my house, skipping, punching and grunting for at least an hour every day.

For guys from other regiments who already lived four or more to a house, and were accustomed to the unforgiving terrain of Nepal, they had the bonus of being able to hill-run together in a 'household group', which they did with massive backpacks weighing fifty-five kilos, they told me.

'I weigh fifty-six kilos,' I said to one once. 'Carry me on your back!'

And guess what, he did.

Zero Johnstone has been a brick since I left. Even when he was working abroad in early 2020, he emailed to see if I was OK when floods hit Hereford hard. Then, a few weeks later, he put a note through my door:

Just come to see how you're doing. Haven't heard from you in a while. I wanted to see if you needed anything from the shops.
If I don't check on you, who will?

I patched things up with Sam, the badged man from Dorset who failed one of his courses and stood me up during it, and when he comes up here twice a month for work on camp he calls in for a coffee or we meet in town. Scott, with his fridge full of nothing but cheese and wine, dropped me round some food during the floods, knocked on my door during the lockdown, offering to get me some groceries from Tesco, and texts from wherever he is in the world to hear how life is in 'H'.

Another of my neighbours from the Regiment, Ross, mended my bike puncture last week. His phone kept bleeping insistently. Eventually, I asked if he needed to go.

'Nah, it's to remind me I've got a cake in the oven,' he said. 'Coffee and walnut.'

'Wow,' I said. 'Secret baking supremo, eh?'

He shook his head and carried on pumping up the tyre.

'Never baked before. Lockdown was a chance to learn new skills.'

He wasn't the only one branching out. Alex McQuoid was stuck at home on standby so he made a compost box for the garden.

'I didn't know you were into gardening?' I said, astonished.

'I'm not,' he replied gruffly. 'I'm going to see if someone else wants it.'

I often think of the well-known poem written by the great American poet Robert Frost in 1916, 'The Road Not Taken', with its famous opening line 'Two roads diverged in a yellow wood.' It has become an emblem of an individual's choice and self-reliance. Many academics and scholars have argued over the poem's meaning, but I believe it suggests that humans are confronted with, and defined by, their choices in life; they can choose only one path and must abide by their choice. The last line of the poem says it all, I think, when he says he took the road less travelled by: 'And that has made all the difference.' Whether that difference is good or bad remains to be discovered.

Frost gave the poem to his good friend, the poet Edward Thomas, who was plagued by indecision, and could not choose between a life writing and teaching in America, or the pull of fighting in France in the First World War. Frost told him 'No matter which road you take, you will always sigh, and wish you had taken another.'

The poem was a pivotal moment for Thomas, struggling with two courses of action. Eventually, in 1915, he chose to enlist in the Artists Rifles Regiment and go to war. 'Frankly, I do not want to go,' he said, 'but hardly a day passes without my thinking that I should. The problem is endless.'

He was killed in action in April 1917.

The men of 22 Special Air Service Regiment, or the SAS as they are popularly known, are members of one of the most specialised, elite regiments in the world, and their mystery and legend are part of the life they must accept. Each one of these men has made his choice to volunteer for the entirely different, arduous and secretive life as a badged member of this fabled military unit. And it is a life, not just a job. The choice to move from their familiar life to the unknown, and the concomitant responsibilities, if not agonising at the time, must be a dilemma when they later wonder if they did the right thing.

For all people who go from a simple, anonymous life to success and riches, the psyche needs to catch up with the reality they've created. This loss of identity can lead ordinary, good people into cycles of chaos; too many marriages, too many homes... Most people who succeed have to differentiate between their home lives and their public lives. For the elite soldier, there's no going back. He makes a choice that can never be changed. When he starts this life, everything will remind him of what he has given up, but he can still find some peace. He has crossed the line from the green army, and the old ways of living no longer apply. Looking over his shoulder he sees bridges burning.

I have been asked if I think that when men leave camp they are burdened by how their role is seen by the rest of the world, but for most, that is not their experience at all. These men have to disguise their identity so completely, never wearing uniform outside camp, getting changed into normal kit to go home just as a mechanic might, but whilst the mechanic can say, when asked, what they do for a living, these men cannot. They can't keep tools, uniforms or anything identifying in their vehicles. They drive out of camp and stow away their security passes, say goodnight to the policemen at the gate and leave all the trappings of their identity behind as they step outside. They are protected by those high fences that keep others out. Very few people have such a tangible separation between work and life as they move from one side of the fence to the other every day. Back and forth between identities.

I think they are truly fortunate.

ACKNOWLEDGEMENTS

I owe many thanks to Orphans Publishing and especially my amazing editor, Debbie Hatfield, who has been patient beyond belief with my manuscript, my tedious arguments over detail and the necessary demands and alterations required by the MOD.

And I mustn't forget all the 'geezers' who read bits of the book and said they liked it, being especially amused at how they were viewed by an outsider but grateful that their story was being told.